THE VIRGIN GAY GUIDE

THE VIRGIN GAY GUIDE

TIM LAMING

This book contains material which some readers may find offensive. Please do not read this book if you may be offended by strong language and accounts of sexual activity.

First published in Great Britain in 2003 by
Virgin Books Ltd
Thames Wharf Studios
Rainville Road
London
W6 9HA

A catalogue record for this book is available from the British Library.

ISBN 0 7535 0752 8

Typeset by Phoenix Photosetting, Chatham, Kent
Printed and bound in Great Britain by Mackays of Chatham, Chatham, Kent

CONTENTS

INTRODUCTION

According to the *The Oxford English Dictionary*, homosexuality is described as 'feeling or involving sexual attraction to persons of the same sex'. Doesn't sound like much to get excited about really, does it? Take a pill and you'll feel better in the morning. But of course there's so much more to being gay than a simple feeling, hence, the following 100,000 words contained in this book. Being gay, lesbian, queer or a faggot, poofta, shirt-lifter, arse bandit, dyke, lesbo, call us what you will (it's not like we haven't heard them all before) is a lifestyle all its own, which we can either immerse ourselves in completely, or simply dabble in, as the mood dictates. There are many lifestyle choices to be made, but fundamentally there is one choice which, as homosexuals, we can't make; we can't choose to be straight or gay. We are what we are – we were made that way.

It's true that some people choose to remain 'straight' even when their instincts encourage them to be anything but heterosexual. Upbringing, morals, religion and peer pressure all have a great influence on the way we act, but it would be dishonest to suggest that anyone could ever actually choose their sexuality. Although there are many crackpot religious groups who claim to be able to cure homosexuality (as if it were some sort of disease), we all know that in reality they simply provide the tools with which to repress true feelings. We are what we are, and our choice is whether to accept (and enjoy) that fact, or to try and be something that, fundamentally, we're not.

We're queer and we're here. But at this point in our history there's no need to be hiding in dark corners because, at long last, we have begun to see the light of a new era in which society no longer regards homosexuality as a taboo, a perversion or a failing. Society is evolving rapidly, and being gay is now neither unusual or uncommon. Thankfully, the stigma attached to the name is almost gone, and we're (almost) free to be who we really are, and who we really want to be. Homosexuality was never anything to be ashamed of, even though society (encouraged by generations of religious dogma) tried to tell us that it was. Being gay is fun; being gay is liberating; being gay is exciting.

We're out of the closet. The door is locked behind us. Let's move on and enjoy the ride.

I decided to write this book for a number of reasons. Primarily, I feel that the time is right for gay issues to be dragged out of the dark 'Gender Studies' corners of fusty book shelves, and out into the brighter light of the high street. For way too long, gay literature has been restricted to specialised publishers and specialist book stores, tainted with an image of brown paper wrappings and men in dirty raincoats. It really shouldn't be like that. We've moved far beyond the days when picking up a 'gay book' had to be done carefully, in case somebody saw you and sniggered. It's time that we finally grew up and gave the subject the same treatment as any other social issue.

I also think we've become victims of our own gay press; we're surrounded by magazines, newsletters and books which tell us what we think. Or at least they tell us what we're supposed to think. The trouble is, if you actually talk to gay people out on the streets, they often disagree entirely with the statements and attitudes which are constantly fed to us by the gay press. So this book represents a fresh, honest and direct look at all aspects of gay life as related by real gay people, rather than the usual line-up of gay commentators, with their dogma and agendas.

Whether you're gay, bisexual, lesbian or straight, I hope very much that you'll find this book entertaining, interesting, amusing and useful. In order to be as comprehensive as possible, it is naturally impossible to dwell on specific subjects at great length, and so I have strived to strike an appropriate balance between what is relevant and interesting, while ensuring that no gay topic is completely ignored. Thanks to the ever-useful internet, it is possible to find more information than you could ever need on just about any subject mentioned in this book, and wherever possible I have included suitable links to the world-wide web. At least with this book, you have a truly comprehensive guide to everything gay, and a starting point from where you can find much more, if you want to.

You might disagree with many of the views which are expressed in the following pages, and of course you're entitled to do so. Neither I nor the various commentators would pretend to have the answers for everything – we merely have a view. If your view is substantially different, then at least this book has got you thinking, and if you really do have something to say on any of the topics in this book, please contact me and tell me. You never know, we might be writing the updated and revised edition at this very minute. Read on and enjoy!

Tim Laming

1: Gay politics, gay power

We might as well start with the heavy stuff. We've come a long way since the dark days of Oscar Wilde, legal and social repression, sex scandals, outings and media slurs. The great gay movement for change began just over thirty years ago in New York, when the Stonewall riots fostered the first gay rights campaigns which ultimately led to the (relatively) liberal society in which we now live over here in the UK. But progress wasn't easy. It's taken thirty years to transform Britain, but even now we've merely achieved tolerance, rather than acceptance. And yet, if you ask just about any young gay guy or girl for their views on politics, gay activism, gay rights and our place in society, they tend to look at you as if you're slightly odd, as if the whole subject is just so last decade.

For example, here's what an eighteen-year-old has to say on the subject:

'It's ridiculous the way that people bang on about gay rights as if there's some great political struggle for survival going on that we should all be joining. I just don't see it. Being gay or straight isn't something which bothers me particularly and it doesn't bother my friends or my family either. I'm just me and that's the way I am, just like other people are straight. You read all this stuff about how gay people are repressed or treated badly and that just doesn't really happen, at least not in the way that activists make out. Yes, you get stupid people who make jokes about being gay or older people who have bigoted views but that's always going to happen, like you get racist jokes and so on. Protest marches and things like that may have been important years ago but now it's just silly and it makes gay people look like they're all weird, as if they've got some point to prove. I wish we could just move on actually.'

On the other hand, throw the same questions at slightly older people (and particularly those who don't live in big cities where there's a tangible 'gay scene') and you get a slightly different response as illustrated by this letter from a Yorkshireman:

'In 1997 I walked through the centre of London on the annual Gay Pride March – and I literally cried. I was surrounded by thousands of other men and women just like me, and for the first time in my life, my minority status seemed to lift from me as though it were on wings. Gay Pride is now depoliticised and called Mardi Gras, but even back then in the late nineties I heard people complaining that the politics had disappeared from the Pride March, and that more and more people were only attending the festival that takes place afterwards. Surely this couldn't be true; there were more people walking than ever had before and more people showing quite openly that they were happy to be living with a

sexuality other than heterosexual. It wasn't until Pride became Mardi Gras that I really started to think about whether a point had been made, and began to see that being allowed to dance through the streets of our capital city in gold lame shorts does not constitute equality.

Where has the fight gone? And I don't mean in the last five years or so, I mean onward from the decriminalisation of homosexuality all those years back in 1967. I realise, of course, that we and society have moved forward in leaps and bounds since then, but did we win any battles to get here, or have things just fallen into place in our favour? Some would say that it doesn't matter, but I would have to disagree; there is always the chance that things may slip and slide into a place where we are no longer regarded as a valid part of society (that's assuming that we are now) but once more thrown back into the gutter with the other perceived "degenerates" of our society. If this were to occur, who would fight? Who is there that would have the strength or will to wage war against our oppressors? We have found ourselves in a state of complacency, so I'm not sure we would be in any position to resist a wave of terror which could very easily pass over us. It seems that as long as we are permitted to have our pubs and our clubs, and our fashion, and our music, then we are happy to let everything else be controlled by the "normal" people. Life goes on around us but we exist only in our ghettos of flashing lights and sex.

That is not to say there is anything wrong with disco and sex; let's face it, sex specifically is the one thing which separates us from the rest; but we have become obsessed by it and even that now has a whiff of compliance. We enter into blessings and strive for a recognised "gay marriage" but why? Aren't there so many more important inequalities to spend our time fighting for? There are far too few people prepared to stand up and shake their fists at the world in defiance for it to be wasted on tokens; an attempt only to prove that we are the same as those that we are quite obviously so different from.

Perhaps my cynicism is unjustified for it would appear that the government and public opinion is on our side, but it must be wrong of us to enjoy the benefits society has afforded us when we are not willing to stand together as a united whole; a race born out of every corner of the earth, to stand and fall as martyrs to our cause; for the right not just to be allowed, or to be permitted, but instead just to be.'

Phew! It's easy to see how there are two distinct points of view defining our current place in society, and there's no clear indication as to which view is right or wrong. More recently we've seen a whole range of laws and reforms being offered up in the greater cause of gay equality. Some have been prompted by continuing political pressure from lobby groups such as Stonewall, although a more cynical observer would suggest that election votes have to be sought, and of course European laws on human rights will ultimately impose many laws upon our government, so it probably looks better if the government appears to be taking the initiative – while they still have it. But whatever the reason for such sweeping changes, the fact is that things are moving in our favour, and moving pretty fast. At long last, you might say.

But what of the future? Does this mean that gay activism and political campaigning is redundant? When all of the proposed changes have finally been achieved, where do we go from here? Veteran campaigner Peter Tatchell commented that 'if anyone thinks homophobia is nearly over, they need their heads examined. We're making progress and that's fantastic, but let's not kid ourselves that the battle is over. Even when we get legal equality that won't mean the end of homophobia and there will still be prejudice and discrimination in the media, the church, business, sport and the day-to-day bigotry of neighbours and work colleagues. Activism will be vital to challenge these other areas of intolerance.'

Likewise, even the lobby group Stonewall accepts that the days of hard political lobbying may soon be over when there is little left to actually lobby for. But changing attitudes within society will take much longer, and it is in this direction which activists like Peter Tatchell, Stonewall and others are now turning their attention. Helen Marsh, a spokesperson for Stonewall, said that 'it is great what is happening but there is still a lot to do. In a lot of places outside London discrimination is still widespread and there needs to be a lot of work done to change people's attitudes.' So the fight for equality goes on, even though the so-called gay and lesbian community seems far from united in its understanding or appreciation of such struggles. The future's bright, but slightly cloudy. Let's take a look at some of the slightly less-than-grey areas of gay politics:

STONEWALL

Largely as a result of the infamous Section 28, a pro-gay and lesbian political lobby group was set up in 1989, employing full-time professional staff who would work towards the advancement of civil, political, economic and cultural rights of lesbians and gay men. Taking their name from the seminal New York riots of 1969, Stonewall was formed, beginning a new era of political activism, as a Stonewall spokesman describes:

'In the early days it was often a question of gaining footholds which we could use to push the principle of equality. Bringing together sympathetic MPs, getting debates and amendments, using each opportunity to push forward our claim for equality. Since then, our work has continued to focus on Westminster, but we have grown and our remit extends to national campaigns, research and information provision. The Stonewall Immigration and Parenting groups were formed in 1993 and 1995

respectively to provide support and advice for specific groups within our community. The initial funding to start Stonewall came from a gala performance of Bent *by Martin Sherman. We have retained that tradition of event fundraising with the annual Equality Show, which takes place at the Royal Albert Hall, where hosts of stars perform for our benefit. About 40 per cent of our income comes from the Equality Show, 40 per cent from our Friends, individual supporters who give at least £5 a month, and a further 20 per cent comes from the corporate sector.*

During 1989–94, the success of this period was the campaign on the age of consent in 1994 which mobilised thousands of lesbians and gay men and created a new understanding in Parliament and society of our identity and aspirations. Although we narrowly lost the vote for sixteen, as one MP said afterwards "the earth moved". We could not be disregarded again. Our age of consent campaign brought the case for lesbian and gay equality into every home in the nation and won support from all sections of society. The campaign was acknowledged as one of the most successful parliamentary lobbies ever. In the summer of 1997 Stonewall launched its Equality 2000 campaign, reaffirming our belief that the lesbian and gay community should enter the new millennium as free and equal citizens. The Equality 2000 campaign consolidated Stonewall's work into the five main campaign areas which you now see on our website. The last century ended with an historic decision from the European Court of Human Rights on the ban on lesbians and gay men serving in the armed forces. That was followed in November 2000 with the passing of the Sexual Offences (Amendment) Act which equalised the age of consent.

In many ways we have been living in a war zone. As a social group, lesbians and gay men have been actively persecuted, punished and excluded. The victories that we are winning now are largely about dismantling that overt discrimination. As the prospect of winning the war comes closer we also have to think long and hard about winning the peace. Winning the peace will mean coming out of the ghetto. We have to bring our needs and aspirations into the public arena and build links with many other groups, organisations and institutions in society. We recognise the need to organise a more systematic programme of education, information, advice and research on lesbian and gay issues to combat homophobia and increase awareness of our communities. Although parliamentary lobbying will remain Stonewall's core activity, research, training, information provision and building alliances will be given more focus and more resources.

Whilst it would be wonderful to one day close the doors of the Stonewall offices having achieved all our campaign objectives, there will be a need for an organisation independent of government to monitor the social effects of legislative change. In this respect we liken our future to that of

the racial equality and disability movement – legislative change being only the start of the long and sometimes tortuous path towards an end to bigotry in all areas of society.'

So much for Stonewall's own self-proclaimed achievements. Undoubtedly, the group has done a great deal since its formation and, in practical terms, it is Stonewall that has quietly but resolutely pushed successive governments in the right direction until significant pro-gay changes have been made. Recent legislation on adoption and new laws on sexual offences and even partnership rights all owe their success to Stonewall's persistence. But, of course, making changes in Parliament only tells part of a much bigger story. Real change requires much more than just new laws, and even Stonewall's own literature makes a hint at this unavoidable fact.

Peter Tatchell, long-time critic of the group, recently said (to the *Pink Paper*) that 'Stonewall has concentrated on the very narrow brief of parliamentary lobbying and law reform, but homophobia also needs challenging in other areas of public life such as the media. Stonewall's agenda should be about transforming society, not conforming to it.'

Peter probably has a good point (as usual), but even he wouldn't deny that law change was very necessary, and it was only Stonewall's patient but persistent lobbying that actually achieved results. However, many long-overdue law reforms are now under way, and Stonewall does need to look to the future, and reinvent itself. As part of this process, it is perhaps a convenient coincidence that its well-known leader, Angela Mason, has stepped down.

Announcing her decision to the *Pink Paper*, Mason commented that her departure would be 'a good opportunity for a fresh face to look at the fresh challenges'. She also went on to admit that relations with the media have never been particularly successful, and that her replacement must have better public relations skills.

In fact, this was something of an understatement as, despite the fact that the group has effectively been the country's leading gay lobby group for many years, Stonewall has never received much attention from the media. Although adept at political persuasion, Stonewall has consistently failed to make any real connection with either mainstream society, or even the wider gay community that it represents. Ask any typical gay man or woman out on the streets, and you'd be lucky to find anyone who has any real clue as to what Stonewall actually does. This kind of image problem is even more of a disadvantage when it comes to gaining air-time on television or column inches in the papers, but if social change is the key phrase for the future, it's the media that will make it happen, and only with our influence. Will Stonewall be at the forefront?

Viewpoints

'I think Stonewall has mostly done a pretty good job, but it's taken such a long time to get even basic changes to the law changed and things should have been done much more quickly in my view. What they've done has been good but I do really believe they could have been much more pro-active and made governments do things much more swiftly instead of being so meek and mild. Angela Mason was the wrong person to be leading them, because she just didn't have the presence or the authority to take on people in debates and stuff. She just sat there and muttered half-hearted replies instead of going for the throat like you wanted her to. The person that takes over will probably be another pushover that nobody listens to. Why can't they get some mouthy lesbian to really go for it and tell the media some hard facts instead of just being so damned polite all the time?'

Brian (postman, 28), Cardiff

'God, it's hard to know what to think really. The trouble is, you just switch off when you hear about Stonewall 'cause you know it's going to be all about rights and equality and so on, which is all very well but it's just endless arguing that's really got nothing to do with my life as it is. I agree that laws should change to make gay people on a level with straight people but badgering MPs is not going to change how people feel about being gay, or stop school kids being bullied for being gay, or anything like that. So I say just forget it. The European Courts are doing all the human rights stuff, so I don't think we need gay rights groups as such.'

Jay (student, 19), Leicester

'Actually I'm not very impressed at all. I agree that Stonewall has possibly helped to get the government to change some laws after a very long time but they've taken way too long to do it, and I don't accept that they have to go for this softly-softly approach. We've had every right to expect equality all along so Stonewall should have kept shouting that at the politicians until they listened, instead of being up their arses all these years going to dinners and stuff. Angela Mason's now got herself an eighty-grand job with the government for her troubles. That just smacks of favouritism and it makes you wonder how much time she spent on gay rights and how much time she spent on getting her feet under the table. I wish all these people would just get their heads out of their arses and really do something.'

Donna (student, 18), Manchester

'It's time we woke up and stopped being so fucking pathetic. Stonewall's done some good work but we should have been doing so much more all these years. These activism groups don't seem to be very active at all, and they spend way too much time on internal politics, I think, instead of

actually getting some results. Every time I hear something anti-gay on television or in the papers, I personally want to know why these comedians aren't out there defending us, if they're really interested in gay rights. When somebody does finally manage to put our case it's always some idiot that either can't speak, or doesn't know what he's talking about, or he just gets talked down. Where are all the people that have got some balls?'

Jill (unemployed, 22), Bedford

Links

www.stonewall.org.uk

Stonewall Lobby Group, 46–48 Grosvenor Gardens, London, SW1W 0EB

SECTION 28

If you ever get yourself stuck in the middle of a gay rights demonstration (which isn't very likely these days, now that pro-gay protest marches are no longer regarded as fashionable) you're almost certain to hear at least a few militant lesbians screaming something about the infamous Section 28, a seemingly insignificant sub-clause in a piece of stuffy legislation which has neatly served to illustrate the hypocrisy and homophobia which is still sanctioned by successive British governments. What's it all about? Well, the whole saga can be traced back to 1986 when dreary old Lord Halsbury introduced a Private Members Bill in the House of Lords which described an 'Act to refrain local authorities from promoting homosexuality'. You'd think he'd have better things to do, but back in the 1980s the country was gripped in a frenzy of anti-gay rhetoric, largely fed by a variety of right-wing religious groups and other alleged bastions of so-called respectability, with lunatics like Mary Whitehouse (God rest her intolerant and bigoted soul) insisting (and people actually believed this – seriously) that the country was being taken over by evil predatory gays and lesbians who were hell-bent on making innocent children become gay (although nobody ever quite worked out how they were going to do this – presumably it involved drugs or hypnotism).

With Margaret Thatcher in power, there wasn't much risk of any of these views being questioned or suppressed but, even so, it's interesting to note that Halsbury's Bill was thought unnecessary by the government, who considered it 'risky and open to harmful misrepresentation'. That was something of an understatement as the following years demonstrated.

Although it was quietly dropped during the run-up to the 1987 general election, the Bill did get as far as the House of Commons, where Dame Jill Knight adopted it, until it was ultimately abandoned through lack of support. Unfortunately, like a dog (or bitch) with a bone, she didn't abandon the subject, and promptly introduced a new clause into a Local Government Bill for 1988 which was going through the Commons at that time. With hardly any fuss, a small amendment was made to Section 28 of the Act, stating that:

A local authority shall not:

a) intentionally promote homosexuality or publish material with the intention of promoting homosexuality

b) promote the teaching in any maintained school of the acceptability of homosexuality as a pretended family relationship.

And so the damage was done. In isolation the legislation was little more than an opportunity for some obscure B-list dame to justify her existence and get her name printed in a few papers, and, technically speaking, few would disagree with legislation which prohibits the promotion of any particular beliefs or persuasions. But, as the government had so woefully and accurately predicted, it was the way in which the clause would be interpreted that would create what has become a fifteen-year headache for both gay activist groups and successive governments.

Not surprisingly, both education authorities and teachers were suddenly terrified of mentioning the H-word. Homosexuality was once again completely taboo, for even the most cursory discussion of the subject could be interpreted (at least in theory) as 'promotion' and lead to prosecution at worst, or an awful lot of trouble at best (for example, the Institute of Education at a London university concluded that the clause created 'an atmosphere of confusion and fear that discouraged staff from intervening to stop an epidemic of homophobic abuse in school playgrounds and corridors').

Thus, the battle lines were drawn between the far right (especially the Church and much of Fleet Street) and the liberal left, supported by gay rights groups. The eventual arrival of New Labour didn't help much either – Blair's new government was perched on the proverbial fence, trapped between its wish to appease the demands for equality made by most clear-thinking individuals and groups and the hatred being spewed from the Church, encouraged by the newspapers that New Labour wanted to keep firmly on-side.

But who were the real victims? Sadly, the only people who didn't get much of a serious mention in the whole debate were the nation's children, the people that the legislation was supposedly designed to protect. Patently, Section 28 didn't protect them at all, quite the reverse in fact, as it discouraged teachers from discussing homosexuality with kids who were inevitably growing up gay. Even more dangerous was the broader development of an atmosphere which encouraged children to believe that homosexuality was some sort of scary perversion which couldn't even be mentioned in class, unless it was for the purposes of a cheap joke (usually aimed at someone gay). This created a 'green light' for school bullying which went almost unchecked. After all, what teacher is going to step in to stop a pupil from being 'accused' of being gay? That could be interpreted as 'promoting' homosexuality. It was a messy and lethal situation which led to countless cases of severe depression and even suicide amongst school children.

In wider terms, the gay community took great exception to the clause, not only because of the implications for a whole generation of potentially confused gay children, but because the very wording of the Act reinforced the notion that being homosexual was in some way inferior to being heterosexual. What else could the 'pretended family relationship' mean? The Act was clearly suggesting that any relationship between people of the same sex was a sham, and didn't really count, whereas 'proper' relationships were made exclusively between a man and a woman. Clearly the notion is complete garbage, but somehow it had become enshrined in law.

The New Labour government readily accepted that the clause was both offensive and damaging, and boasted that it would quickly be scrapped. However, 'quickly' was presumably a subjective term as far as Blair's government was concerned, and it wasn't until February 2000 that legislation to repeal the Act finally reached the House of Lords, where (despite the will of the House of Commons, who voted in favour of repeal) everybody knew that the process would come to a grinding halt. The out-dated and prejudiced views of the unelected House were sure to defeat the will of both the Commons and (therefore) the nation. And they did.

Listening to the House of Lords debate was both fascinating and repulsive. Some of the speeches were undoubtedly based on wisdom and logic while others were little more than barely disguised monologues based on the teachings of the Church. For example, Earl Longford (who was, to some extent, pro-gay) spouted the following clap-trap:

'Homosexuality is against Christian rules, as is any sex outside marriage. Homosexuality can have terrible, tragic results. Whatever else it does, it deprives people of the supreme joy of marriage and children. Helping a young person to become a homosexual means that he will never be married and never have children. That is a terrible burden to inflict on a child, although it is no worse than the behaviour of a heterosexual man who has five mistresses. I do not say that one is worse than the other. They are both against the rules. They are both sinful.'

Of course, a five-year-old could have pointed out that it's not homosexuality which deprives gay people of marriage and children – it's the government. Likewise, Longford is probably right in claiming that being gay can have tragic results, but his twisted logic implies that it's the very nature of homosexuality which causes the tragedy. More likely, it's the beating on a street corner or the murder in a darkened park which is really responsible. Even more comical is his concept of 'helping a young person to become a homosexual' as if being gay was some kind of bizarre fashion. If it wasn't patently hilarious, it would be tragic.

But, of course, it was the infamous Baroness Janet Young who embraced the continuing debate with relish until her timely demise in 2002. Her House of Lords speech was, like most of her utterances, specious, in that it superficially addressed all the prejudices of the Church and Fleet Street without appearing to be overtly offensive. Unless you happened to be gay, that is:

'I have said publicly on many occasions that, like the right reverend Prelate the Bishop of Blackburn, I believe that marriage is best; that marriage is the right way to live. The right reverend Prelate did not say this, but I believe also that there is no moral equivalence between homosexual and heterosexual relationships. As a teacher and a parent I feel that we need to set in front of children an ideal by which they should live. They may not live up to it; I do not live up to ideals either. But I have an idea of how I ought to live. That is what we should strive for. That is what we should put in front of children. To say to children that there are alternatives in life which are equally valid is not right. One needs to be careful what one says to vulnerable children growing up uncertain of the way. What one says to adults and what adults do is a completely different matter and the two points should not be confused.'

So there we have it. Baroness Young neatly categorises every gay man and lesbian as being inferior to the rest of society, just because we don't fit her neat (and grossly confused) view of the world. There are no alternatives. God is right (or at least her god is, it seems) and we are wrong. Go figure.

But if Janet Young's tambourine-rattling sounded (at least superficially) merely misguided, there were more colourful comments from others, such as the delightful Cardinal Thomas Winning (Scotland's most senior Roman Catholic – gasp!): **'It pains me to use the word perverted when discussing the homosexual act but that is what it is.'**

Presumably the endless stream of abuse cases involving the Church means that his comments don't apply to his colleagues. No matter, he died in June 2002. Shame.

But even Winning's pious remarks pale in comparison to those from former tabloid journalist Jack Irvine (now the Director of a Scottish PR company), who referred to '. . . slobbering queers who want to get their hands on young boys' arses . . .' How sweet.

But things were slightly different in Scotland, where, in contrast to national opinion polls which suggested that most people were in favour of abandoning Section 28, the Scottish were very much in support of its retention. Peter Stanford wrote in the *Independent on Sunday* that 'The Sassenachs may, in this black and white world, have lost sight of what is right and wrong, but a poll last week in the *Daily Record* suggested a two-to-one majority of Scots in favour of keeping Section 28.' He went on to say that 'Just as the English have apparently moved on, with the Blair government matter of fact about its openly gay cabinet ministers, the Scots are making their play for seeming the most sexually repressed and intolerant people in Europe.'

Things were not, of course, quite as simple as they seemed. It's probably true to say that Scottish attitudes towards homosexuality are some years behind those of England, but many people didn't really have a view on Section 28 at all, and simply responded to the poll based on their limited knowledge of the meaning of the Bill and its implications.

And then there was Brian Souter, the sour-faced owner of the huge Stagecoach company who (for reasons which are still unclear, but he obviously has some personal issues to deal with) decided to embark upon a mission to abandon plans being made by the Scottish Parliament to repeal Section 28. With his sizeable financial resources, Souter was able to create and back a huge 'Save Section 28' campaign which, with the help of allies such as Cardinal Winning, promoted their anti-gay hatred in direct defiance of the view being expressed by the Scottish Parliament. Indeed, when Souter appeared on BBC's *Question Time*, a questioner did suggest that if he had such a good case to make, Souter ought to abandon his businesses and seek election as an MP.

Boy George was also on the show, and, although he made a sensible and clear defence of the case against Section 28, he didn't exactly savage Souter, as many (including the BBC presumably) had expected. George later commented that he was 'very conscious of the fact that going on *Question Time* and being a bitchy, queeny type would have defeated my purpose. Anyway, I would hate to be thought of as a gay activist.' Fair enough. But it's also fair to say that we expected a little more from someone who is, unquestionably, on our side.

Souter's campaign began to falter as his hatred was brought to the attention of the wider public. His campaign Freepost facility was targeted by his opponents, who quickly realised that not only letters of support could be mailed to Souter, and he would be obliged to pay for them all. It was closed down. Undeterred, Souter funded a private referendum which (unsurprisingly) yielded a pro-retention result. But, of course, the referendum could hardly be described as fair. Souter had loaded the question and still only managed to achieve a response of just over 30 per cent. Sensibly, most Scots had chosen to throw his ballot paper in the waste bin.

Thankfully, the Scottish Parliament ignored both Souter and Winning, and finally scrapped Section 28. Ironically (and you couldn't have made this up), one of Souter's deputies (Chair of his UK buses division) was later charged with soliciting for a male prostitute.

Meanwhile, back in England, Section 28 remains firmly in place. Blair insists that his government remains committed to the repeal of the clause but there is no sign of any attempt to force the issue. A group of left-wing Labour MPs pledged to force a vote unless the government included removal of the clause in the autumn 2002 Queen's Speech but it didn't happen, and where it will all ultimately lead remains unclear.

Even more disturbing is the way in which the whole subject is now being clouded by talk of education guidelines, rather than the straightforward removal of Section 28. Home Secretary David Blunkett has already issued guidance on sex education, stating that teachers should have no role in promoting any sexual orientation. He insists that children should be taught about the 'importance of marriage, family life, love and stable relationships in bringing up children'. All very nice, but he still doesn't challenge Section 28's inference that a homosexual relationship is inferior to a heterosexual one. Or maybe Blunkett believes this is true.

Discussions with ministers, Lords and Church leaders supposedly continue, although there doesn't seem to be much consultation with any representatives of the gay community other than Stonewall, who evidently claimed that they (and, therefore, we) could 'live with' an amendment proposed by the Bishop of Blackburn, which would have required schools to promote marriage in sex education lessons (although Baroness Young immediately dismissed the idea, as it 'failed to prevent schools from promoting homosexual relationships'). Some would argue that we might not want to 'live with' any amendments, nor any 'fudging' by the Home Secretary.

Section 28 can be dressed up or glossed over, but while it remains part of the country's law, it will offend gay people, and ultimately result in violence towards children. While Baroness Young did the decent thing and died during 2002, the wait for Section 28's repeal continues. As Liberal Democrat MP Evan Harris said, 'Don't hold your breath.'

Viewpoints

'It means nothing, and yet it is believed to outlaw the speaking of homosexuality to anyone of an age below that of consent. It is nothing more than a piece of fear-mongering. Since its application, it has succeeded with its desired and diabolical effect. There is not a school in the country that has the courage to speak of it; it portrays homosexuality as a society-decaying disease, a morally abhorrent lifestyle, and it is unspeakable. This at least is what our nation's children are led to believe. The beast we must slay, the animal we have named 'Section 28' is like the mouse portrayed as a tiger. It doesn't say schools can't talk of gay people,

or even of gay sex. It doesn't say that bullying or taunting (because the victim is believed to be gay) is to be ignored or to be tolerated; in fact, it says the very opposite. It doesn't say a pupil going through a crisis of sexual identity should be shrugged off; told it is a phase, a growing pain, or something to be hidden. There is nowhere in the legislature where it reads that a teacher cannot advise, console and offer relevant information and help to a student unable to find his or her way through the shredding thorns of alienation, homosexual guilt, and the ever present torture of puberty.

So why are our educators dangerously silent? What is it that our schools are afraid of? All the clause actually says is that a local education authority cannot promote homosexuality as a preferred lifestyle or a pretend family unit; meaning basically that it can't say that gays are better than straights; and that it can't spend its money on projects for gay, lesbian and bisexual students while neglecting those of heterosexual incline. And that's it – that is all it restricts – but the fear of overstepping the mark, and landing themselves in court has frightened councils and their schools into a corner, and turned the whole subject of alternative sexuality into a taboo. The fact that something so insignificant can cause so much damage is the very reason it must be removed from the statute books forthwith. It is a homophobic ruling which poisons our nation at its roots, bringing forth new generations of ignorant and bigoted populous to carry on the country's most revered traditions: hate and intolerance.'

Leon (writer, 24), Wakefield

'It's quite absurd really, because Section 28 doesn't actually say much at all, other than that schools shouldn't actively promote homosexuality. In many respects that's not such a bad thing to say, because schools shouldn't be promoting any particular type of lifestyle. But the way that the clause is worded, and all the baggage that has been attached to it by bigots in the House of Lords and in the media, has encouraged schools to think that they just can't even discuss the subject without running the risk of getting into big trouble. In fact, nobody has been prosecuted under this Act, but it illustrates how damaging the clause is. It has to go, because it stops teachers from discussing homosexuality with pupils, leading to bullying or even suicides in some cases. And just as importantly it sends out a signal to society that homosexuality is somehow wrong. It's a poisonous piece of legislation which should have been thrown out a long time ago.'

John (writer, 28), Manchester

Links

news.bbc.co.uk/1/hi/uk/613023.stm

www.sbu.ac.uk/~stafflag/lawsection28.html

STONEWALL RIOTS

Back in the dark days of 1969 while most of the world was still wallowing in the hippy culture which was supposedly all about peace, love and understanding, there wasn't much love or understanding being given to homos. Being gay (particularly in Britain) meant living a secret. It was a life of hush-hush liaisons, knowing looks, furtive assignations and seedy back-street gatherings.

In America, things were no better; in fact they were a whole lot worse in most US states and, even amongst the bright lights of New York, the gay community wasn't exactly welcomed into society with open arms. They were tolerated, grudgingly, but the gay scene was still a world of back-street basements with blacked-out windows, shuttered doors, police raids and beatings. New York's police regularly marched into gay clubs and closed them down. Only a few survived, and amongst these was the Stonewall Bar on Christopher Street – a dark and dowdy shell of a building which had merely been repainted after having been virtually destroyed by arson a year previously. It was a dump, but it was pretty much all that the gay community had, and it was hugely popular. Even the grubbiest of venues could soon come alive with some pumping disco music, lots of alcohol, more than a few drugs and hordes of homos.

But on 28 June 1969, the police came out on another almost ritual raid. As ever they burst into the bar, switched the lights on and arrested the staff for selling liquor without a licence. It was a common sight, and the punters were pretty much used to it, but they were in an ugly mood, what with the constant hassle from the police, and the country-wide sadness at the death of Judy Garland a few days previously (Judy was a huge gay icon at that time in history). As the drag queens, lesbians and bartenders were packed off into police vans, the crowd pelted the police with coins. And then bottles.

Patience had broken. The drag queens, in typical feisty fashion, had seen and heard enough. The endless intolerance and intimidation had finally reached a breaking point, and the girls weren't taking it any longer. They fought back and a full-scale riot ensued. The police retreated into the bar to defend themselves from the crowd but the punters were furious and smashed their way back inside with a broken parking meter. The police held out until armed reinforcements arrived and the arrests began, while the riot spilled out onto the surrounding streets where gay men and women gathered, shouting slogans, throwing bottles and starting fires in trash cans. It was absolute mayhem and, as the police tried to round up the crowds, they merely retreated into side alleys, only to reappear behind the police line. The chaos spilled over into the next day, and the day after, finally ending in more casualties and arrests some four days after it had first begun.

It was an ugly business, but an historically important milestone in our gay history. For the first time ever, gay people had stood up and decided that they would take no more. The Stonewall riots were a turning point, creating a catalyst for gay rights activism, and the beginnings of all that has happened ever since. The very fact that, at long last, we can live relatively freely as gay and lesbian people within mainstream society is ultimately a direct result of the Stonewall riots. We have a great deal to thank those drag queens for.

Links

www.qrd.org/qrd/misc/text/stonewall.history-ADVOCATE

www.planetout.com/pno/news/history/archive/06211999.html

OUTRAGE!

Gay political activism might sound like a phrase from the seventies, but, of course, campaigns for equality and gay rights still continue. While Stonewall has, rightly or wrongly, become our accepted political representative, there are other groups that have done (and continue to do) a great deal on our behalf, even though their efforts tend to go largely unnoticed by both the gay press and national media.

Amongst the range of campaign groups which are still very much in business, OutRage! is possibly the most well known and certainly the most controversial. Advocates of in-your-face activism, OutRage!'s policies and beliefs are a direct contrast to Stonewall's softly-softly diplomatic approach. Formed during the late 1980s OutRage! is the home of in-your-face confrontation. OutRage!'s David Allison explains:

'Not everyone loves OutRage!, not even some of us who have been involved for many years. Like most groups we have the mad, the bad and the sad. We've had those who were out to push their own agendas and those who sought to further their own careers. But there have been many others who got involved simply because they cared and wanted to contribute. Those people will always be the soul of the group.

The media is important. There is no point in staging an action unless it gets coverage and, consequently, encourages public debate on the subject that you are trying to raise awareness of. London witnesses a demonstration of one sort or another almost every day. Most are ignored. Marches are boring unless you can bring hundreds of thousands on to the street. Using the media successfully was and is an integral part of our activism. Setting up photo opportunities with camera-friendly subjects in an attractive, relevant location makes life easier for the people behind the cameras, and is therefore more likely to get our message into print or on to television. Similarly, remembering the rule of "who, what, why, when and where" gives us the chance to give journalists what they want

quickly, and still leave time aplenty to sink a couple of pints with them before they return to the office. How better to get them onside?

OutRage! has been accused of seeking publicity for its own sake. We would not deny that we have had our fair share of media queens who can hear a camera click at a hundred metres but, fortunately, most of them have been able to make a persuasive case too. Having people who are articulate, informed and confident is an obvious pre-requisite to ensuring that our message gets across on the air. Over the years we've done some pretty outrageous things that have put us below the salt in the eyes of the more polite and respectable individuals within the community. Many of them would prefer a softly-softly approach. We respect that. In practice we are separate branches of the same tree – we rely on each other.

Bashing MPs and PMs, pop stars and presidents has reminded the country that gays are not a crowd of limp-wristed, handbag-swinging, mincing poofs. In many cases, our confrontational approach has persuaded homophobes to give in and talk to the "nice" guys rather than endure OutRage!'s in-yer-face vulgarity. A prime example of this is the reaction of the Church of England to our intrusions into its life. For nearly twenty years the leaders of the Lesbian and Gay Christian Movement had tried to get the Church to talk to them, but met with total silence. Then we started questioning the sexuality of a number of bishops and invading Lambeth Palace at embarrassing moments and suddenly the LGCM was being invited round for tea and sticky buns. The Archbishop of Canterbury had looked into the abyss and seen Beelzebub in an OutRage! T-shirt. Compared to that, the LGCM was the Choir of Angels, even if they were singing "Jesus wants me for a bumboy"!

Careful planning and attention to detail has contributed to the success of many of our actions, as when we invaded the National Executive Committee of the Labour Party in the heart of their headquarters in the Walworth Road. While one member of the team distracted the security staff, another team, dressed in smart business suits, headed for the meeting room (we had obtained a plan of the building and other details from an insider). When the team walked in on the meeting, one member went straight to the bewildered David Blunkett to reassure him that we were not an IRA active service unit and that he was in no danger.

Another unsung activity is providing information, support and back-up to the thousands of individuals who contact us. Because of our high profile, people in small towns and villages, many of whom have no access to the gay press, are able to track us down and make contact. We do our best to put them in touch with any relevant gay groups and often maintain personal contact by letter, phone or email. At the moment, in addition to this country, we are in ongoing contact with individual gays in rural France and other parts of Europe, in Indonesia and China . . . we share experiences and learn from all these people, and from other activists across the world. We have provided speakers for schools, universities, political groups, trades unions, youth groups and religious organisations – always listening as well as lecturing. OutRage! tries to be part of the community; we don't lord over it.

We also give lots of help to students writing dissertations, essays or projects, usually via face-to-face interviews. We never say no. These young people, gay or straight, are the future, so we do all that we can to ensure that they are as well informed as they possibly can be – not only about OutRage!'s philosophy in so far as we have one, but, much more importantly, about the issues that affect our community. We are honest with them, whether it is about those who have fought homophobia using controversial tactics or those who have succumbed to the ghetto mentality; whether it is about those who have contributed to the community by giving their time, energy and money, or those who are attempting to drain every last penny from us, in exchange for over-priced and inferior goods and services. They get the whole picture, warts and all.'

Viewpoints

'I don't like the kind of thing that OutRage! does. Going around trying to "out" people just for the sake of it is wrong I think 'cause it's up to the person to decide whether to come out or not. You can't just make somebody do that and it makes us look bad when they start accusing people. I think that OutRage! are probably doing the right thing in trying to fight for our rights but they're just doing it the wrong way, and in any case I don't think there's anything that important to fight for now. We've got the age of consent and things like that, so they'd be better off just campaigning properly without making gay people look like lunatics.'

John (unemployed, 20), Ipswich

'OutRage! just doesn't get enough support in my view. They do a fucking good job and I wish they'd do more. The sheepish way that Stonewall carries on is just so embarrassing and it doesn't do us any favours at all. It's taken years and years to get even a few laws changed, and when Stonewall start crowing about how they've campaigned for us, it makes me sick 'cause I think it's their approach that has made things move so slowly. OutRage! have really been the people who have got the media's attention and, at the end of the day, it's the media that influences things in this country, not the politicians. Modern politics is all about reacting to the media. If you can get the media on your side, or at least get them to talk about you, then you're talking to the public, and that's what matters.

People are allowed to say whatever they want about gay people and we need more activist-type groups to give back some of our own views so that we're treated with more respect. I don't think it's about equality because I don't think we'll get equality for a very long time, if ever, when people are still brought up to believe that being gay is wrong or weird.

But we should at least fight to get respect instead of just rolling over and letting people do or say whatever they like about us.'

Mark (builder, 38), Swindon

'I get sick of hearing people saying that we've got equality and rights and stuff, when gay people are still treated like second-class citizens. OutRage! used to get on the news all the time but now you hardly ever hear about them which is a crying shame. They were right to try and "out" famous people, because I think anyone that accepts fame should also accept that they forfeit the right to privacy about their sexual preferences; it's that simple. If you're going to seek fame then you shouldn't be allowed to lie about being gay because that kind of attitude allows discrimination to continue and it fosters the idea that there's something wrong with being gay. If it wasn't seen as somehow wrong, then nobody would lie about it, so OutRage! are ultimately right to make people come clean for all our sakes'.

Lisa (student, 19), Birmingham

'Fucking brilliant. I love that kind of stuff, especially from the Church people that keep on trying to peddle the gay-equals-sinners crap. It's great when the Archbishop gets embarrassed and has to confront gay people instead of hiding away to preach hatred. I'm all for it; the in-your-face thing is a good idea and there should be more of it. I haven't got any time for this "oh we should be quiet and persuade people to accept us" stuff; it's just shite. We need to stand up for ourselves whenever and wherever we can and stop letting the world treat us as if we're not important. Black groups have always had the balls to stand up and we should too. These days it's just sad to hide away and come out with all that crap about being one big happy society. Everyone knows it's bollocks really. These people that say they're so accepted wouldn't dream of going round some dodgy housing estate telling everyone they're gay 'cause they know they'd get killed. They just like to kid themselves that they're fitting in when really they're not at all.'

Mark (mechanic, 28), Leeds

Links

outrage.nabumedia.com

OutRage! PO Box 17816, London, SW14 8WT

LESBIAN AVENGERS

Direct action girly style, the Lesbian Avengers were formed in 1992 and, although they now have sub-groups all over the world, their in-your-face activism seems to have almost ended. Shame really 'cause they did it so well.

Think tits-out, public snogging and bus raids . . . Their last great public display of queerness was back in 2000 when the girls poured pink paint over a bus owned by Stagecoach homophobe Brian Souter. Wicked – more please!

Links

www.lesbianavengers.org

SISTERS OF PERPETUAL INDULGENCE

Created in San Francisco (quelle surprise!) but very much alive over here, the Sisters are a group of gay boys dedicated to Aids prevention and gay activism. Boys in habits. Cool.

Links

www.thesisters.org

ARMED FORCES

Don't ask and don't tell. While the rest of the country slowly gets over the whole gay thing, the armed forces still lag way behind, and still haven't quite learned how to deal with homosexuality. It's probably not surprising when you consider that, even after consensual gay sex was legalised in 1967, the new law still didn't apply to the armed forces, where as many as ten or more arrests would be made every year, and victims could be imprisoned for up to eighteen months. The service chiefs simply chose to pretend that homosexuality either didn't exist or, if it did, it was some kind of peculiar perversion that had to be stamped out. The ugly nature of this attitude is illustrated by the story of Mike, a former Royal Air Force serviceman:

'I always fancied boys, probably from as early as about the age of eleven or twelve. That's when I think it first happened. I was only twelve years old and at school I sent lots of Christmas cards to all the boys that I fancied. Not surprisingly I was outed at school for this crime, and all my friends knew because the Christmas cards I sent to the boys had messages written inside them describing the explicit details of what I'd like to do to them and it went around the school like wild fire. It became common knowledge that I was a fucking poofta! So that was it, I was out at school. My friends knew, but none of my family did at that time.

Later on in life, after leaving school when I was just sixteen years old, I went into the Royal Air Force. At that time I was technically straight, not actually having any sexual connection with any other boys, but I was actually gay because I still fancied boys. In the early years back at school I

was as happy as hell. I was having a great time but like I said I went into the air force and remained more-or-less straight until I got kicked out, and when that happened my family found out that I was gay. Then I went through a really big sort of depression. I was about twenty years old and I thought that I was the only person in the world who was gay. I didn't confide in anyone or talk to anyone. I took it out on myself in a big way and I even put a hosepipe up the exhaust of my car and tried to gas myself. I spent three days in a coma and then twenty-three weeks in a mental hospital. By then my parents and everyone knew about me. I was still living at my parents' place in Kent and the police found me there and informed them of what had been going on.

It feels fabulous being attracted to both sexes. I love sex. What better way to enjoy sex than to have it with everyone. The best of both worlds I guess, but I prefer to have sex with boys though. Nature attracts me to both guys and women. But it's not a physical attraction as such. To me it's a mental attraction. Yeah, I can look around and see some really cute guys and there are some really fit birds out there, but they've got to have a personality and intelligence to turn me on more. Sex is better with a guy though. They know how to give good blow jobs. Girls really don't have a bloody clue but then that's understandable. I don't intend to marry a man or a woman. What's the point of marriage? Most marriages end in divorce anyhow. What's the difference between bisexual and gay? If a guy is bisexual, he's effectively gay anyway because he shags boys. So bisexual is gay in any case. What you're trying to get at is the difference between a gay man and a straight man. In my experience there's no such thing as a straight man anyway, as all fucking men are bisexual, even though they just don't admit it. Those are the ones who are the liars, not the gay men. At least gay men come out with it and say they shag boys or that they shag boys and girls. Straight men do shag boys but won't fucking admit it. I've had plenty of so-called straight boys.

But back to the Royal Air Force. I have to say that I couldn't have felt discriminated against at any time when I was actually in the RAF because it wasn't an issue for me when I was serving in the air force. When I wanted gay things or gay experiences while I was in the air force, I just used to go out and buy magazines. There always used to be a newspaper shop near the base that sold gay magazines. Nobody really knows why, but there's always a shop like that no matter what base you're at, probably because there's so many men altogether and there must have been loads of gay blokes on the base, but I certainly didn't know any.

I used to buy all these magazines and eventually, as you might expect, the military police found them. It all started because some bloke in the barracks lost his (expensive) watch. So they decided to do a barracks search from room to room. They got to my room, which I shared with another five blokes. By the way none of them were in any way good-

looking . . . They came to my locker, went through my main locker and found my big black box trunk, which was padlocked. They asked for the keys to the padlock and I said, no, that I'd left them at work in another part of the base so they said, fair enough, we'll break it open. They did so and it was crammed full of gay magazines. So then I got arrested for being in possession of pornographic literature of a homosexual nature.

I was shit scared. I was locked in the guardhouse for two days, and then I was released from the guardroom, charged and sent back to work. A new station routine order came out the next day reminding everybody that it was illegal to be gay and do this and that and the other. Then everyone looked at me, obviously thinking that if I'd spent two days in the guardroom and now a routine order comes out mentioning all this stuff, then I was connected with it. So word got out round camp that I was a fucking poof. Some things they said hurt me really bad. It wasn't just said, it was physical as well. I was beaten. I was beaten up so badly one night I had to spend the night in the medical centre.

Then about three days later at about ten in the morning, two SIB special investigators turned up at the base and arrested me from my work department, and they read out the charges in front of everyone, so that everyone knew for a fact that it was me who was the gay one. I was then taken away to RAF Newton where I was what they called "interviewed" but it's what I call a fucking interrogation into the details of my sex life. Back then RAF Newton was where they trained all the military police. They're like the CID but much worse bastards.

Because of the charge I was on, they put me in a twelve-man barrack room. Only it was empty except for me, as of course I might infect other innocent men in the forces. I was locked in the room and I was told to get a good night's sleep and this is about six in the evening. They said they'd be interviewing me in the morning. However, at two-thirty in the morning they barged in, woke me up, dragged me out of bed, made me get dressed, took me over to the station headquarters and put me in an interview room. In this room was a desk, a two-way mirror and a video camera in the corner of the room. They said they were going to go and get a cup of tea and left me there for three hours. I started to fall asleep because I was tired, but, just as I fell asleep, they started to interview me and this went on for fifteen hours!

They wanted to know what I'd done with other members of the air force, and the answer was nothing because I hadn't of course. I was still technically a virgin. Even though I had some experiences when I was twelve with my friend, I was still a virgin, so I was telling them the truth. A lot of the questions were just ridiculous, like asking how do you lubricate a man for anal sex, and suggesting that I lick his arse and so on. Personally, back at that time, I did not have a clue about rimming and oral sex or things like that, and it was all alien to me. Even though I was gay, I hadn't actually done anything about it, and the whole idea of it I found disgusting. It was really totally degrading. I was thinking, how did they know all this stuff anyway?

I don't want any compensation or an apology. What's the point? I've been out of it now for nearly twenty years. I could fight it in the courts and have a six-year drawn-out battle with the government. I don't want to drag it all up again. It's in my memory box. I can think about it now and again when it comes up, like when I get asked about it.

But it changes the way you think about things. It made me think. I ended up involved in the age-of-consent demonstration in the Houses of Parliament. I can't remember the year exactly but it was about ninety-six or seven and I was there with some mates and it was quite a big crowd there, but the police hadn't really laid on any extra staff. They thought it'd be a nice quiet Passover. This was when we were trying to get the age of consent down from twenty-one to sixteen. The tossers in Parliament did not want to make it sixteen, only to eighteen, and then only with some reservations so nobody was happy with that. I mean, why the hell shouldn't we have an equal age of consent? You can shag a girl and get her pregnant and marry her, but you can't shag a bloke? It's ludicrous.

Anyway loads of "OutRage!" people were there and, no, I'm not one of those OutRage! people, because I think they're a bunch of wankers. Anyway, loads of people sat down in protest and the police threatened to charge everyone with obstruction. I was right behind the press pen on St Stephen's Gate and a couple of OutRage! guys behind me kept saying, "Let's storm the Bastille!" So I said, "Are you lot ready?" and they said, "Yeah, we're ready." I noticed that the lock was undone on the press pen gate so I thought, here we go, and I ran forward, did a drop kick on the doors to St Stephen's Gate, kicked the doors open and ran halfway up the stairs and got to the House of Commons and six coppers pounced on me. Then I was locked up for two hours in the Palace of Westminster police station.

Later on I was taken by van to Vine Street police station and was originally charged for inciting a riot, causing an affray and criminal damage. The charge of inciting a riot was eventually dropped because at the end of the day the police only managed to arrest ten people and apparently they have to nick twelve to make it a riot. So I got done with criminal damage for kicking the gates and causing an affray. Then I appeared in Bow Street Magistrates Court and four weeks later I was fined a hundred and fifty pounds and a further three hundred in costs. Capital Gay *which is now a defunct newspaper, paid for all the costs though and I think it's a shame they're gone, because they paid for everything and they had nothing to do with it. I suppose I have views on most aspects of gay life, based on my experiences.'*

(Interview by Craig Paul Johnson)

It wasn't until 1991 that the Armed Forces Select Committee finally heard evidence from Stonewall about gay men and lesbians in the armed forces and their experiences. This led to the Committee's recommendation that the ban on homosexuality should be dropped, and the law was changed in 1994 to match the same laws that apply in civilian life. However, this contradicted the Ministry of Defence policy which stated that 'Homosexuality is incompatible with military service' and all gay men and lesbians still faced automatic dismissal upon their discovery, leading to a loss of their job, pension and home, and a very public outing to their families and friends. However, when a group of former servicemen and women took their case to the European Court of Human Rights, it was judged that the MoD's position was unlawful, and in January 2000 the Defence Secretary announced that the ban on gay men and lesbians serving in the armed forces was officially lifted. But, of course, a change in the law doesn't necessarily change attitudes and perceptions, and while gay people can now openly serve in the RAF, Navy, Marines or Army, most people prefer to keep their sexuality to themselves in an environment where any deviation from accepted behaviour would be frowned upon, if not actively discouraged. Even now, three years after the ban was lifted, it's a brave man (or woman) who is out in the forces.

Links

Rank Outsiders (Armed Forces Lesbian & Gay Association)

www.rank-outsiders.org.uk

BCM Box 8431, London WC1N 3XX

CHRIS MORRIS

Think of gay rights campaigners and, rightly or wrongly, you inevitably imagine middle-aged men with beards or lesbians in dungarees. A significant exception to the cliché was a young and handsome Chris Morris who, at the tender age of just sixteen, was asked by Stonewall to become their representative for a test case in the European Court of Human Rights in support of the campaign for an equal age of consent. Chris willingly agreed, and spent much of the following two years being interviewed by media across the UK and Europe about his case:

'I tried to be honest. I believed that the root cause of most prejudice was ignorance and that the solution was therefore education. I wanted to challenge the stereotype of "dirty old men" chasing "vulnerable children" and persuade people that the unequal age of consent did not protect young gay people. Far from it, in fact the inequality created a climate where teenagers could not ask for advice, felt isolated and risked a criminal record for doing the same things that their straight friends

were doing quite legally. There was a symbolic message in that too: that being young and gay was wrong while being young and straight was right. By changing the law I believed we would be one step closer to smashing that belief.'

In order to support the campaign, Morris created a youth group called Youthspeak with additional support from Neal Cavalier-Smith (founder of Prowler Press) and actor Sir Ian McKellen. As part of their political efforts, they managed to get hold of Europe's most powerful display laser and beamed a huge '16' on to Big Ben, causing a great deal of media interest and more than a little attention from the Metropolitan Police (who ultimately only gave the group a parking ticket). As a result, the group received more than a thousand letters of support, and quite a few new members.

Ultimately, the case never reached Europe, after Home Secretary Jack Straw asked Morris to settle out of court, in order to avoid the difficulties and embarrassment of the government being found in breach of the European Convention of Human Rights. He promised the group that Parliament would schedule a vote on the age of consent, and some two years later, despite a rough ride in the House of Lords, the age of consent was finally lowered to sixteen in November 2000, just a few months after Chris's twenty-first birthday. Quite a present.

Morris also became co-creator and editor of a current affairs magazine called *Outcast*, a fascinating newsletter-style production which acted as a forum for gay activism and an outlet for honest debate on political matters. The mainstream 'free' and commercial gay magazines rarely gave much column space to gay activism (and still don't), and *Outcast* stirred up some proverbial hornets nests which other groups (and magazines) had carefully tried to steer around. Unfortunately, too much truth was a bad thing, and *Outcast* was eventually killed off by lack of advertising support, the potential sources of revenue being too scared to associate themselves with a magazine that was just that little bit too honest. Not surprisingly, after having (successfully) taken on the government and after having experienced the sometimes tragic hypocrisy and falseness of the so-called gay community, Morris eventually abandoned his interest in activism, and drifted away into the world of media production; a great shame and undoubtedly our loss.

Links

www.chrismorris.com

c/o 4d Media, 72 New Bond Street, London, W1S 1RR

DEREK JARMAN

A name from the past but one which should be remembered. Derek Jarman was an accomplished film maker responsible for some of the more controversial imagery of the seventies. His first film (*Sebastiane*) caused a huge stir when it was screened on television (it dealt with homosexuality in Roman times – you can just imagine), only to be upstaged by his 1977 production *Jubilee* – a no-holds-barred swipe at the monarchy with appearances from the likes of Adam Ant and Toyah Wilcox.

After announcing that he had been tested as HIV-positive, Jarman went on the offensive, and spoke openly and excessively about the subject, mostly to an establishment which really didn't want to listen. He continued his work with gay activist groups such as OutRage! while creating yet more controversial films such as *Caravaggio* (for which he won a Turner Prize) and the bizarre film *Blue*, which featured a plain blue screen, complete with voice-overs (symbolising the invisibility of the Aids virus). He died in 1994 but his legacy as a tireless and outspoken supporter of gay rights and Aids activism remains with us.

Link

www.sbu.ac.uk/~stafflag/derekjarman.html

OUTCAST

While the gay press continued to follow its own agenda, some parts of the gay community began to wonder when some alternative views of gay life might be heard. During the summer of 1999 a group of activists, who were frustrated by the quality of debate in the gay press, decided to set out and create a voice of their own, as an *Outcast* writer explains, 'Our dream was to create a magazine where no issue was off-limits; a magazine that dared to challenge the stereotypes and ask the questions that other queer titles were afraid to ask. None of us had any experience of running a magazine and only a few of us were published journalists, but we had plenty of energy and enthusiasm, and even more idealism. Some would call it naivety!'

The first issue hit the streets in September 1999, the *Observer* describing it as 'a band of brave souls confronting the culture of the gay ghetto'. Some 500 copies were sold and more than 6,500 given away, and, with such a good response, the team decided to continue for at least another six months. Established writers came on board and even politicians began to show some attention, with articles being submitted by the likes of Ken Livingstone, Ben Bradshaw and Charles Kennedy. Community groups were given space to promote their activities in each issue, in order to encourage recruitment and fundraising. But behind the scenes, things weren't so optimistic.

'From day one, our few advertisers were told that supporting Outcast *would mean that they would no longer receive special deals from other gay magazines. Rumours that we were going bust were constantly spread so that companies would not pre-pay for their advertising, making our cash flow position almost impossible. Yet, we survived financially with a handful of core supporters. Legal threats were our other main worry. When we dared to question the big players on the gay scene, their lawyers hit back hard. These people were not used to being criticised. We had several battles with lawyers who threatened to sue us over articles we published even though both articles were completely honest and accurate. We persuaded David Price, a well-respected libel expert, to fight our corner for free, and won the battles.*

Although we never lost a libel case, these long disputes ate at the heart of Outcast. *They undermined our morale and made people wary of getting involved – after all, they didn't want to be sued. Our original printer refused to print the magazine because he was afraid of "reprisal attacks" or legal action. We had to indemnify a new company, and the financial fallout meant that the magazine had to go bi-monthly from then on.* Outcast *collapsed almost exactly two years after it had begun. After the roller-coaster ride, most of the key people involved felt they'd done enough. Apart from our proof reader everyone had given their time for free and we'd neglected our jobs, partners and social lives as a result. We needed to move on to new challenges.'*

Viewpoints

'Foolishly, Outcast *refused to pay the protection money demanded by the all-powerful gayest cartels who have kidnapped homosexuality and chained it up in a boutique of bad taste, self-serving dogma, cringing advertorial and Geri Halliwell fanzines.'*

Mark Simpson (writer)

Link

www.outcastmagazine.co.uk

BARONESS YOUNG

Oh bless, poor old Baroness Janet Young died at the age of 75 in September 2002. If it was anyone else we might have had a twinge of remorse or sadness at her departure, but this lady was different. On the face of it, she was a sweet old dear, devoted to her religion and her belief in the traditional values of marriage and families. All very worthy, of course, and her colleagues lined up to praise her political achievements. Lord Strathclyde stated that she carried out her job (as Leader of the House of

Lords) with 'deep respect for a Parliament she truly loved'. Unfortunately her respect didn't extend to homosexuals, and her years in the Lords were largely devoted to fierce opposition to anything and everything which supported gay rights. She was the woman who fought to keep Section 28 and to retain an unequal age of consent, and she was planning to cause even more mayhem by fighting new gay adoption laws, partnership rights, employment rights and partnership equality. She was, by any standards, a thoroughly nasty piece of work.

But no matter, she's dead now and, as columnist Sebastian Sandys commented (after announcing his delight at her death), 'We are not required to be sad that she died. The silly notion that you should not speak ill of the dead doesn't apply.' He's right. Baroness Young devoted the latter years of her life to spiteful, hateful and hurtful discrimination against gay people. She made no apologies for doing so, and consistently boasted that she was right to defend her hatred of all things gay, simply on the basis that her religion (supposedly) condoned her action. But thankfully even her most energetic attempts to sway media and public opinion failed miserably, thanks to one development which even she couldn't manipulate to suit her own ends – she died. Go figure. There really should be bus tours to go and dance on her grave. Good riddance.

Link

politics.guardian.co.uk/politicsobituaries/story/0,1441,787506,00.html

ANGELA MASON

Born in 1944, Angela has long been the public face of campaign group Stonewall, although she's been involved with gay rights activism since the 1970s, and was most famously accused (and acquitted) of being a member of the Angry Brigade bombing campaign. Unusually, Angela was in fact married (to scriptwriter William Randolph Mason) but later began a long-term relationship with fellow Gay Liberation Movement member Elizabeth Wilson. Awarded an OBE for 'services to homosexual rights' in 1999, Angela is undoubtedly a nice person. But the jury is firmly out as to whether she was possibly just a little bit too nice for the job that she actually did.

Stonewall is at the forefront of gay rights campaigning and Angela Mason is regularly called upon to speak on behalf of Stonewall and, therefore, the gay community. Putting our case clearly and politely on the television news was her forte but perhaps ultimately we need someone with a bigger mouth and a slightly harder attitude. In a world where politics-of-the-megaphone rule, maybe 'nice' is not such a good thing?

Angela has moved on to a seriously well-paid job with the government (the DTI) as the Director of the Women and Equality Unit (whatever that is), a significant development which has encouraged more than a few anti-Stonewall cynics to suggest that the group's relationship with the government is bordering upon incest. But more important is Angela's successor. Let's hope that Stonewall make the right choice.

Link

www.sbu.ac.uk/stafflag/angelamason.html

THE CHURCH

It doesn't take much understanding of global history to conclude that most of the world's major wars, mass murders and generations of institutionalised hatred have been created and nurtured by the Church. Religion might be a personal thing but it's also everybody's problem when people get killed or persecuted because of it. Homosexuality has traditionally been one subject which the Church has loved to hate, and even today, in the supposedly enlightened new millennium, the Church is the last bastion of homophobia. While the whole country seems to have moved on and perceptibly 'got over' the national fear or dislike of the whole gay thing, the Church resolutely clings on to its medieval hatred and sanctimony. The very best you can hope for is a 'we don't hate you but we don't approve of what you're doing' pronouncement. How fucking generous of you. Who asked for the Church's opinion anyway? What right does the Church (of whatever religion) have to cast us as sinners? Did God give them a written certificate of authority? Nope, we suffer Church-fed national hatred on the basis of a slightly dubious book.

Maybe one day the Angel Gabriel will descend at the head of a Pride March (but what would he wear?) and say, 'You guys pack that in right now.' Can you imagine the 'I-Told-You-So' parties in every church hall? In this debate, which has gone round in ever-decreasing circles, only one thing is certain; nobody, but nobody, has ever had so much as an email from God, so why do we even have to listen to these deluded, drag-obsessed hymn singers?

Link

www.rainbowquery.com/Categories/Religion.html

www.stonewallrevisited.com (nauseating religious 'gay alternative' site)

www.bibble.org/gay/religious.html (religion and homosexuality)

BRIAN PADDICK

It's not often that you get a policeman telling the whole world that he's gay. OK, we all know that there are just as many gay people in the police force as in any other walk of life, but like so many other supposedly 'macho' professions, you're supposed to be straight and act straight. Being gay isn't (or at least wasn't until recently) an option. But things are changing and, when a senior (and rather dishy) commander announces that he's gay, you know that something significant is happening.

Unfortunately for Brian, his relaxed and open attitude towards his sexuality also applied to other parts of his life, leading him to advocate the now infamous 'softly-softly' approach to cannabis use in Lambeth which effectively saved the police a huge amount of time and money. Sensible though the move undoubtedly was, the media lapped up the story with glee and, when Brian's former lover thoughtfully revealed that Brian had (allegedly) smoked cannabis and allowed it to be smoked in his home, the *Daily Mail* and all the other media vultures swooped down on their prey. Of course, it wasn't so much the drug use that got the *Mail* so excited; it was the fact that Paddick was gay, happily and openly so, and nobody even cared (and how frustrating was that for so many anti-gay commentators?). The *Mail* (and others like them) simply used the cannabis story as a stick with which to beat him, and they succeeded.

Paddick's moved on to a desk job and the homophobic newspapers have scored another victory. Some things never change. But we can take some encouragement from the saga. Paddick was the police force's most senior openly gay officer, and there must be many more men in the police's hierarchy who will have noted that, in the final analysis, being gay wasn't the actual reason for Paddick's downfall. We'll just wait for a few more closet doors to open.

Links

www.urban75.org/paddick

www.partyvibe.com/articles/brian_paddick.htm

www.mpa.gov.uk/issues/paddick/default.htm

CIVIL PARTNERSHIPS

Just when we had all resigned ourselves to the fact that New Labour had spectacularly failed to do anything to support gay rights, a whole raft of measures have suddenly appeared, all aimed at providing equality for gay men and lesbians. One of the most significant is the plan to amend partnership laws, so that registered couples can be afforded the same legal rights as a married heterosexual man and woman. What would this mean? Well, it would enable a gay partner to be recognised as a legal next-of-kin, so that hospital visiting rights and decisions on treatments can be made (at present, partners are only admitted to hospitals on a discretionary basis). It would allow same-sex partners to register a death, and it would allow automatic inheritance of property which would currently be passed to blood relatives. Even with a will, the transfer of property would currently incur an inheritance tax of 40 per cent, but with the new law, property would be transferred without tax, as within a normal marriage. Likewise if a partner who is in receipt of a public sector pension dies, a recognised partner would still benefit from it.

So, there are many advantages to the status of marriage which currently don't apply to gay couples but, with a change in the law, we will finally be treated equally. Ironically, the new law may not apply to unmarried straight couples, on the basis that they do have the option to marry should they wish to do so. It's not often that a law discriminates in our favour, is it?

Viewpoint

'It's time that we were finally treated the same. I have never been interested in the "gay marriage" thing because it's just stupid and embarrassing. It was always just for show because it had no legal status, and besides it just seemed like gay people were just trying to imitate straight people. But a recognised partnership for legal reasons makes much more sense. I don't suppose we're all worrying about whether we get property left to us or whether we can visit a partner in hospital, because we tend not to think about things like that. But I suppose it's the principle that we will be treated the same as any other couple which is the important thing.'

Ian (32, labourer), Manchester

Links

uk.gay.com/article/news

www.christian.org.uk/pressreleases/2002/december_6_2002.htm

SEX LAWS

We've endured ludicrously unworkable sex laws since 1885 when sex between men officially became illegal. Strangely, lesbianism was never covered by the law, supposedly because dear ol' Queen Victoria steadfastly refused to believe that dykes even existed. But while the ladies could legally have some girl-on-girl action, the nation's gay men were subjected to over a century of persecution. Finally, it's all about to end. The act of cruising (hanging around with the intention of picking up a guy) will no longer be illegal, nor will the act of 'procuring a homosexual act' (that's 'cottaging' to you and me). Likewise, buggery (eek!) will also be legalised between consenting couples and it will also become perfectly legal for a gay couple to perform a sex act in an 'isolated place where one would reasonably expect not to be observed'.

Indeed, the aim of the law reform is to sweep away all of the ridiculous old rules and replace them by a simple all-embracing law that covers both gay and straight couples, making 'overtly sexual behaviour in public' an offence punishable by up to six months in prison. But, of course, the new laws will still have to be interpreted and it will undoubtedly be fascinating to see how the police and judiciary handle things.

It seems pretty clear that the new laws will enable the police to forget about the expensive and time-wasting business of chasing guys who cruise parks and toilets late at night, on the basis that such places are clearly defined as 'isolated' at least at night. On the other hand, it suggests that any overtly sexual goings-on in the same place during daylight hours might be treated rather differently. But the reforms have a vague smell of common sense about them and, even if the definition of 'overt sexual behaviour' is open to debate, at least there will no longer be any opportunity to apply the definition purely towards homosexuality. So maybe we have finally made some progress after all.

Viewpoints

'The law's always been stacked against gay men, and a change has been a long time overdue in my view. These days it's just absurd that the police are overstretched trying to combat crime, and at the same time they're sending people out to catch two blokes having sex in a park in the middle of the night. How stupid is that? I think the only possible problem with new laws is that you might get some spiteful bastards complaining to the police that somebody's engaging in overt sexual behaviour in a place where they can expect to be seen, like if they stand on a ladder and look over a hedge or something. You know how petty some people can be. But I think a change in the law will encourage the police to just move on and forget about cruising and cottaging and all that crap. It doesn't go on as much these days anyway, so we might finally just forget about it.'

Stephen (39, unemployed), Bristol

'Did anybody ever have any logical reason why you could get arrested for having a wank with some bloke in a toilet? Why would that be an offence? It was between the two people who were doing it so it was just objectionable that you had police entrapment and monitoring going on as if there was some big criminal activity going on. There are shootings, drugs, muggings, robberies, and all the police can do is check if some bloke's got his knob out in a park? It's about time the law was changed and the police found something better to do. I don't know how this "overt sexual behaviour" thing will work but as long as it applies to straight people too then I see no reason to object. I've seen plenty of straight

people screwing so maybe they should start nicking them instead, that would be a twist.'

Nigel (25, driver), Newcastle

Link

uk.gay.com/channel/news

ALAN DUNCAN

It's questionable whether an MP deserves a mention in any book just for being gay, but Alan Duncan deserves a comment if only because he was the first Conservative MP to come out of what must be a fairly crowded closet. He announced that he had no regrets about coming out and that he hoped 'the reaction this has prompted will make some in the Conservative party realise that we do need to design a social agenda for the modern world which includes a proper understanding of issues such as this'. Sadly, he also added that being both gay and a Tory didn't necessarily mean abandonment of policies such as Section 28, military service or gay marriages. 'Some of the demands made by the left over the last few years are not necessarily ones which we need to share.' Oh dear, maybe it's naive to expect too much too quickly. But it's a start.

Viewpoint

'It's a bit sad really that some MP announcing he's gay is even worthy of mention. It just illustrates how homophobic the Tories are, and while you have to congratulate the guy on saying he's gay, you just know it doesn't make the slightest bit of difference to anything. The Tories are always going to cater for church-goers, stuffy old gits, **Daily Mail** ***readers and all the sad old people in society who think they can blame all the country's problems on homosexuality. You can feel a bit of compassion for the younger Tories who believe in equality but you have to wonder how deluded they are if they think that the Tories are anything but institutionalised homophobes. That's not to say that Labour is any better because they're not really. They're not anti-gay but they're so terrified of media opinion that they're frightened to do anything pro-gay in case the papers object.'***

Sam (student, 19), Manchester

Link

www.alanduncan.org.uk

HATE CRIMES

The Crown Prosecution Service has finally decided to do something to support gay victims of crime. For many years, while racial attacks have been dealt with effectively and severely, gay hate crimes have largely been overlooked. A survey revealed that some 38 per cent of the gay community has suffered at least one homophobic incident over the previous twelve months and, of those, only eighteen per cent actually reported the crime to the police. Attorney General, Lord Goldsmith QC, said, 'Homophobic crimes strike at people's right to feel safe and secure, and to abuse someone because of their sexual orientation and gender identity is a hate crime that cannot be tolerated. The CPS is sending a clear message to those who commit such crime that they will be dealt with firmly under criminal law.' Cool.

Link

www.cps.gov.uk

OSCAR WILDE

You could probably fill a whole book exclusively with details of all the great and famous people throughout history who have dabbled with partners of the same gender. But some people have to be mentioned, simply because of their influence on our lives. Ignoring his celebrated career as an outstanding writer, Oscar Wilde is the shining example of out gayness, defiantly camp and effeminate in an age when homosexuality wasn't even mentioned for fear of persecution or prosecution. But, of course, the real Oscar probably didn't live up to the larger-than-life image which modern gay society tends to attach to him. It's worth remembering that he married and had two sons, and lived a shady life of closet rendezvous with rent boys until meeting his long-term lover Lord Alfred Douglas, the infamous 'Bosie'.

Oscar's flamboyant attitude, outrageous wit and sarcasm, plus an all-too-obvious liking for boys, managed to get him embroiled in court actions; the first trial was a libel case against Bosie's father, the Marques of Queensbury, who accused Wilde of 'posing as a sodomite'. After the defence named ten young men who could testify to Oscar's various acts of indiscretion, the Marques was cleared of the charge, but it was clear that the muck-slinging of the first trial would lead to another, now that the details of Oscar's private life had been publicised. Even the Marques expected him to flee the country (he sent Wilde a note stating that he would 'not prevent your flight but, if you take my son with you, I will shoot you like a dog') but Oscar stayed, and he was arrested and charged (the so-called Labouchere Amendment made any act of indecency between two men illegal, if the jury were suitably offended). His defence was a speech which, even for Oscar, was particularly eloquent:

'The Love that dare not speak its name in this country is such a great affection of an elder for a younger man as there was between David and Jonathan, such as Plato made the very basis of his philosophy, and such as you find in the sonnets of Michelangelo and Shakespeare. It is that deep, spiritual affection that is as pure as it is perfect . . . It is in this century misunderstood, so much misunderstood that it may be described as the Love that dare not speak its name, and on account of it I am placed where I am now. It is beautiful, it is fine; it is the noblest form of affection. There is nothing unnatural about it, and it repeatedly exists between an elder and a younger man, when the elder has intellect and the younger man has all the joy, hope and glamour of life before him. That it should be so, the world does not understand. The world mocks at it and sometimes puts one in the pillory for it'.

Great words indeed, but the speech illustrates how Oscar still didn't exactly shout to the world that he was actively having sex with other men. The trial was abandoned but restarted some time later. Wilde still avoided any admission that he had engaged in any sexual activity and it wasn't until he admitted to not kissing a boy 'because he was ugly' that the case began to turn against him. When testimonies of sex with male prostitutes were given in court the case was made against Wilde and he was sentenced to two years' hard labour.

Oscar served his sentence before going into exile in Paris, but his years in jail had taken their toll, and an ear infection eventually led to the development of meningoencehpalitis, from which he died in November 1900. Oscar's life was a testimony to the cruel and evil attitude towards homosexuality which existed in Britain a hundred years ago. It's slightly disturbing that even as recently as 1994 the then Home Secretary Michael Howard refused to seek a Royal Pardon for Wilde. So maybe we haven't progressed quite as far as we like to think we have.

Links

www.oscariana.net

www.showgate.com/tots/gross/wildeweb.html

PETER TATCHELL

Unquestionably one of the most influential figures in gay politics, Peter Tatchell is the *bête noire* of the modern British gay scene. Unafraid to ask the most difficult of questions, Peter rejects all notions of assimilation, acceptance and integration. He's all about rights, activism and defiance. His brand of in-your-face gay confrontation is a hard pill to swallow but, while we collectively cover our eyes and ears, Peter meets the challenge head-on.

No wonder the gay community wrestles with its conscience every time Peter's name is mentioned. Do we love him or do we despise him?

Although Australian by birth, Tatchell is very much a British institution. Inspired by the 1969 Stonewall riots, he first came out in that same year at the age of just seventeen and, after moving to England (having refused to participate in the Vietnam War), he joined the Gay Liberation Front in 1971.

The GLF was Britain's first political movement of openly gay people, committed to actually changing society, rather than assimilating into the status quo. Rejecting pleas for tolerance, they demanded acceptance – but on our terms. With more than a little help from Peter, the GLF began all manner of disruptive, attention-getting activities ranging from pub sit-ins (in venues where they had refused to serve 'lezzies and puffs') through to protests and demonstrations in all the right places.

In 1972 Peter was manhandled out of a lecture being made by one of the world's leading psychiatrists (Hans Eysenck), who advocated the use of electric shock treatment to 'cure' homosexuals. But following this (and protests in Harley Street) the medical profession eventually were persuaded to drop the designation of homosexuality as a mental illness.

A year later, Peter was in East Berlin at the World Youth Festival, where he smuggled thousands of gay rights leaflets into the oppressive communist state. Despite attempts to drag him off stage, he made a defiant speech on gay liberation at a Youth Rights conference. He also tried to lay a pink triangle wreath at a former concentration camp but the government blocked the action. He was interrogated (and assaulted) by the East German Police, and he narrowly avoided arrest when he carried a homosexual liberation banner through Alexanderplatz – the first such act in a Soviet Bloc country which ultimately led to the first gay rights groups in the GDR (and indeed any communist nation).

Famously, Tatchell stood as a Labour candidate in the 1983 Bermondsey by-election. He suffered assaults, abuse, media smears, dirty tricks; people displaying his election poster had their windows smashed; and even his home address and telephone number was advertised through anonymous leaflets, denouncing him as a traitor, a queer and an extremist with the accompanying plea to the reader to 'have a go'. Sweet. Bermondsey became a by-word for bigotry. But no matter, the whole episode simply inspired Peter to devote himself full-time to campaigning for 'queer human rights'.

Following the onset of the Aids crisis, Peter produced a trail-blazing self-help book (*Aids – A Guide To Survival*) which offered hope to many while convention offered only defeatism and fatalism. His work helped change views on Aids, and he also founded the UK Aids Vigil Organisation – the first movement to campaign for civil liberties for people living with HIV and Aids.

In 1988 he helped co-ordinate a 12,000-strong candlelight procession at the World Health Minister's Summit on Aids in London. In 1990 Peter co-founded OutRage! – a direct-action group sceptical of both mainstream society and orthodox gay culture. His research helped explode the myth that homosexuality had been legalised in 1967 by revealing that prosecutions in 1989 were almost as high as in 1954–55 and encouraged the police to de-prioritise action against gay behaviour. He also pressed the police to do more to curb queer-bashing incidents and he was instrumental in setting up the first liaison forum between the police and the gay community, and the first police monitoring and recording of homophobic attacks.

In 1994, Peter hit the headlines again with the publication of his book *Safer Sexy*. It was the world's first truly comprehensive guide to safer sex for gay and bisexual men and it was the most sexually explicit book ever published in Britain (gay or straight). Controversially, in the same year he began campaigning for the age of consent to be brought down to fourteen for everyone, on the basis that young people's first sexual experience often took place around this age, and that it was wrong to criminalise people for consensual behaviour. Even more controversy surrounded Peter later in the year (and in 1995) when he and OutRage! declared their intention to 'out' public figures who attacked the gay community. Outside the General Synod of the Church of England, OutRage! staged the most successful outing campaign ever, naming ten Church of England bishops who were accused of hypocrisy and collusion with homophobic policies. The media turned on Tatchell, but within two weeks the Church began its first serious dialogue with the gay community. For eight years, the then Archbishop of Canterbury Dr George Carey refused to meet with lesbian and gay organisations and, on Easter Sunday 1998, Peter (and six other OutRage! members) famously interrupted the Archbishop's Easter sermon and walked into the pulpit with protest placards. This shaming of the Archbishop encouraged Carey to have his first meeting with gay groups, and also to tone down his public advocacy of discrimination against homosexuals.

In more recent years, Peter has turned his attention to the homophobic policies of Robert Mugabe, ambushing his motorcade in London in 1999. He attempted to arrest Mugabe under charges related to the 1984 UN Convention Against Torture, but, needless to say, the police arrested Tatchell instead. However, his action gave gay rights in both Zimbabwe and at home some welcome attention, and many media commentators who had habitually criticised Tatchell for years suddenly hailed him as a hero.

His activities continue, and nobody can predict where Peter's unique style of political debate will take him next. His confrontational attitude might make many lesser mortals wish he'd make a little less fuss, but his direct approach has been effective – possibly more effective than some other gay rights groups (and the gay media) might care to admit. But whether or not you agree with his tactics, you can't disagree with his views or his aims. He's our hero.

Viewpoints

'A national hero'

Sunday Times

'Heroic . . . an example to us all . . . the Peter Tatchell left bruised and bloodied in a Brussels gutter is a better man than the EU politicians who have been fawning over Mugabe . . . Mr Tatchell has the courage of his convictions. They owe allegiance only to hypocrisy.'

Daily Mail

'Peter Tatchell has done more to keep gay rights on the agenda over the last decade than anyone.'

Time Out

'His impact has been immense . . . brave, honest and absolutely sincere in his determination to build an unprejudiced world.'

Lord Hattersley

'He's very necessary . . . incredibly brave . . . doing good work in a world where most people are too timid.'

Sir Elton John

'I hate him. Who the hell elected Tatchell as gay people's spokesman, and who is he to go about outing people and saying what we should and shouldn't do? It's not his business who wants to come out and who doesn't, and when he starts protesting and getting on the television I think he just embarrasses us all.'

Terry (unemployed, 23), Cardiff

'He's a fucking hero that guy. All these bleeding hearts that go on about how he shouldn't protest and show us up, and how he shouldn't out people and all that. I just think "get a fucking life" I mean, he's doing it for us and he's made things happen. The media loves people like Tatchell because he makes a scene, and that's got to be good for us, if it gets gay rights on the agenda.'

Mike (clerk, 26), Birmingham

'I think it's just become fashionable to hate Tatchell, like he's a part of history now, but what he does is in order to get justice for gay people, so it's no good just wishing he'd not campaign like he does, because it's his way and, even if you don't like it, you have to accept that he's made things happen. So good on him I say.'

Mark (unemployed, 22), London

'That man deserves an award. He gets nothing but crap from gay people and the gay press, and all the national papers hate him, but he just keeps on making a stand. You have to admire his guts. The only reason gay people often hate him is because he's too in-your-face and they're all like part-time gays that pretend to be straight most of the time, and they don't like what he stands for. But Tatchell's got his head screwed on right; it's these pissy closet types that need to sort themselves out and stop knocking a bloke for doing some good.'

John (designer, 33), London

Links

www.petertatchell.net

www.tatchellrightsfund.org

PTHRF, PO Box 35253, London, E1 4YF

MARGARET THATCHER

Bad old Maggie, we hate her; she's the devil incarnate. Well, OK, that's the message we get from the gay press every time her name is mentioned, but that's just lazy homo journalism for you. Somebody decided that they didn't like Maggie and that was it – we all jump on the bandwagon without a moment's thought. OK, she was a prize cow, and if you don't agree with her politics then that's fine, you don't have to.

She was famously responsible for overseeing the introduction of the much-hated Section 28, but let's not imagine for a minute that she personally wrote the clause. She supported it undoubtedly, but you've got to accept that she had a point of view based on her upbringing and values. Agree with her or not, Margaret knew how to make things happen. She was a matriarchal icon, a defiant, stubborn battleaxe wrapped up in patriotism, and love her or hate her you had to respect her. Unlike so many other prime ministers, Margaret had balls. She said what she thought, and she did what she said she'd do, and that kind of approach is pretty rare in British politics. So let's get off this stupid notion that if you're queer you've got to hate Maggie Thatcher. It's so last-decade.

Links

www.margaretthatcher.com

www.margaretthatcher.org

IAN MCKELLEN

Sir Ian certainly doesn't need any introduction unless you've avoided television, cinema and theatre for the past thirty years or so, but perhaps more significantly (at least as far as us homos are concerned) he is one of a very rare breed of celebrities who are not only firmly out of the closet, but also happy to say so loudly and proudly. He has, in fact, been open about his sexuality for a very long time although at one stage he didn't discuss the subject with his family or the media, as he recalls: '. . . neither of whom showed much interest in my sexuality, whatever it might have been. Probably because for most people in England, sex is a tricky topic.'

However, in 1988 he was involved in a BBC Radio 4 discussion on the subject of the then new Section 28 clause and during the programme he effectively came out to the whole nation, and almost from that moment he became an enthusiastic activist, as part of the wider on-going movement to change UK laws that discriminate against gay men and lesbians. He was a co-founder of Stonewall and he still regularly supports many of their projects. He's also now very happy to discuss homosexuality with the media, although he still tries to avoid too much detail of his private life, on the basis that it involves other people: 'I prefer to restrict my public views to what I know best – acting and activism.' Most recently he took a swipe at Tony Blair's government, accusing them of being no better than their Tory predecessors, who he described as 'woefully ignorant'.

Ironically it was Margaret Thatcher who awarded Sir Ian his knighthood as he recalls: 'I'll always be glad I was offered it after I'd come out and Maggie knew she was giving it to an openly gay man – not a species she is renowned for favouring.' A well-deserved knighthood if ever there was one.

Links

www.mckellen.com

ROBERT MUGABE

Where do you start with an arsehole like Robert Mugabe? This is not the place to discuss his human rights record, suffice to say that he's a truly nasty little pig-faced dictator, with a thing about homosexuality. He makes no apology for outlawing homosexuality in Zimbabwe (we're worse than pigs, according to Bobby), and makes all manner of grand pronouncements about how vile we are, and how we're worse than animals, and how we should be punished, blah, blah . . . Well, at least we don't spend our time killing people in the pursuit of political power.

But even though we should worry about repression in other countries, Mugabe is, thankfully, really not our problem. The trouble is, he's a player on the world stage and he's occasionally welcomed to our shores by our deliciously two-faced government, who haven't got the guts to tell him to, er, fuck right off.

Peter Tatchell famously likes to risk injury or even death by making a fuss whenever Mugabe sticks his ugly head outside of Zimbabwe, and the free world should be grateful to him for doing so, because somebody surely ought to highlight the hypocrisy of our government, and Tatchell seems to be the only guy with enough guts to actually do it. Ironic really when you consider that Peter is supposed to be one of the girly 'limp-wrist' brigade, according to the newspapers, and he turns out to have more integrity than the media and the politicians put together.

What is it with Mugabe anyway? What's his problem? He's even started accusing Tony Blair of being a little bit pink. Maybe this evil little sour-faced dictator has some personal issues to deal with? Who knows, he probably dances round his Presidential suite in a pair of red stilettos and a blonde wig when he's all alone. Not a pleasant thought, is it?

Link

mugabe.netfirms.com/index.htm (not an official site as you'll see)

EMPLOYMENT RIGHTS

Together with new laws on partnership rights, hate crimes and sex offences, employment rights for gay men and lesbians are also receiving some long-overdue attention. Officials are currently consulting various bodies about the creation of a new employment law which will make it illegal to sack an employee because he or she is gay. Additionally, the new law will also apply to an employment environment where employees are able to take action if they are in a bad workplace culture where nobody is doing anything about the problem, even if no anti-gay action is being made directly against them.

But as you might imagine, it's not going to be completely plain sailing. The government also proposes including an opt-out clause for 'genuine occupational reason'. This means that religious groups in particular will be able to refuse employment if they can offer a legitimate reason as to why a gay man or woman might not be suitable for the job. Stonewall believes that it will be very difficult to justify such refusals but many religious groups will, of course, be able to use their beliefs and teachings as plausible excuses for refusing work to gay people. Likewise, Terry Sanderson of the Gay and Lesbian Humanist Association comments that 'the government is encouraging faith groups to take a greater role in running welfare and support services. This means that many more jobs that are nothing to do with religion will fall under their control. The jobs of gay people in some of these organisations will be at severe risk.' Interesting times are on the way.

Links

Lesbian and Gay Employment Rights (LAGER)

www.lager.dircon.co.uk

Unit 1G, Leroy House, 436 Essex Road, London, N1 3QP

Gay & Lesbian Humanist Association

www.galha.freeserve.co.uk

MICHAEL CASHMAN

Best known as the actor who played the part of an openly gay character in the BBC soap *EastEnders*, Cashman is one of a rare breed of celebrities who are openly gay and proud to say so. He was a founding member of Stonewall and became their Chair in 1988. His interest in politics led to his election as a (Labour) Member of the European Parliament in 1999 and he continues to support gay rights as part of his political career. He's also had the dubious distinction of living with death threats, having been put on the National Front's 'hit list' (how's that for an honour?) following his outspoken stand against Section 28. The police also informed Cashman that he was being targeted by George Rees, a delightful character who was eventually locked up for the attempted murder of a gay man. Who said gay politics were dull?

Links

www.michaelcashmanmep.org.uk

Terry Duffy House, Thomas Street, West Bromwich, B70 6PY

2: Sex

Sex is the defining subject which we can't escape but which we still carefully tiptoe around. By definition, it's what 'gay' is all about, and yet we dismiss the subject as if it's just a minor part of our lives. Unless we're between the sheets, that is. We share a huge variety of conflicting views on sex, as illustrated by the colourful comments of Leon, a Yorkshire-based writer:

'Sex. Messy, isn't it? Well, it certainly should be in my opinion, or else you're probably doing it all wrong. All those fluids splattering about, and bodies throwing themselves around; sweat mixing with sweat, saliva with saliva, and all culminating together in one great big sloppy, sticky, oily mess. As far as I know, I think that is the way it is supposed to be, the way it was meant to be when sex was originally accepted as a method of sharing intense pleasure.

However, in my not too limited experience, that isn't the way things seem to be with many people. Anything exciting or interesting seems to have been outlawed somehow, and instead of good fun we have a whole list of unwritten rules. Sex, it seems, must be simple, quiet, clean and completely lacking in any form of passion or excitement. Isn't that how straight people do it? As gay men and women I wonder whether we shouldn't be pioneers, as we are with many other aspects of life like fashion, music, art and so on. But no, it seems not and, for now at least, the majority of the gay community (although do we actually have a community?) loftily frown on those that still take pleasure in all the 'naughty' things, like the dangerous but exciting act of public cruising. It shouldn't ever be forgotten that this form of meeting between gay men is in fact our heritage, whether we want to accept it or not, but we have reformulated our position within society and carefully reinvented ourselves as pseudo-straights. It's like politics. Once it was Labour against the Tories, but now there is a grey middle ground with New Labour. Likewise, once there were gays and straights; but now we are watered-down shadows of the majority. The New Queers.

Our ways of sexual contact and fulfilment have always been worlds apart from the 'others' but now we're expected to conform and integrate. In the light of a new century, in order for our sexuality to be acceptable, we find ourselves forced to conform to straight sexual values in as many ways as possible. We don't talk about anal sex (bumming, sodomy, buggery or whatever the straights delight in calling it) and we certainly don't talk of actually enjoying oral sex. Imagine. Likewise we pray that nobody ever asks for the precise details of rimming.

We even seem to take on full responsibility for the evil that is HIV and Aids. Of course, we didn't invent it, and we are certainly not the only section of the population which has been affected by it. But as a way of seeking a tolerant treatment we collectively bow apologetically in front of our heterosexual counterparts; an apology for something over which we had no more control than anyone else.

Believe me I have nothing against straight people or their sexual practices. Why should I? But they aren't us, and we're not them, so why should we limit ourselves to their ways and mind-sets? Why should we even try? Maybe I am a rebel, but I take sexual pleasure, quite unashamedly, in anything that turns me on, regardless of acceptability and no matter how it may look in the eyes of the 'normal' people. We are different, when it comes to sex at least, if not in any other aspect. We have different moral values and differing ways of looking at the very purpose of sex, let alone the actual act.'

Indeed. Take a deep breath and dive into the wild world of gay sex.

ABSTINENCE

Without doubt, the safest sex of all, abstinence is the way to go if you're unsure about your sexual preferences, scared of health risks or just too damned choosy. Just don't do it or do it all alone and make love to someone who you will respect in the morning. You'd be forgiven for thinking that abstinence was a dirty word in gay circles, but lots of gay men and women choose not to, thank you very much. For whatever reason, the choice is there, and let's be honest, there's a whole world of stimulus out there (books, magazines, internet, videos) for those of us who don't dig dating.

Link

www.self-improvement-personal-development.com/p_sex.html

AIDS

Where do you begin? Back in 1959, in fact, when the first cases of pneumocystitis crinij pneumonia (or PCP if you don't want to get tongue-tied) was recorded in the Congo. The disease attacks the victim's blood system, destroying T-cells resulting, as we all now know, in a breakdown of the body's immune system, so that even relatively mundane viruses suddenly have the potential to kill. Ten years later, a teenage prostitute in the USA died after developing Kaposi's sarcoma (a hitherto rare form of cancer). A further ten years on and gay men in both the USA and Sweden developed the same disease, followed by more cases of PCP in America just a year later. By 1980 it had been established that both types of disease were effectively connected to a wider epidemic, which finally received a name in 1982 – Acquired Immunodeficiency Syndrome or Aids.

Research established that this huge world-wide problem first developed in Africa (where more than 15 million people have since died as a result) but first reached continental USA via just one man, often referred to as 'Patient Zero', a Canadian airline steward called Gaetan Dugas who is presumed to have contracted the virus which leads to Aids (HIV or Human Immunodeficiency Virus – first isolated by the Pasteur Institute in 1983) while in Africa, and brought it back to Canada, from where it rapidly spread through the USA and beyond.

By 1983 the media had got hold of the Aids story in a big way. Large numbers of gay men were being killed while thousands more were contracting HIV. It was a gift to homophobes, right-wing bigots and religious leaders across the world. Here it was – the Divine Judgement, the Great Gay Plague. By the mid-1980s the first Aids-related deaths had occurred in the UK – the epidemic was out of control with no cure and no way to even halt its progress.

It wasn't until 1987 that the first drug appeared which was designed to combat the effects of HIV – Zidovudine (or AZT Retrovir) with a price tag of $10,000 for just a year's supply, making it the most expensive drug in history. This led to even more controversy, with accusations of profiteering and political genocide.

Things got ugly. President Bush called for mandatory Aids testing; San Francisco bus drivers wore face masks (thanks to ludicrous press reports that HIV could be contracted through airborne transmission) and Delta Airlines banned Aids victims from their aircraft (although a boycott quickly got them to change their minds). US Immigration closed the US to people with Aids and civil disobedience was widespread as gay activism groups took to the streets. In Britain, every household received a copy of the now infamous 'Aids – Don't Die of Ignorance' leaflet which did more to terrorise the public than actually educate them. Meanwhile, Princess Diana opened the first English hospital Aids ward (and, controversially, dared to shake patients' hands without wearing gloves).

The epidemic continued unchecked. Amongst gay communities across the world, safe sex messages were everywhere, but of course there was no way of knowing how many people had already become infected with HIV in the days before the safe sex message had been hammered home. By 1991 more than 10 million people were estimated to be HIV-positive.

But what of the present? The climate of Aids hysteria has subsided, even though the number of people infected with HIV continues to climb. Why the change? Primarily, it's the development of drugs which has enabled the disease to be kept under control, even though there is still no actual cure.

The results have been tangible; not so many years ago, most gay men knew somebody who had died of Aids, and we became almost accustomed to people suddenly disappearing from the gay scene, only to later learn that they had, as feared, died from an 'Aids-related illness'. But thankfully those dark days have largely gone and most HIV-positive people manage to live with the virus, although some manage to do so more comfortably than others. Drugs are controlling the epidemic but they're not curing it, and a daily cocktail of pills is no picnic – the side-effects can be pretty severe.

Even more disturbing is the way that the control of Aids has encouraged people simply to ignore the whole subject: after all, if you don't know anybody who has actually died from the disease, then it must be 'sorted' and so why should we care? The truth is that the disease thrives unchecked, and the relative ignorance of a new generation is allowing the notion of unsafe sex to become almost acceptable. You can see the way that things have changed if you just log into Gaydar's member profiles. How many times do you read the 'Practise Safe Sex?' line, and the profile's owner has replied, 'sometimes'. What is that all about? What is going on? Safe sex is no longer mandatory? It's no wonder that infection rates are beginning to rise again.

Another concern is the even more significant rise in HIV infection amongst straight people. In some ways it was vaguely gratifying that the Aids crisis should have crossed over to mainstream society, as it finally killed off the media- and religion-fuelled notion that gay-equals-sex-equals-Aids-equals-death. No longer could the virus be pinned on the evil ways of the gay sinners. It was remarkable how the wider public never grasped how the virus could so easily be spread by unsafe heterosexual sex in the same way as it spread through the gay community. Certainly the media helped to reinforce the idea that it was a 'gay disease', but straight people also tended to close their eyes to the fact that they were also regularly engaging in the same acts of unsafe sex as the gay men were (including anal intercourse in particular). But as ever, the gay community was just rather more honest about what we were getting up to in our bedrooms.

The result is that the Aids crisis has crossed a line, and become public property in a way that it never has been throughout its history. In some ways this could be a step towards finding a real cure (now that it really concerns everybody, not just a 'minority'), but in other ways it creates an even bigger danger that the gay community will simply choose to believe that Aids is no longer our problem. Just when we looked like we were controlling the epidemic, the consequences of this new thinking could be just as devastating as the first time round.

Viewpoints

'I know when and how I got infected. It was my mistake. I know it was stupid but there's no point in constantly beating myself up about it, when

there's nothing I can do about it now. We all make mistakes in our lives but some of us get lucky with the consequences, but in my case I didn't, and I went to get tested and found out that I was positive. I don't know what it was, but I'd already sort of told myself that I would be positive – I just sort of knew somehow, so when they told me it wasn't really a big shock or anything. It's not like on television or in the movies where you have this big scene and you start sobbing or anything. You just have to deal with it and get on with things the best you can. At the time it did seem like a death sentence because everyone who was HIV-positive eventually dies because of it, but now things aren't that straightforward, and you really don't know what your future will be. The endless pill-popping isn't much fun though, and it can sort of take over your life if you're not careful, so that you're constantly worrying about forgetting your drugs, or worrying if you're getting ill, and then there's side-effects so that some people can be really ill just because of the drugs they're having to take. So it's not so great, but at least you're alive and you just have to get on with your life'.

Steven (unemployed, 36), Bradford

'The way that unsafe sex is starting to come back all over the country is just terrifying. I just don't know how anyone can even think of having unsafe sex with someone if they don't know whether they're positive or not. I mean, if you don't know, then you have to assume that they are positive, just for your own safety. I know positive people who have had safe sex with people and not told them they had HIV until afterwards, and I think even that is wrong. They should always be honest and let the other person make the judgement as to whether they have sex – safe sex – or not. Then there's positive people that have unsafe sex with other positive people which I suppose you can't complain about; after all, it's not like they're risking anything any more, but I think it just blurs all the areas around the subject so that nobody knows who is positive and who isn't, and there's no real understanding that, if you're going to fuck with someone, you need to use a condom every time, no matter what you think or what you've been told by the other person. I'm HIV-positive and if I had my time over again I'd be so much more careful about who I was shagging. There's so much brave talk about how people will take risks and if they catch HIV then that's that, as if it's like getting a cold or something. It's just ridiculous: you're gambling with your life. People do still die of Aids'.

Martin (clerk, 43), Norwich

'The current trends are really worrying. I'm a sexual health worker and I see what's going on all the time and it's really scary. Gay men, particularly young gay men, just don't seem to understand the risks they're taking. You talk to them and they seem to think Aids isn't a serious disease any more. Lots of people actually believe it can be cured.

It's frightening. Then I talk to HIV-positive men who say that it's up to their sexual partners to look after their own protection and decide what risks to take, so they don't even bother telling them that they're HIV-positive. What kind of attitude is that? Some people really are playing Russian roulette. The really bizarre thing is that it's straight people who seem to be more clued-up about Aids than the gay people are now, and, when you look back at the past twenty years, you wonder whether we're just right back where we started on the Aids problem.'

Ian (sexual health worker, 28), Leeds.

'I'm no slag, but I've slept with quite a few lads, and I'm not HIV-positive 'cause I got tested again only a couple of months ago. There's lots of different ways you can look at the Aids thing, and I've got mates who have been fucked without a condom quite a few times, and they haven't had a clue whether the guy that's shagged 'em is positive or not. They've been lucky I suppose, but it's the way things are. You get pissed out of your brains or you drop an E in a club, and you stop thinking about things – you just do what you feel like doing, and I know how easy it is to forget about things like condoms. I've only ever been fucked once without a condom and that was by accident – he was already shagging me before I even realised that he hadn't got a condom, so by then it was too late and I just got on with it. That was the reason I first got tested and I've been tested twice since then just so that I know. If I had my wits about me I'd never fuck without a condom again, but I'm not gonna say it'll never happen 'cause I can't say that for certain. I'd do oral sex though, and I have done lots of times, as they say that it's not really a risk when compared to anal sex, so you have to just decide in your own mind what is a real risk and what isn't, and what you're gonna do or not do with a guy. To be honest, I think the only time I'd be happy about fucking without a condom would be if I had a boyfriend who I knew didn't sleep with anyone else, and I knew had tested negative, and that I could trust. Then I'd be OK with it, but otherwise I wouldn't do it. What's the point of taking such a risk for the sake of just using a condom?'

Brian (shop assistant, 26), Glasgow

'To say that gay people are generally obsessed with the way we look might be an understatement. We continually worry about our outward fitness, but we seem to lack interest when it comes to such things as our actual health: we smoke, drink and use recreational drugs probably more than any other section of society. As well as this, many of us indulge in sexual interaction with others as a hobby or pastime giving little regard to our sexual health status. We quite happily go about our everyday lives with some of us carrying those nasty little pests about with us; the ones that appear in those late-night government-funded health education broadcasts which now invade our televisions come the twilight hours. And then, there is still the big one;

Satan in viral form. Flesh decaying, debilitating, life eating; the monster which has already ravaged a proportion of the population is still there lying in wait in the silent but deadly form of HIV. Secretly going about its business, quietly eradicating those important cells that defend us from the tyranny of disease, until we are unknowingly without the strength to fight a chill, and then, Bang! The worm turns, that sneaky little thing that was HIV mutates into a demon of gigantic proportions; its jaws are open, its teeth dripping with bloodthirsty drool, and from out of the darkness it leaps for its prey and down we come; our faces in the mud, our flesh splitting at every seam and the long, slow, painful death where every day we look that beast in its eyes while it stands growling at us in laughter, until one day our exhausted bodies finally give up the fight and lie motionless waiting for the peace to come and take them away.

How can we fight such a force? Where is the weapon that can able our victory against such a foe? Silver bullets don't work, neither do crucifixes, wooden stakes, needle-fed poisons or any other commonplace weapon generally used against the armies of darkness. No, not this time, for this creature there is only one magical shield to protect us from this devastation: a scrap of latex; a sheath of rubber. This wonder drug is not ingested; it is not difficult to apply, and it is readily available, but for some unfounded reason the only known virtually successful protection against this beast is not always used; a folly of the highest degree when the consequences are the possibility of a fate worse than death.'

Leon (writer, 24), Wakefield

Links

www.aids.org

www.gmhc.org

www.ejaf.org Elton John Aids Foundation

www.metromate.org.uk Gay Men Fighting Aids

www.tht.org.uk Terrence Higgins Trust

www.positivenation.co.uk *Positive Nation* magazine

BAREBACKING

A relatively new fashion which has gradually found its way across the Atlantic, barebacking describes the act of performing anal sex without the use of a condom. It hardly seems worth outlining the potential risks involved in this kind of activity, and yet the gay scene seems to have become astonishingly tolerant of the practice, as if it were just another sexual deviation which should be either indulged in or simply ignored. This particular form of unsafe sex is relatively common amongst monogamous couples (where the risk of contracting a sexually transmitted disease is virtually nil) and there are many people who, even if not advocating it, would at least understand the motives of HIV-positive men engaging in the activity, but there are always some serious questions which need to be asked. Are monogamous couples truly monogamous? Do HIV-positive men only engage in unsafe sex with other HIV-positive men?

Those who practise barebacking have some interesting, if slightly specious, arguments to offer us: the sex feels better without the rubber; the sex is more intimate; it's cheaper (you don't have to buy condoms) and it promotes monogamy. OK, the sensations might be better, but at what price? As for being more intimate, well, STDs thrive on intimacy. Cheaper? Well, you can walk into almost any gay pub or shop and stuff your pockets with condoms for free. And as for promoting monogamy? A pretty weird way to try and tie your partner down, don't you think, unless you're planning on being tied to a hospital bed, that is.

Viewpoints

'I don't use condoms 'cause it makes sex really dull if you start messing around putting condoms on. It's a risk you take but you should always know whether the bloke you're with is positive or not. You'd expect him to tell you I guess but if you have any doubt then you'd ask him. But I can't have sex with a condom on; it just doesn't do it for me. So I suppose it's just a choice I've made, and I have to live with the consequences if there ever are any. Sex is a two-way thing and both people know what they're getting into, so if either person is uncomfortable with what you're doing, you should just stop. I know all the risks but everything is a risk and you'd never get out of bed if you worried about everything like that. You have to decide what you will do or will not do.'

Simon (unemployed, 20), London

'This barebacking thing is just disgusting. I can't believe that, after all the years we've had of people dying of Aids, there are still stupid arseholes out there who think it's either acceptable or fashionable to go around engaging in unsafe sex. I don't care about this rubbish about the sensations being better without a condom 'cause what's the point of slightly more exciting sex if you're gonna kill yourself as a result, or kill somebody else. If you don't think fucking is exciting with a condom then don't do it; there's plenty of other things you can do. On the other hand, if you really can't bring yourself to use a condom, then get yourself a partner and wait until you both know for sure that you're both healthy

and that you're not sleeping around. Then have as much unsafe sex as you like 'cause it won't be unsafe then if it's just between you two.

I can't see why anyone is incapable of restricting unsafe sex to a monogamous relationship, and only engage in safe sex with anyone else. I don't think anyone has the right to put anyone else at risk no matter what the circumstances. After all the money that has gone on Aids research and all the losses, the tears, the heartache that has come from illness and death, I think the least that any responsible human being can do is to stop condoning stupid acts like barebacking. If I met anyone that did that sort of stuff, I wouldn't touch 'em with a barge pole, in fact I'd probably tell them what I think of 'em in no uncertain terms. It's a disgrace.'

Tony (17, student), Bristol

Links

www.thebody.com/sowadsky/barebacking.html

www.managingdesire.org.scarcebtb.html

BEADS

Not the ones you hang round your neck. These beads are much larger and purchased from sex toy suppliers. Basically, you shove 'em up your arse or into your vagina (as appropriate) and at the point of sexual climax you (or your partner, or some passers-by) pull them out, thus heightening your sexual pleasure. Sounds like a cheap conjuring trick but you can bet you'll never see Paul Daniels doing this one with Debbie McGee.

BEARS

Big, burly and hairy. You got it, that's a bear, but we're not talking about the four-legged variety. The term is widely used to apply to guys who fit the general description, but as you might imagine, there are all kinds of variations on the theme. In its widest interpretation, a bear epithet could apply to a man with a hairy chest (something which is frowned upon in some gay circles, on the basis that everyone should – for some peculiar reason – be shaved smooth), but with the hairy chest there can also be a beard or a moustache, cropped hair, or no hair, a beer belly, leather chaps or a leather jacket, body piercings, and so on. There's also the bear lover – a guy who isn't necessarily a big hairy type himself but likes that kind of guy – and the bear cub – a description which can apply to both Bear fans and younger lads who are just getting into that kind of 'look'. Of course, when the gay scene fosters the notion that everybody should be slim, eighteen and smooth, the average bear often fails to fit in too well at your average gay club, so special bear events have sprung up all around the country, and many gay pubs and clubs hold regular weekly or monthly bear nights. Expect hair, faux butchness and lots of leather, but don't let the moody faces or the macho attire put you off – most of the guys are just as girly as everyone else.

Link

www.geocities.com/bcbearsmc

BISEXUALITY

There are straight people and there are gay people. Or so we're told. There's also a strange and fascinating breed of people who identify themselves as bisexual, somewhere between the two poles, being attracted to both the opposite and same sex. Well, maybe not so strange really, as some very learned psychiatrists have consistently acknowledged that sexuality is a fairly fluid state, and, even if you identify yourself as defiantly gay, you'd probably be deluding yourself if you didn't accept that you might have harboured the notion (just once or twice, you understand) of doing it with 'the other'. In fact, it's probably more realistic to assume that there is no rigid definition of sexual preference and that we're all essentially bisexual. It's just that some of us are more straight or more gay than others, that's all.

As ever, it's society (or more precisely the media) which encourages us to label ourselves, and bisexuality just doesn't fit in with any mainstream notion of acceptability. Even the most anti-gay individual accepts that gay people exist, but bisexuality is often regarded as nothing more than confused thinking or just a simple cop-out. Straight people will tell you that it's merely a term that some (straight) people use when they're growing up, or when they're trying to make themselves sound colourful and interesting. On the other hand, gay people often regard bisexuality as a cop-out too. They'll tell you that it's a term that (gay) people use when they won't admit to themselves (or others) that they're actually gay or when they're trying to make themselves sound colourful and interesting . . .

Sigmund Freud probably got it right when he suggested that we're all bisexual, but that we simply repress the side of our sexuality that we're least comfortable with. Even the gayest of gay people can sometimes cross the line and that's fine – there are no rules. What is slightly offensive, however, is that we're led to believe that it's a one-way street: gay people might occasionally dabble with the opposite sex, but straight people don't even so much as think about same-sex possibilities. Of course, it's bullshit of the worst kind, but the media (and of course religion) insist that the world is black and white, even though we know it's actually lived out in glorious colour.

Link

www.bisexual.org Bisexual Foundation

BLOOD

Just when you thought prejudice against gay people was on the way out, you stop to marvel at the Blood Transfusion Service, who beg us (quite rightly) to donate blood. But guess what? They don't want your blood if you're gay! Many groups who the BTS considers to be at risk of transmitting HIV are, not surprisingly, prohibited from donating blood. Those who have recently had a body piercing, those who have had (straight) sex in Africa, drug users, prostitutes, those with medical reasons such as CJD, and so on. The list also precludes a man who has had sex with a prostitute or a woman who has had sex with a man who has had 'gay experiences' (watching Graham Norton on TV?).

But, despite such zealousness, the BTS doesn't ask any questions about straight people's sexual activity, such as their number of partners or whether any safe-sex precautions were taken, even though the rate of HIV infection is now higher amongst straight people than gay people. As campaign group OutRage! comment,

'We're not asking the Blood Transfusion Service to stop taking sensible precautions. We're simply asking that it recognises that there is a huge diversity amongst the gay community. If the Service considers it OK to take blood from a highly promiscuous straight man, why not from a gay man who practises safe sex? Why not a gay man in a long-term relationship who has had an HIV-negative test? Why not a gay man who has not had sex for thirty years? We are asking for consistency and a policy based on medical facts, not public hysteria.'

OutRage's Peter Tatchell comments that

'this policy of the Blood Transfusion Service is endorsed by most Aids organisations including the Terrence Higgins Trust. It agrees that no gay man, whatever his sexual history or HIV status, should donate blood. Safer sex is not, according to the THT and the BTS, safe enough to protect the blood supply from contamination by gay men. This begs the question: if safer sex is not adequate to safeguard the blood supply, why have Aids organisations been saying that safer sex is adequate to protect the lives of gay men? Either safer sex works or it doesn't.'

Tatchell goes on to say that

'what is also offensive about the blanket ban on gay blood donations is that it is based on crass generalisations about the whole gay community. It colludes with homophobic stereotypes, lumping all gay men together without differentiation, as if we're all the same. We're not! There's a huge diversity of gay sexual behaviours and lifestyles which the BTS and most Aids organisations fail to acknowledge. Some gay men are at risk from HIV and others aren't. If the BTS and THT were to apply a similar sweeping judgement on the Black or Jewish communities there would, quite rightly, be an uproar. It is a fact that the vast majority of gay and bisexual men do not have, and never will have, HIV. Those who have long and rigorously practised safe sex, and who have since tested HIV-negative, can safely give blood and there is no justification to ban them from doing so.'

Link

www.blood.co.uk Blood Transfusion Service

BODY IMAGE

It's slightly ironic that while straight women are notoriously prone to body-image issues ('does my bum look fat in this?') things are turned upside-down in our homo world. Rarely do you hear about lesbians who are trying to starve themselves into a skimpy piece of dental floss; the girls seem to have the whole size thing sorted. It seems that in dyke-land you're either a big and butch dyke, or you're slim and sweet, the archetypal Lipstick Lesbian. But things are so different for the fellas . . .

The simple fact is that we're all image conscious. OK, you can stick your head in the sand and insist that the way somebody looks is irrelevant, and it's what the person is like inside that really matters. That's very true, but it's also painfully obvious that, when it comes down to the plain and simple matter of sexual attraction (and let's face it, sooner or later it usually does), it's the way that you look that ultimately counts for everything, and for gay men it's become an unpalatable truth which some people find harder to swallow than others. You guys can skirt round the issue and you can delude yourself as much as you like, but if you're going to be brutally honest with yourself, what is it that attracts you to somebody else? What is that 'phwoar' factor? It's never anything to do with personality, at least not initially – it's about the way somebody looks, what his face is like, what his body is like, and the way he's dressed. It's so incredibly superficial it's almost embarrassing, but there you have it – that's the horrible truth.

As if that wasn't bad enough, gay men have also become victims of so-called body fascism; this is all about the obsession with the body beautiful, the six-pack abs, the bulging pecs and the big biceps. The media (particularly the gay media) consistently tells us that we're really not that shallow, that you don't have to be an Adonis to be socially acceptable. Fat is fine, and skinny is cool. But, as you flick over the magazine page and see another perfect image of another set of rippling abs muscles, you've got to wonder just how serious these commentators are. Maybe they should stop trying to fool themselves by thinking that we're believing even a word of it. We know how it is, and we're not fooled for a second. If you don't have the right kind of body, you just don't fit in. It stinks, but what can you do?

There are two schools of thought when it comes to looking for solutions to the problem. The first way out is to forget about the whole body-image thing and just be yourself. Ultimately, people will like you for your personality, and for being you, so who cares if some shallow wanker doesn't give you the eye just because you're not as drop-dead gorgeous as he is? OK, it might mean that the options for regular, meaningless one-night stands might be severely reduced, but does that even matter? Isn't a relationship more important than just a shag? And since when have relationships ever lasted on the basis of how pretty the two partners are? Exactly, so pass me the pork pie . . .

Then there's the other option; you surrender to the pressure and you conform. If you're lucky enough to be naturally as fit as the proverbial butcher's dog, then you've got it made – the whole body-image thing is never an issue (it never is if you're beautiful, funny that . . .) but if you're not exactly model material, it means a constant battle with diets, gyms and guilt. It's surprising that so many gay men have the time or energy to put so much effort into looking good but, when you've got a stereotype to live up to, you either make the grade or you don't. You hear all those guys who tell you they go to the gym five times a week just to keep fit, or because it 'feels great'? It's crap; they go down to the gym because they want the pecs, the abs and the arms that (gay) convention tells us we've got to have. And good luck to every one of 'em if that's what they want. We shouldn't criticise them for their efforts, in fact they're doing us a favour – they provide the eye candy when they whip their shirts off on the dance floor. They're not fooled by the whole body-image thing either – they know that it's superficial and it means nothing, but they've made a choice, and they know that if you want to get off on the attention, and you want to pull the guys every night, then you have to work for it in sweat.

But, at the same time, there's the rest of the gay world, and all those people that can't find the time or the motivation to pump iron. The people who are too old to worry about gyms, and people with disabilities that haven't even got the options that the rest of us have. Does it mean that they all have to be excluded from our clubs and pubs, just because they don't conform to our standards? Of course not, in fact you can bet your last penny that the guy with the most captivating personality, the most interesting stories and the sweetest nature will probably be the fat lad hiding in the corner, not the muscle-bound hunk gyrating in front of you. There's room for everybody, and we should embrace our diversity. Vive la difference.

Viewpoints

'I hate the attitude you get from people if you're not some muscular hunk. I mean, it's not everybody, but you can see the look on some people's faces, like they think you haven't even got a right to be in the same club as them if you haven't got a thirty-inch waist or something. It's not as if I'm expecting to sleep with 'em, in fact I wouldn't even want to sleep with someone with that kind of personality, but I just hate that kind of people that think they're untouchable or special or something just because they look good. Why can't they just be themselves and grow up?'

Martin (unemployed, 24), Sheffield

'There's no way I'd say I was drop-dead gorgeous, but I think I look pretty good, even though I've not got big muscles, and I get plenty of attention. I admit it's flattering to get stared at and chatted up, but I don't think that's some sort of crime. I just enjoy it while I can. I have lots of friends who are lots older than me, and some would happily tell you they're overweight or whatever, but I don't think you have to surround yourself with beautiful people. In reality your friends are your mates because you just like them for the people that they are, no matter what they look like, and, even if you're looking for some hunk to cop off with, it doesn't mean you can't be friendly and polite to anyone.'

Paul (driver, 30), Manchester

'I'm only eighteen and I look good. I don't have to hide that. I like buying designer clothes and dressing well and I don't care if anyone else has a problem with that. I don't like the way you get older people and ugly, fat people staring at you like you're a piece of meat, and I think they're really sad, as if I'd even be interested in 'em. Why don't they just go after their own kind of people and stay away?'

Jordan (student, 18), Manchester

'I used to be really quite skinny, and I got sick of feeling inferior to other people, that's all it was. I started going to a gym and I hated it, but I kept going, and now I look way better than I used to. I'm nothing special but I do get lots of people saying I've got a good body and it's nice to get compliments, especially when I worked pretty hard to get this way. I admit I'm one of those lads that always has his shirt off in clubs and stuff, but why shouldn't I? Most people like looking and I like the attention, there's nothing wrong with that. If you don't like it then don't

look, that's what I say. I know that I'm not shallow or anything, I do have a brain, and I just chose to try and be more like the kind of people I'm attracted to, I suppose. I think too many people look down on fit-looking guys as if they're stupid or really shallow, and that's unfair because they're not. They just know that if you want to get the guys you have to sort of conform to a look. It's their choice that's all.'

Jay (office administrator, 27), London

'The really funny thing is the way that there are so many really good-looking lads out there who don't have muscles and don't get into the whole gym thing. And when you talk to them they all think they're really unattractive and they give off this whole inferiority thing. When I say to 'em that I think they look great, they nearly always say that I can't really think that 'cause guys think muscular men always fancy muscular men and that's that. It's stupid because I don't, and lots of people I know don't either. I'm pretty muscular but I think a slim or even a skinny lad is way more horny looking. You go to Trade or Crash or whatever and it's always packed with big guys all stripped off, but I'd like it more if there were lots of skinnier people flashing their bodies more. But they're just too shy, I suppose.'

Steven (driver, 29), Southend

'Oh I so wish I was really fit and good-looking, but I'm not at all. I'm just normal and a bit overweight. I sometimes think about going to a gym or dieting more but then I just think it's silly getting into all that just to try and get some man into bed. It's just meaningless. I'd rather have a proper boyfriend and I'd never plan to spend my life with someone who was with me just because I was good looking. That would be a bit shallow, so I figure that, when I finally meet someone, they'll like me for the person I am, no matter what, as I would with them. But I admit I do like watching all the really fit people when I'm out clubbing, as it's good fun to just look and imagine. And I think most of them get off on the fact that they're being looked at anyway.'

Sam (unemployed, 22), Leeds

BONDAGE

All part of the sado-masochism scene, bondage is (as the name implies) all about getting tied up. But that's a simple description of a complex subject. Bondage can be much more than simply having your hands tied behind your back while somebody gives you a blow job. Apart from the obvious *Carry-On* images of being tied by hand and foot to your bed, things can get much kinkier than that. How about being wrapped in cling film? Or handcuffed and clamped to a dungeon wall? It does happen, and more often than you might imagine. If you want to take things even further, there's also a whole world of rubber hoods (complete with oxygen mask and a funnel for inserting fluids – we won't go there), one-piece rubber suits and, for the real deluxe experience, a coffin to lie in. Bizarre stuff, but then sex has always been about exploring your boundaries, and, while some of us might settle for a quick fumble while we're watching *Emmerdale*, there are many others who like to make sex a little more theatrical and eventful.

But what is the thrill of bondage? It's all about control or, more precisely, giving up control and being totally helpless, at the mercy of your sexual partner. It goes without saying that it can require a good supply of mutual trust (it's probably not a good idea to let a total stranger tie you up) but, if you like the idea of letting someone have complete control over your body, it's worth thinking about. A positive boon for the lazy 'cause, let's face it, you won't be going anywhere for a while.

Link

www.boyfetish.com

BUTT PLUGS

Similar in concept to the dildo, a butt plug is rather smaller and usually made of rubber. The deal is that you insert it in much the same way as a dildo (up your butt) and then, well, you leave it there basically while you wank, engage in vaginal intercourse, watch television, go shopping . . . it's your call. Ask the right people and you'll be surprised to learn that quite a few folk have ventured out to work with a butt plug keeping them company. And you wondered why that guy sat opposite you on the bus was smiling.

CANNABIS

Call it what you will (spliff, marijuana, ganja, weed, skunk, hash, blow) it's all the same; it's the drug that finally came out of the closet. Although it's been around forever as a sort of underground drug that everybody knew about, it was always something that other people did, and strangely nobody ever actually did it themselves. Of course, everybody was puffing away, but we had to keep up the pretence of ignorance. Finally, after the government realised that we couldn't keep up the sham forever, they effectively decriminalised the drug by downgrading it to a C-category substance, enabling the police to allocate its resources to things rather more important than booking people for smoking a spliff. It's now pretty common to see drinkers smoking weed in pubs and clubs, and it's unlikely that the police would now bother to even caution anyone for smoking the drug.

It is, of course, a relatively safe drug to consume, inducing feelings of relaxation, a loss of inhibitions, helpless giggling and even has a reported beneficial pain-relieving effect on Aids, cancer and other illnesses. But much depends on the way in which the drug is ingested. Smoking cannabis creates all the dangers associated with inhalation of tobacco, indeed it could be more dangerous if smoked through an unfiltered joint. It can, however, simply be eaten, and the infamous coffee houses in Amsterdam know all about cooking space cakes and space buns, or sprinkling weed on other food. The results are less immediate than through smoking, though, and also, therefore, less predictable. The risk of dependency is very low, and the only real risk of overuse is the possibility of being really, really boring to your sober friends.

Links

www.cannabis.com

www.cannabisnews.com

www.ukcia.org

CIRCLE JERK

Definitely not involving Jamaican spices of any description, this term basically describes a group wank, if you will. And, yes, it does go on, not least in bastions of heterosexuality such as rugby clubs and military barracks where repressed urges are occasionally relieved by 'wanking competitions' (who shoots the most, the fastest, slowest or furthest) or as part of a seemingly age-old ritual of ejaculating on a biscuit, with the last one to make his deposit being forced to eat the aforementioned biscuit. No, really. In strictly gay terms (by comparison), circle jerks were certainly very popular in America during the height of the Aids crisis (a group wank is the safest sex imaginable) but never particularly popular in Britain, probably thanks to good ol' British reserve. Well, it's not something you can advertise on the pub's bulletin board, is it? Definitely a good party game if you can persuade everyone to join in, but not so good if you haven't bought that laminate floor just yet.

CIRCUMCISION

Not a subject that would interest the ladies all that much (female circumcision is possible and does happen, but only in the most obscure of societies) but, for gay men, circumcision is always a topic worthy of debate. Over in the USA, circumcision is performed as routine on almost every new-born child, while other religious groups (for example, Jews) perform circumcision as a rite of passage, rather than for any strict medical reason. Over here in the UK, however, most men remain uncircumcised unless there's a practical physical reason for performing the operation (notably, having a foreskin which is too tight to withdraw).

But fashions change, and certainly over the past couple of decades (possibly since we have gleaned a better understanding of day-to-day life in the USA for example) lots of gay men have expressed a desire to 'get the op' purely for cosmetic reasons, and this can be done, but usually only through private treatment. There's no particular advantage to having a circumcised penis other than the fact that it looks somewhat neater but, then, how many people are going to be seeing it?

There's circumstantial evidence that there may be some medical advantages to circumcision, as the removal of the foreskin may avoid the development of some diseases, but there are no hard facts on this. Undoubtedly, a circumcised willy is easier to keep clean, but whether that's a good reason for an operation is another matter. Other medical research has suggested that circumcised penises can contribute to loss of erectile performance, but once again there is no hard evidence to support this theory.

On the other hand, there's a view in some circles that everyone should have the right to remain 'as created' without being circumcised, and that parents who agree to such procedures have effectively abused their child. Nice idea, and you'll not be surprised that it's an American thing, linked to the notion that you can sue for just about anything these days.

In reality, whether to be cut or uncut is a personal choice, and one which is likely to be made on medical or religious grounds rather than for any other reason.

Links

www.cirp.org

www.geocities.com/HotSprings/2754

Viewpoints

'I was circumcised when I was in my twenties because my foreskin was too tight. I didn't know then but it's a very common problem but most people are just too shy to do anything about it. I think it's a bit stupid really, because there's no point in being shy with a doctor who has seen it all before, but then you're gonna be with a guy and he's gonna be looking at it much more than a doctor, so why not just go and do something about it if you need to. If you've no actual need to do it, I suppose it's your choice.

I'm so glad I had it done 'cause sex is so much better now. Most of all I'm not shy about anyone seeing my cock now because I thought it looked

kinda stupid before. After it was done and I had to go to the doctor a couple of times later on, I just whopped it out without a thought, and now I'm a real exhibitionist with it. I'll probably get arrested eventually, heh heh.'

Lee (sales assistant, 34), Birmingham

'I'm not saying I'm a slag or anything but I've been close enough to more knobs than I can count, including lots of straight men, and let me tell you there's an awful lot of blokes who need to wash their dicks, it's really quite gross. Blokes with circumcised dicks are quite rare but they're clean and look way better I think. I was done when I was a kid, but I've spoken to blokes who were done later and they do say you lose a lot of sensitivity, so maybe that's not so good, but I think I'd rather everyone was like that instead of being minging.'

Richard (unemployed, 23), Manchester

COCK RING

Not to be confused with cock fighting (now there's a mental image), cock rings are suitably sized hoops of metal, leather or rubber which are slipped over the penis while in its flaccid state. Once positioned beneath the testicles, sexual activity (masturbation) allows the penis to become erect, and the restrictive nature of the cock ring enables the wearer to maintain an erection without further stimulation. Having got blood into the penis, the cock ring serves to keep it there in a way which is similar to the age-old trick employed by strippers, whereby they tie off their erection with a tight band (you didn't think they naturally stayed that big, did you?).

Although the cock ring doesn't fulfil any particular sexual function other than helping to maintain an erection, they are popular with both gay and straight men, especially those who are into bondage and other sado-masochism activities, seeing as the ring provides a very useful attachment point for harnesses, chains and other goodies. On the other hand, if your sexual activities are rather less ambitious, a cock ring can also be worn as a pendant or attached to a jacket, or . . . well, you choose.

CONDOM

Sometimes referred to as a Johnny, rubber, French letter or more euphemistically as 'precaution', the condom is still the simplest and most effective way of preventing the spread of HIV or other STD infections (other than by abstinence). Primarily used during anal intercourse, the condom is placed at the tip of the (erect) penis and unrolled to cover the entire penis prior to penetration. Although easy to do, lots of gay men insist that wearing a condom during intercourse lessens the intensity of sensations which can be felt, but whether this is actually true (bearing in mind the tissue-thinness of the rubber) or if it's more of a psychological perception is still open to debate. What is more certain is that anal sex without a condom is a sure-fire guaranteed way of spreading either a common STD or HIV, and the question of sensitivity, or the old argument that 'putting on a condom kinda kills the moment' thing, just doesn't compare to the potential risk of getting yourself an incurable and inevitably fatal disease.

Condoms are (rarely) used for oral intercourse too, although it's not hard to understand the reluctance to chow down on a piece of rubber, even if it is mint flavoured. Given the extremely low risk of HIV transmission through oral sex, it's hardly surprising that few people bother to use condoms for anything other than downstairs business.

While straight men can justifiably claim that using condoms is an expensive business, gay men have easy access to an endless supply of free condoms in most gay pubs and from any sexual health centre. So there's really no excuse for not using a condom, is there?

COTTAGING

A term which conjures up black-and-white images of dark figures lurking in seedy toilets, hiding from the law. It used to be like that and in some places it still is, even though there's no longer any real reason for gay men to be seeking sex in your local public loo. With the advent of phone lines and the internet, it's never been easier for guys to meet other guys, and the practice is undeniably slowly dying out. But there are those who still get a buzz out of the prospect of no-strings, no-talk, no-questions-asked anonymous sex.

Viewpoints

'I've been cruising and stuff since I was about nineteen or so, and I'm twenty-five now. It's good fun really if you're into that kinda thing, but I know that lots of people aren't, and they think it's really sleazy and sad which is OK, but I don't like the way they make judgements. I mean, if they don't approve that's fine 'cause I don't need their approval, but I just hate their attitude like they're somehow superior beings just because they don't go looking for sex. That's crap really 'cause they're not better or anything; they just choose to do things differently. I suppose a lot of it has to do with the way that you look at sex, and whether you think of it as just being fun, or whether it has to be this big expression of love thing. I know it can be a really intimate thing like that but most of the time most blokes aren't looking for some romance or anything like that, they just want to have sex, so why should they go through all the crap of meeting

someone, going on a date and all that stuff just to get to the bit where you get naked. It's stupid when you can just go out to a toilet and meet some guy and just do it there and then. For lots of people sex is just about satisfying the need most of the time; it's just for fun, and it's got fuck-all to do with love or romance.

Another thing you have to remember is that you get lots of blokes who are married or with girlfriends, and they don't have any other way of meeting other men, unless they go to toilets and stuff. It's a bit sad but it's a fact of life that lots of married guys want to have sex with blokes and they're either too scared to get out of their relationship or they want to keep their relationship but they want to go with guys at the same time. There are lots of fucked-up people out there but you can't go around making judgements about people. They do what they have to do, so it's mad to start saying that the police should kick blokes out of parks and toilets 'cause they've got nowhere else to go unless they're gonna start kerb crawling and looking for prossies and stuff, which is no better, is it? And at the end of the day, nobody's making you go cottaging or cruising, so if you don't approve, just don't do it and keep your views to yourself.

I dunno what will happen now that this law thing is gonna get changed so that it's supposedly legal for two guys to be doing stuff in a toilet if you can prove that you didn't think anyone would be upset by your actions or whatever. I can't see how that would work really, as the police would just call you a liar and that you knew someone would take offence. But if it's late at night or something, I guess somebody will fight it and say that nobody is gonna be in a park at night unless they were up for it. Should be quite interesting to see what happens. I don't think it's that important really 'cause the police don't really bother about that sort of stuff any more. I think they've got more important things to do, and they say that they only act now if somebody makes a complaint. I guess they do still go around trying to catch people in toilets and stuff but it doesn't happen that often now, and I think it will probably become a thing of the past. The way I see it, most councils have closed most of the public loos anyway, so most of the ones that are left are in really obscure places, and most people know what goes on in them.

Why do I do it? Well, like I said, it's an easy way to meet people without having to get into all the crap about dating or whatever. If I was after a boyfriend (which I sometimes am, and I've had two before), I'd go to clubs and pubs or whatever, but for sex it's easier to go to a park or some other cruising area. All I do is, like everyone else, I just hang around and see who is there. You see guys walking by and then they'll stop and come back. Then you can just walk to a quiet place or somewhere where you can't be seen and, if the other guy is up for it, he'll follow you. Then you just go for it; you don't even need to speak really, just do what you want to do and that's it.

Other guys will go into a toilet and they'll just stand at the wall like they're taking a piss. Somebody will come in (or they'll already be there) and you just have to stand there and see what happens. If you see the other guy wanking, you know what he's after and you just join in, until you're both doing it to each other. You have to be careful in case someone comes in while you're doing it, but that doesn't happen much, especially at night. In fact sometimes you can have more than one guy there anyway. I've wanked off two guys at the same time, it was mad.

It's a laugh really and, if you've got nothing to do or if you're pissed-up or something, it's good fun, although sometimes you can stand around for ages looking for someone you fancy. I'm a decent-looking lad so I don't think I'd ever put anyone off, but you get lots of old guys and fat blokes and stuff like that, so most of the people you wouldn't want to touch with a barge pole. But you can't start slagging them off for being there 'cause they're human too and you just have to give 'em the brush off. They probably can't get it anywhere else so you just have to ignore the ones you don't fancy and wait for someone you like.

I suppose it could be a bit risky sometimes though. It's not to do with the police or whatever 'cause that sort of thing rarely happens now and, even if the police do turn up, they usually give people a warning rather than go through all the arrest crap. So you just leave and stay away for a bit until it blows over. The real risk is from thugs who are out to mug people or just go on the anti-gay thing. It happens a lot, especially in big cities where you get groups of Asians or whatever going round trying to be hard kids, and it's an easy target to go into a park and start picking on blokes, especially as there's probably no police there to stop 'em and nobody to see what they're doing. I know people who have been stabbed and beaten in parks, so you have to be careful. If you see anything dodgy your best bet is to leave. It really stinks, because they always get away with stuff like that, probably because the police probably think we deserve it for being there in the first place. But a crime is a crime and they ought to do a bit more to stop violence like that even though they probably never will. Mind you, it's not like you have to go into a dark park or whatever, as you can always pick up guys in all kinds of places. I've cruised guys literally out on the street and ended up going behind buildings and stuff.

Will I ever stop cruising? Well, I don't know. Maybe if I get a boyfriend I won't want to do it any more, but I know lots of lads who are in relationships and they still go out looking for other men, so I can't say for sure. Most of 'em do it behind their boyfriend's backs, and I suppose it's just human instinct at the end of the day, so, if you know that you can get it somewhere easily and for free, you're gonna go and get it, aren't you? I don't see that there's anything wrong with it and, OK, I know it's a bit sleazy hanging round in toilets and stuff, but that's just the way it is

and, if you get what you're looking for, then who gives a shit about the surroundings? And like I said before, if you don't like it then don't do it 'cause nobody's making you. And I don't want to hear any of this crap about us giving gay people a bad reputation either. Straight blokes are no better – they just go with prostitutes or shag women behind their wife's back, and, as I said, lots of blokes out in the parks are straight anyway, so it's got nothing to do with giving gay people a bad name. We're no better or worse than anyone else.'

David (call centre worker, 35), Birmingham

CP

Corporal Punishment is yet another deviation from the sexual norms, and one which is enjoyed by all kinds of people both gay and straight. Essentially, CP involves all the sort of things you can imagine that the description implies, ranging from whipping, caning and flogging through to more severe beatings with sticks, bats or just knuckled fists. More commonly, however, CP is often a euphemism for spanking, a pastime which seems to be astonishingly popular with people of all persuasions, although the fascination is hard to identify, if you're not one of those people who actually likes giving it or getting it. Although gay men and women are no more likely to engage in 'offbeat' sexual activity than their straight counterparts, discussion of such interests is undoubtedly more common among gay people, who are, almost by definition, rather less inhibited when it comes to exploring sexual taboos. Certainly, a look through any adult magazine or website will display an astonishing array of CP interests, and most gay chat rooms will include a section for CP enthusiasts, which is always very popular. So if you have an uncontrollable urge to relive your school days and get a free spanking, it's surprisingly easy to arrange. Even more bizarrely, there are lads out there who will happily arrange for you to kick and punch them for pleasure. Go figure.

CRUISING

Absolutely nothing to do with the *QE2* (although, some of those cabin crews . . .) cruising is all about picking up. It's pretty much a male thing too, as the girls just don't seem to do this sort of thing (and nobody knows why). How does cruising work? Well, first of all you need a location, be it a toilet, a park, a nightclub or a bar. Anywhere, in fact, if you spot somebody that you fancy. It's a skill that most gay boys learn almost by instinct – all part of that strange ability we've got to spot when someone is 'up for it'. Somehow or other you just catch a glance, or a stare that lasts just a little bit too long to be unintentional. Things like that.

What happens? Well if you're doing the cruising you need to stop, and make it pretty obvious to the other guy that you're interested. Sometimes it's just a case of passing one another on the street. A little glance and you wonder, 'is he or isn't he?' Take another couple of steps and look back . . . he's turned to look back too. Bingo! Then you just have to use your judgement. Hang around and see if he comes and talks to you, or you go and ask him for a light, or the time, or whatever comes into your head.

In clubs it's all much easier simply because cruising (or at least copping off) is what most people are there for. It's about exchanging glances, making the eye contact last just a little longer than necessary. It's about getting close, dancing nearer and nearer. And it's about waiting outside at closing time. You could just be really pushy and walk up to anyone and say, 'Do you fancy a shag?' but that wouldn't be half as much fun, would it? They say it's all in the thrill of the chase.

Viewpoints

'I've never, ever been any good at cruising anyone. I know how to do it – it's not exactly rocket science, but I haven't got the nerve to do it right. If I gaze at someone and he looks back at me, I'll immediately look away 'cause I'm too shy. The trick is probably to make sure the other fella knows that you're interested but I'm not brave enough to be so forward. I'll just shy away and he'd probably think I wasn't interested and disappear. The only times I've ever copped off with anyone in a club is when they've come and started talking to me. I always wish I was a bit less shy.'

Terry (postman, 29), Brighton

'Cruising can be a good laugh, even if you don't actually want to get off with someone. I love places like Canal Street in Manchester, especially in summer when everyone's outside the pubs drinking and talking. You can sit there or walk up and down and just be eyeing up lads all day, and they're giving you the look back. It's really funny sometimes, and it's a good ego boost when you get someone that's so obviously cruising you. I often think it's like you're having sex without actually making physical contact – you do all the foreplay and that's just enough really, so that you know you could have gone further if you wanted to, but why bother? You got your ego flattered so move on.'

David (office worker, 28), Manchester

'There's different kinds of cruising, of course. There's the really intentional stuff that goes on in some parks and places like that, and then people are obvious about what they're doing, lurking in bushes and behind walls and so on, waiting for you to follow them. In clubs it's the same sort of thing with people staring at each other then chasing each other into corners and stuff. But just out on the street it's more a chance

thing, when you just see somebody that you fancy, and you know that they like you. I've met guys out on the street like that a few times, just when I've been out shopping or whatever, and we've ended up having sex in car parks and all over. I don't know if they've been gay or bi or straight, but you can always tell when somebody is up for it. Most of the time you just sort of glance back at people, and you'll just keep on walking, but if I'm in the right sort of mood then I'll just go for it and see if the other guy is really interested or not'

Mark (unemployed, 22), Swindon

CUNNILINGUS

No, not an Irish airline, it's actually the rather fancy latin term for . . . well, 'cunnus' is latin for vagina and 'lingus' means tongue, so you get the picture. Undoubtedly it's one of those slightly taboo areas of sexual activity which is enjoyed by both lesbians and straight couples, although they might not necessarily tell you about it in the cocktails bar. Likewise it's not something which enters the conversations of gay men all too often. Not surprisingly.

CURIOUS

You can dig out a dictionary to get yourself a proper definition if you need to but, in gay parlance, the term has a slightly different meaning. It first appeared in personal ads in magazines and newspapers describing straight or bisexual men and women who wanted to explore the bounds of their sexuality (or, in plain speak, get it on with someone of the same sex). Since the development of internet chat rooms the term 'curious' has taken off in a big way, and it crops up time and time again. Trouble is, it's lost some of its meaning, because you know only too well that most of the guys in the chat rooms who describe themselves as 'curious' don't have much to be unsure about – it's become an overused term for straight-ish bisexuals and gay men who want to have a bit of a fling with a gay guy, but don't want the whole thing to look too, er, gay. By using the term 'curious' you can give the impression that you're just looking to experiment, and when the messy business is over you'll still be straight, which, of course, makes everything just fine and dandy. Unless, of course, you're experimenting every other night . . .

CYBER SEX

The very name conjures up all manner of images of stainless steel androids, blinding white surfaces and flashing display screens. The reality is rather more mundane, and probably involves nothing more glamorous than a seedy bedroom, a home computer and a much-used box of tissues. The whole point about cyber sex is that it's pure fantasy. The internet enables you to be anybody that you want to be, your looks, age and personality (even your gender) only limited by your ultimately limitless imagination. The proliferation of online chat sites created the new phenomenon – a way of having sex without actually having sex, a sort of enhanced wank, if you will. Dissatisfied with the one-dimensional gratification of the pornographic image, you could now communicate with another human, and explore your wildest fantasies person-to-person, or within a 'chat group', saying whatever you want to say – all that stuff that you'd never have the nerve to say in the flesh, so to speak. It's all about creativity and the ability to suspend belief. Nobody (unless they're incredibly naive) enters a cyber chat room and expects reality. You know that the other gay who says he's a fit, slim-built blond twenty-year-old might well be a fat, ugly, seventy-year-old married vicar, but you just have to go with the moment and believe that he is what he says he is. You never know – those profile photos might just really be him and, if they are, he might have taken them within the last decade. But while the whole idea of talking yourself through a live wank fantasy might seem almost as tragic as the masturbatory use of a porn magazine, it's safe sex at its best; it certainly doesn't harm anyone, and it's cheap (in more ways than one), if not free. It can also be quite compulsive; you know how some of your mates never want to bother going out any more?

Viewpoints

'I think most people who have got into using chat rooms have got into cyber chat in some way or other. Sometimes you can't help yourself because it's fun to talk about all kinds of sex stuff which you just don't really discuss in real life. If somebody starts talking to you, and he's got photos and he looks really sexy, then what would you do if he starts telling you what he'd like to do to you? You just have to go with it sometimes. I don't think anyone is daft enough to believe any of the crap that you come out with, but there you go. It's harmless.'

David (unemployed, 26), Cardiff

'God, I've had some right laughs in cyber chat. I like going into straight chat rooms and finding some straight lad who's got a webcam. If you give 'em enough bullshit you can get 'em to do anything, so you give out some story about how your camera is broken, but you'd so like to see him on his webcam. I say I'm a really hot girl and describe myself, and get into all the stuff about what I'd like to do with him if we met up. Next thing he's sat there in front of his camera and he's got his clothes off and his knob out, wanking off to this gorgeous shag that he's talking to, thinking you're some tart with big tits. But I suppose he's having fun too, so it's

not like I'm really using him, is it? Or if I am then sod it, I don't care. It's good fun.'

Steve (office administrator, 33), Manchester

'There's no way I'd admit it to anyone in real life, but I've done cyber sex lots of times. I'm nearly in my fifties now and there's absolutely no way I could go out and hope to pick up anyone, so I wouldn't even try, as I haven't got the looks, age or confidence to be doing that sort of thing. To be honest it doesn't bother me any more, and cyber chat is just an easy way of getting a sort of sex, even if it's make believe. I can pretend to anyone that I'm somebody that I'm not, and we can fantasise about sex. That's all it is, and it's more fun than rewatching a porn video, or buying dirty magazines.'

George (sales assistant, 48), Lincoln

'I don't think many girls do cyber sex, or if they do then I don't know about it. I think it's just something that horny blokes do when they want a wank. I honestly don't know why the same idea doesn't appeal to women as much, but maybe it's because we're more touchy-feely than men and just talking about sex isn't as big a turn-on for us. The whole chat-and-meet internet thing is really male dominated but I don't know why; it just doesn't seem to be that big a pull for girls. Even when you do find sites where girls are in chat rooms, they're talking about politics or support groups or something, and it's never about sex really.'

Sue (unemployed, 25), Leeds

CRYSTAL METHS

The full name is Crystal Methamphetamine, sometimes referred to as krank, tweak or ice. The use of crystal meths as a recreational drug began in the USA, where the gay folks latched on to it long before mainstream club culture took over. Originally it was truckers and bikers that found the drug useful as a way of keeping awake and alert over long distances. Snorted or injected, the drug produces a feeling of euphoria which can last from between two and sixteen hours, and is notorious for its capacity to give you the urge (and ability) to have wild sex for hours, maybe even days (eek!). On a more mundane level, it's good for keeping you awake on the dance floor all night.

The down side? Well, crystal meths can cause paranoia, short-term memory loss, wild rages and mood swings. It can also damage your immune system, and of course the possibility of throwing yourself into a day-long sex frenzy with a complete stranger can lead to other health problems which don't need explaining here. Psychological dependence on the drug is common and, if you're really unlucky, even a small dose can kill.

Links

www.urban75.com/Drugs/meth.html

DARK ROOMS

A creature of the seventies, dark rooms first appeared in clubs over in America as a means of enabling gay club-goers to do, shall we say, a little more than just dance, without upsetting the other customers. The concept is simple – you get a room, black it out completely or put a dim bulb in a corner and away you go – the guys walk in, do whatever they want to do and leave. The dark room eventually spread around Europe and the rest of the world, although they never really took off all that much in England, probably because of a combination of our distinctly British attitude to anything too wild, and the constant threat of getting locked up if you got caught sort of killed the excitement. They've also lost much of their popularity since the first days of the Aids epidemic, when the idea of having anonymous sex suddenly didn't seem like such a good idea. They do live on, however, and although they're probably illegal in just about any country where you might find one, they're still to be found, and there are still plenty of guys who are more than happy to take a walk on the dark side. Great idea if you're uncontrollably randy and not too bothered about whose bits and pieces you're touching, but definitely a bad risk if you're too choosy – the guy who you saw going into the room might not be the same guy that you're fumbling with in the dark. That's the whole point in fact; dark rooms are an opportunity for everyone's looks and age to become redundant, so remember that before you close the door.

Viewpoints

'Years back I did dark rooms all over the place. You can still find them in some places but it's not very common now. A long time ago just about any kind of sex you can imagine would be going on in the darkness, but now I'd say that just about everyone is either wanking or sucking and that's all. Aids stopped nearly all the unsafe sex, but I know it still goes on. It's good if you see someone that you really fancy and they're up for it. But, yeah, you do have to be careful that the bloke you want to get is the one that you actually get when you get in the dark. Lots of people don't care when they're pissed, but you have to have your wits about you if you're cruising someone in particular.'

Charles (office administrator, 29), Manchester

'I've been in a dark room when I was on holiday, when I was totally smashed. I saw people going in and out and I thought I might as well go and join in. It was nearly completely dark and I think there must have been five or six people in there, and I just remember standing there with all these hands on me, and someone sucked me off before I came out. God knows what they were like but I didn't do anything stupid. It was just a drunken thing.'

Barry (designer, 30), London

DENTAL DAM

An old classic for the ladies, dental dams are (or at least were) specially manufactured squares of latex material which were used to provide a barrier between one's lips and tongue and your partner's unmentionables. A child of the Aids crisis years, dental dams sounded like a good idea in theory but the act of sloshing a piece of rubber around in front of your mouth surpassed the absurdity of even the most ludicrous acts of performance art. Needless to say, dental dams have virtually disappeared and you'd be hard pressed to find a gal who admitted to ever having had one. A good one for the mantelpiece though if you have neighbours who ask questions.

DILDOS

The most famous of all sex toys, dildos are commonly bought and used by gay men, lesbians, straight women, in fact just about everybody. It doesn't take much imagination to work out what they're used for, and a dildo can be invaluable for livening up a sex session either with a partner, a group or all on your own. In fact, dildos are particularly useful if you're thinking about trying anal sex, but you're a bit worried about just going for it with another guy. A dildo is a convenient way to, er . . . get used to things, before you try out the real thing. If you're a little more adventurous, bear in mind it's not a good idea to share a dildo with anyone else, unless you either put a condom on it, or scrub it clean before use – the possible risks of infection ought to be fairly obvious. On the other hand, if you still don't fancy the idea of shoving anything up your butt, it's worth remembering that dildos come in an astonishing range of sizes and colours these days, and they make fascinating ornaments, especially if you like to amuse your (straight) guests.

DIPPING

Here's a new one which we seem to be in danger of importing from the USA. Another gloriously effective way of spreading HIV infection, dipping is all about engaging in penetrative sex but withdrawing before the point of ejaculation. Nobody seems to have pointed out that, even without actually achieving orgasm, penetrative sex is still the number-one way to transmit HIV, as pre-ejaculatory fluid (now colourfully referred to as 'pre-cum') carries the virus in much the same way as semen does. So let's get the message clear, OK? Don't do it without a condom, unless you want to risk killing yourself.

ECSTASY

Our love affair with ecstasy (sometimes called pills or doves) continues, even though its days of high-fashion are long gone. You know when somebody is E'd-up; he's the guy that walked in to the club fully dressed with a scowl on his face, and now he's only wearing boxer shorts, sweating as if he's in a sauna and smiling like he's just won the lottery. Famous for its ability to make you just want to get up and dance, ecstasy is the love drug that makes everything look fabulous, and even the straightest thug is suddenly just plain gorgeous. You want to hug everybody if you can only stop dancing. Aww bless.

Of course, it's not all as rosy as the drug might have you believe. The main risk with ecstasy is that it removes your feelings of tiredness and thirst, so you can happily dance for hours without even thinking about cooling down or drinking (and that means water, not alcohol). So, if you are dancing yourself silly, it's important to remember that you need to replace your fluids at about a pint every hour. On the other hand, if you're not dancing to the point of exhaustion, taking in excessive water could be just as dangerous, even fatal.

There are no definite health risks which can be attributed to ecstasy, although it goes without saying that dodgy pills are common and they could be potentially fatal. Likewise there's no guarantee that long-term side-effects won't eventually be discovered. But, treated with respect, it's a drug which isn't as evil as the more irresponsible newspapers would have you believe. The trick is to take things easy as much as you can, get some water occasionally and get your clothes off – for once that really is a good idea.

Links

www.ecstasy.org

www.aromadome.com/ecstasy.html

ESCORTS

Escorts, rent boys, street workers, prostitutes, the name changes but the profession remains the same. They say it's the oldest profession and it's certainly one that endures both for straight and gay men and women. Traditionally, rent boys have worked almost exclusively in London, and had much to do with old-fashioned notions about the capital: you know how it goes – if you're a kid and you want to run away to London, you'll end up on the streets selling your body. In more than a few cases there was more than a grain of truth in the cliché, but it would be wrong to suggest that most boys (and men) enter the world of prostitution by force.

These days it is a career choice for many, particularly younger men without jobs or students on low incomes. Selling yourself can be a lucrative business. And now that it's possible to advertise your services easily through free papers, phone lines and the internet, the business is expanding. Most of the country's larger cities now have their own (smaller) groups of escorts and, while men are willing to pay for their services, they'll continue to exist. Should we frown upon such activities? What's the point? Given that rent boys almost always do their thing by choice these days, it's literally nobody's business but theirs.

Viewpoints

'When I look back at how I got into doing rent, it was because I was friends with a couple of other lads who were already doing it. They made lots of money and they kept saying I should do it too but I had this image of dirty old men slobbering all over me and that put me off. It wasn't any sort of moral thing; it was just that I didn't like the idea of having to have sex with someone really horrible. It took me a while to get my head round it and I realised that it was my choice who I decided to go with, so I didn't have to have sex with anyone if I didn't want to, so I put an advert in a newspaper and, when people called me, I made sure they weren't nasty old men before I said they could come round. It worked too and most people I've had have been OK. I wouldn't say there have been many that I've liked, but on the other hand there's only been a couple that have been nasty and I told them to get lost because they'd lied about what they were like on the phone.'

Lee (23), London

'The thing is, people think you're being used but actually it's the other way round. You're in control and you do what you want to do, and the punter has to pay you to do it. I have had lots of men who have been fairly old and lots of fat blokes, bald, smelly even, but I've told them to get a bath before I'd go near them. You have to just forget about whether you like them and just switch off, and go some place else in your head. I imagine I'm getting shagged by someone gorgeous but most of the time I

don't think about anything much. To be honest I'm probably thinking about what to buy for my tea while I've got some punter fucking me senseless but it's easy money really and I don't see how I'm being used or abused. I'm just providing a service that somebody wants to pay for. They're happy and I'm happy so there's no problem. I'll probably get sick of it before long so when I've got some decent money saved I want to get a regular job, but for now it's working out OK.'

Johan (21), London

'The dirty details? Well, you'd be surprised because I think most people assume that the punters want to fuck you and, OK some do, but I'd say that the majority I've had have wanted me to fuck them, or they've wanted to suck my cock. The other thing people don't realise is that most of the people you get are straight guys, often married, and they want to get it on with another man. I hear all the stories about how their wife doesn't want sex or doesn't want to do it enough, or how they've started thinking about sex with a man, or how they've realised they're gay or bisexual. You get all sorts of mad stories but I just take it in my stride; it's not my problem. Basically there are just lots of fucked-up straight men in the world who want to get fucked. It's quite funny or sad depending how you look at it.'

Paul (21), London

'Yes, I have used escorts quite a few times but I'm not ashamed to say so. I have a good job so I can afford to do it quite often and so I just call up an escort a bit like a treat sometimes if I just feel in the mood. I'm not ugly or anything, so I could go out and pick up guys if I wanted to, but it's easy to pay someone to do what you want them to do, and then just leave without any consequences. There's plenty of choice too, so you can pick someone that is just the right type; in fact I've seen a couple of escorts more than once because they're good and it's just no-strings sex. We're like friends really and they just do the business and they go which is perfect. I don't go around telling people what I do because I don't think it's socially acceptable in most circles, but it's my choice.'

Martin (clerk, 40), London

FELCHING

Just when you think you've heard of every truly gross sex act, along comes felching, which (apparently) involves sucking recently ejaculated semen from the recipient's rectum. No, really, it does. Still, it's not necessarily a uniquely gay activity, so they can't blame this one on the homos. Good one to mention at parties, not such a good one to mention in church. Although . . .

FELLATIO

A fancy name for the good old-fashioned blow job. Just in case you're the only person left on the planet who doesn't know what it actually involves, it's the simple act of stimulating a man's penis in your mouth. And you thought oral sex was all about talk?

Like any sex act, it's something which you either love or hate and, while accepted gay fashion would have you believe that every gay man likes sucking dick, it's not necessarily true, in just the same way that not everybody is obsessed with anal sex.

What does appear to be clear is that guys are almost inevitably better at doing it than girls. Why? Well it seems to be down to the fact that a man knows what the sensation feels like, so he knows precisely what proverbial buttons to press; a case of doing unto others what you would have done unto yourself. The country's bars are always rife with stories about girls giving seriously bad head, and for once it would seem that the beer talk is actually true.

Things get more complicated when you consider what's gonna happen when the guy ejaculates. Do you stop before things get messy, do you keep going and spit out the evidence, or do you swallow? Again, it's down to personal choice and, while lots of gay men will claim that just everyone likes swallowing spunk, there's lots of guys that really just don't want to go there, thank you very much.

If it is your thing, there's conflicting information as to whether it's actually a good idea. Research consistently indicated that the risk of HIV infection from oral sex was virtually negligible, but later information revised this thinking quite drastically, and suggested that it might actually be a risky activity. The most recent research contradicts this view yet again, however, based on the assumption that accepted statistics contained some rather dodgy facts which had been based on asking HIV-positive men what sex acts they had actually engaged in (a surprising number of people claimed that they only had oral sex when in fact they'd actually had anal sex but felt that it was somehow better not to say so).

Current thinking is based on the most recent statistics, and the general view is that around five per cent of all annual HIV infections in the UK can be attributed to oral sex. That equates to around 65 cases per year out of a total of maybe 1,400. So it's fair to say that you would be very, very unlucky to pick up HIV through sucking cock, even though it can (and does) happen. Further research seems to indicate that almost all of the people who have been infected in this way have either swallowed semen or at least had it in their mouths, so current health advice is to make sure you don't have any cuts, bleeding gums, ulcers or other mouth infections if you're going to engage in oral sex. Of course, a condom can also be used, but it's not a practice that many (if any) men seem very keen to pursue. The basic lesson seems to be that common sense is all that is necessary. But try telling that to the pissed-up guys outside the clubs on a Saturday night . . .

Viewpoints

'I always thought that every gay man was into sucking cock 'cause everyone just thinks that they are, but I've been with lots of people now and I know that's not how it is. I think most guys seem to enjoy doing it but some don't and I just don't really. I don't think there's anything exciting about having some bloke's knob in your mouth at all; I just can't see the thrill; it's gross really. But then I probably sound really two-faced 'cause I enjoy being sucked off by girls and lads, but ultimately I don't think I have to make any excuses for how I feel. I'd never make or expect anyone to do anything sex-wise, only do what they wanted to do. I do think that girls are crap at giving blow jobs though, or at least most of the girls I've been with have been. They don't seem to enjoy doing it really. I think they feel like they're performing a duty or something, and they have a nasty habit of getting their teeth in the way.'

John (unemployed, 26), Rochdale

'You kidding me? Sucking cock is awesome. I love it and I always have done. I'm not sure what the actual turn-on is really but I think it's to do with making the other man lose control and you just like giving him real pleasure, something like that anyway. All I know is that it's good fun, that feeling when you can sense he's just about to come, and then when you feel it in your mouth, just incredible. I'd do it all day if I could. Straight men are the best I think 'cause they're always up for it if you can just get them into the position where they think they can get away with it without their girlfriend knowing or whatever. And I know for a fact that lots of straight men like sucking cock too, even though they'd never admit it to anyone, but I know what goes on in toilets, with rent boys and on phone lines, internet and what have you. It's like straight men make out to their friends that they would be disgusted at the idea of doing something like that but actually lots of 'em are gagging to. It's mad, but that's straight people for you.'

Ian (student, 20), Doncaster

FISTING

Another surprisingly graphic term (famously used to such great effect by Julian Clary) for a sex act which is definitely not for the faint-hearted. Basically, it's all about inserting your hand into your sexual partner's butt – the whole way in until you've actually made a fist inside his arse. Ouch! You'd be forgiven for thinking that apart from being hideously painful it would be physically impossible, but, astonishingly, the muscles and lining of that part of your anatomy are much more flexible than you'd ever imagine. If you want to find out just how flexible, the advice is to use lots of lubrication (and that means specially produced lube like KY Jelly) and to take things very, very slowly, starting with a finger and working your way up. Although it's not the kind of thing that every man might fancy trying, some guys find the experience seriously stimulating and erotic.

Unfortunately there are some risks, not least the ease with which the inside of the anus can bleed and be damaged quite severely (things are pretty delicate in there), and hospital outpatients nurses will delight in telling you the countless tales of embarrassed (and often straight) men who have shoved all manner of household goods up their butts, only to be unable to get them out again. At least a hand is removable.

Viewpoint

'We used to do fisting quite regularly but we haven't done it for a while now, so maybe we just got bored with it. I used to do it to my partner and he loves it. Obviously you have to be in the mood for it and it's not the sort of thing you want to do in five minutes while you're cooking supper. You need to have plenty of time to relax and have fun. I suppose it does inevitably hurt, at least that's what he says to me, but not so much that he doesn't want to do it. It's one of those things where you can actually get off on the discomfort, I suppose. But, yeah, it's not something that every bloke would want to do, and I don't think I'd ever fancy having it done to me for starters.'

Neil (care assistant, 29), Bristol

FROTTAGE

Here's an obscure one which you've probably actually experienced, even though you didn't know there was a name for it. Frottage describes the act of rubbing up against another (clothed) person as a means of obtaining sexual gratification. You know when that bloke on the tube is brushing against you just that little bit too much? Well, at least you have a name for it now and, no, it doesn't have anything to do with French cheese.

FRUIT PICKER

A relatively new and delightfully descriptive term for straight lads that like to dabble with queer boys. Just don't ask why because the excuses can be either very unconvincing or just plain embarrassing. They're curious, or their girlfriend doesn't understand them, or they're just really, really drunk and, the next day, well, they can't remember anything about the night before. Whatever, we all know the truth that they just want to get it on with another guy but for some reason they just can't deal with that simple little fact. It's no big deal, you guys, get over yourselves. Oh, and does it mean you're, er . . . gay? Yeah, it does, actually, at least that's what the dictionary says. Is that a problem then?

GLORY HOLES

One from the distant past which still, remarkably, endures in one or two places. In short, a Glory Hole is the name given to a small hole which is drilled into the dividing wall of a public toilet. You can guess the rest . . . Why? Well, the holes were (and sometimes still are) an excellent way of achieving sexual contact between two men in a public toilet, without attracting so much as a frown from the more everyday users of the facility. In purely sexual terms, the set-up provides a turn-on for both the man who is receiving the attention (he can imagine it's the most gorgeous hunk on the planet sucking his dick) and the guy who is doing all the work on the other side, who can also imagine any kind of person he likes is attached to the member that's sticking through the hole. Of course, it's more likely that either one or both parties is less than jaw-droppingly beautiful, but that's part of the fun, or at least it is if you're good at suspending belief. With the arrival of modern building materials, toilet walls can rarely be punctured these days, so the appearance of Glory Holes is now relatively rare. For those that remain, it might be interesting to know how the law looks at their use in the future, now that the rules on public sex are being changed. After all, if the cubicle doors are closed . . .

KETAMINE

Another relatively recent addition to the gay clubber's drugs cupboard, Ketamine is a short-acting general anaesthetic drug (often used on horses, would you believe) which creates hallucinogenic and pain-killing feelings, and quite often results in physical incapacitation (you know the ones who are collapsed in a corner and you just can't get them to walk? Well . . .) as well as numbness or nausea. There don't appear to be any significant health risks connected with the drug, but taking an anaesthetic tells you that it's not the kind of thing you ought to try at a children's party. Ketamine's affects can be unpredictable and, as you might expect, it's possible to injure yourself quite badly and not even know about it until the next day. A really bad trip could cause unconsciousness and cardiovascular failure. Likewise, Ketamine has unpredictable effects with other drugs and shouldn't be taken with alcohol. Stick to Pro Plus, there's a dear . . .

Links

www.leda.lycaeum.org/?ID=148

www.erowid.org/chemicals/ketamine/ketamine.shtml

MUSCLES

What do you do? You can't deny that, for any gay lad, a fit-looking guy with bulging pecs looks damned sexy. But how sexy? And does it make him more sexy than a skinny guy or a fat guy? It's all very subjective depending on personal taste. The media feeds us images which have trained us to believe that, if we want to get some attention, we ultimately need to have a body like Jean Claude Van Damme's; you've got to have biceps like Popeye's to get ahead, or so we're told in a not-so-subtle way. But then, just as we've been visually trained to accept that big-is-best, the glossies start bombarding us with images of scrawny lads with 28-inch waists and ribs poking through their skin, looking like they haven't enjoyed a square meal since 1985. What are we to think? We are victims of fashion, and even unconsciously our heads (and therefore our dicks) are ruled by our eyes, and what we see ultimately tells us what we like or dislike. We are victims of media manipulation and we are at a crossroads in our collective perceptions of what is desirable and what isn't. While generations of gay men have accepted that we should strive to be big and butch, a new generation is being force-fed a different image – that we should be svelte, slightly femme and positively undernourished. What's a guy to do?

Viewpoints

'The whole thing about being really sexy if you've got muscles is a bit mad because it's totally subjective. There are big, pumped-up blokes that are really ugly and then there are some really gorgeous ones. It's stupid the way the media generalises things, and then it encourages us to automatically make out somebody is great just because he's got muscles. Personally I don't think the really big body-builder types ever look sexy. They look a bit stupid sometimes.'

Craig (unemployed, 24), Leeds

'I'm at university and I think it's true that lots of people in my sort of age group don't automatically think that you have to be big and muscular to be sexy and attractive. In fact I think more of us would be inclined to go for people with just normal slim bodies if they had a choice. I agree that a man with a really good physique will always look hot, but I don't think there's as much emphasis on the body-builder look as there might have been in the past.'

Simon (student, 19), Manchester

PHONE LINES

They were so big back in the nineties it was like the whole gay male world was sat on the other end of the line. The infamous phone line took over from the personals adverts in newspapers and magazines and gave us all, male and female, gay and straight, a much easier and more effective way of contacting each other. All very nice, but it didn't take too long before everyone realised the potential for doing a whole lot more on the telephone than just arrange a date. The age of the Phone Wank was born when the concept of creating verbal porn was first realised in the 1980s; a limitless opportunity to talk dirty without fear of ridicule or discovery was discovered by advertisers across the world as a way to get your rocks off without the bother of even leaving your house. The world, it seemed was hooked.

Not surprisingly, the sex-sassy gay guys locked on to the idea in a big way and gay magazines suddenly blossomed with page after page of adverts for filth on the phone. Pay your money and take your choice from an endless variety of pre-recorded smut, designed to whip you into a frenzy of passion, ultimately consummated by your right hand. Wipe up and hang up, that's all there was to it. But listening to pre-recorded pornography was a one-dimensional world compared to the one-on-one chat lines, where you could either discuss your dirtiest fantasies with another living, breathing person or, better still, arrange to meet up and do it for real. The possibilities were limitless.

Of course, the reality of these phone-induced romances was often less than satisfying; it was all too easy to oversell on the phone, and the 'twenty-something athletic dude' often turned out to be a forty-something balding bank manager. Voices can be very deceptive. But there were plenty of successes to outweigh the disasters, and phone meets became a common activity, matched only by the insatiable desire to talk dirty for hour upon hour, with no aspiration other than orgasm. Harmless fun maybe, but the cost of the premium-rate calls created a whole society of gay men with staggeringly expensive telephone bills. It had to stop. And it did to some degree, with the arrival of the internet and the option for easier and cheaper (sometimes even free) conversation via the world-wide web. The phone line companies competed with lower prices, but their monopoly on masturbatory fulfilment was forever stolen by the lure of visually enhanced virtual sex on the net.

Viewpoints

'God, phone lines have cost me a fucking fortune. Lots of people got stung by phone lines because they never realised how much they were paying for the calls until the bills came. Or sometimes you did know it was expensive but you always told yourself you'd stay on the line just a

few more minutes, just in case someone great appeared, and next thing you'd have been on the line for an hour or more. It was so mad but it's compulsive if you're bored or horny and the opportunity is there.'

Sean (unemployed, 27), Liverpool

'I think the phone line thing gets a bad press unnecessarily really, as it's just a bit of fun, and what is the point of getting snotty about people who go on phone lines. If you don't like that kind of thing then don't do it, that's all there is to it. I've been on phone lines for ages 'cause you can find some cheap ones if you look carefully enough. It's just a bit of fun, that's all. I never meet anyone off the phone because you can't be certain that they're anything like they say they are when they describe themselves. They may be OK but they could be an axe-murderer or something. I just go on lines when I've got nothing else to do, or when I'm feeling really randy. There's always other people on there that are feeling just the same and you can just talk about what you'd like to do to each other – be really rude and it's fine. It's great if you're in the mood, just wanking and having some other lad listening to you while you're laid on your bed spurting all over. It's wicked.'

Anthony (student, 20), Blackpool

'Years back I did sometimes meet people that I'd spoken to on the phone line, and it was OK, I suppose, but I never met anyone that I was really into. They were all just quick fumbles really, but there you go. They were never as nice as they sounded, but I think you kinda expect that because everyone tries to make out they're great just to get you to meet up. There was only one bloke that I actually refused to go off with when we met. He sounded really OK on the phone but when we met up he was about twenty years older and looked a right mess. I told him to fuck off, as if I was into necrophilia, 'cause I was really annoyed I'd gone for nothing. After I felt a bit guilty that I'd given him the brush-off like that, but then I thought I shouldn't feel guilty 'cause he was the one that had lied about what he looked like and how old he was.'

James (teacher, 30), Birmingham

'I used to work for a phone company for a bit. You got paid to take calls all day from people who just wanted to talk dirty. It wasn't the chat-and-meet type of line, it was the ones where you knew you were just calling up to talk filthy and have a wank. I needed the cash because I was a student at the time, and I didn't mind doing it, although it took up way too much time for not very much cash. It was crazy really just pretending to be really horny all day for all these blokes who you knew were just sat there wanking themselves silly. I just tried to switch off and kept saying the same old stuff about how horny I felt, and all these wild sex things I'd do to them if we were together. You just kept it up until they came and hung up. God, I became so good at making it sound like I was coming, it

was hilarious. I had mates with me sometimes and it was hard to stop laughing out loud because they'd be sat giggling at the crap I was coming out with. Oh well, it was a crap job.'

Mark (office administrator, 30), London

POPPERS

In response to James Dreyfus screaming that he was 'very big on the gay scene' in an episode of *Gimme Gimme Gimme*, Kathy Burke famously said that 'so are poppers, and they both smell of old socks'. She wasn't wrong, of course, and that little bottle of Amyl, butyl, liquid gold, or whatever you call it, has become a common accessory on the gay dance floor. Snorted through the nose or inhaled through the mouth (a good way to avoid eventually burning your nose), poppers produce an instant high – everything is full-colour and fantastic. The drug causes instant dilation of your veins and arteries, so your blood rushes through your body much faster, and you're buzzing big time. Of course, the same effect can be quite exciting in the bedroom, doing in a couple of seconds what Viagra might take an hour to achieve.

On the flipside of the coin, its effects are very short lived (like, a minute or so), and the next morning you'll probably have a headache like you just don't wanna know. More seriously, poppers should never be combined with Viagra, and shouldn't be used by people who have glaucoma, anaemia, breathing or heart problems. Longer term, some scientists have linked poppers to Aids and forms of cancer, but the jury is out as to whether there is any hard evidence to back up these findings. It's probably fair to assume that poppers certainly don't do you any good, but in moderation there could be worse things to stick up your nose.

Links

www.allaboutpoppers.com

RIMMING

Nothing to do with bottle opening, rimming describes the act of stimulating your partner's anus with your tongue. Undoubtedly one of those things that either excites you or makes you gag, rimming remains surprisingly popular with lots of people, both male and female, even though there is an undeniable risk of STD transmission if you're not very careful or just plain unlucky. Good way to get someone's undivided attention.

SAUNAS

Let's be honest here, saunas have virtually nothing to do with getting hot and steamy. Well, maybe they do in a completely different sort of way, but it would be misleading to suggest that gay men go to saunas to simply open their pores. With few exceptions, gay saunas are about cruising and sex; they're a no-nonsense way to meet guys who are up for it, without having to stand in a cold park, chat endlessly on a phone line or type for hours on the internet. You can see what's on offer and join in whenever you get the urge. Anyone that tells you saunas are for socialising is either telling fibs, or he's been to completely the wrong place.

Viewpoints

'Saunas are pretty good if you're looking for sex. You get lots of different people, so even if you're not into older guys or fatties, you can usually find someone that you like. It's all about going at the right time though 'cause for lots of the time saunas can be empty, so you have to know when to go. It can be really good though, and I've had some good fun, either just with another bloke or with people watching us, or I've been watching them. You can do pretty much whatever you want, and if you're horny it's perfect.'

Jason (sales assistant, 25), Manchester

'I've never been to a sauna and I don't think I'd want to, judging by the tales I've heard. As far as I can work out, they're grubby places full of old, fat geezers who are looking for sex. I know a mate who worked in a sauna and he told me all about stuff that goes on, like the colour of the jacuzzi water, and crusty towels that haven't been washed. It's just gross.'

Ian (unemployed, 22), Sheffield

SCAT

And you thought you were unshockable? Yes, some people go that extra mile and get into the malodorous world of scat, or shit as it's more commonly described. Exactly why you would get off on even the idea of someone taking a dump on you (or you on them) is hard to imagine, unless you're one of those gifted individuals that finds something erotic about poop. But it does go on and, while it's fair to say that things like scat are of equal interest (or disgust) to straight couples, you're probably more likely to hear about it within gay circles, simply because gay men and lesbians tend to be rather more open about the very mention of sexual taboos. Thankfully not the kind of thing that you're ever going to come across by accident but, if anyone mentions scat to you, don't imagine for a minute that you're going to a Cleo Laine concert.

SIXTY-NINE

Yet another one of those visual descriptions that works oh-so well. The ol' sixty-nine is basically two guys or two girls attending to each other's bits at the same time. It's also another act which is just as popular amongst straight society as it is in gay circles, even though only the more laid-back hetties might care to actually admit it. A great pastime for a thoroughly absorbing sex session, but there's a school of thought that suggests you might be ignoring a lot of pleasure when you're busy taking care of your partner's. Better to take things one at a time maybe?

SPEED

Sometimes called whiz, blues, base or sulphate, it's all more or less the same stuff. Speed makes your heart race and you're bursting with energy, ready to dance all night. Snorted or dabbed, it causes a dry mouth and sometimes a strange urge to grind your teeth. It kills appetite and good-quality speed could keep you buzzing for up to six hours, although police tests show that most speed has a purity of way less than 10 per cent. Tolerance to speed builds quickly so that more and more is required to achieve the same effect. The bad news is that anyone on speed could bore for England, embarking on endless rambling conversations about the colour of gerbils, or a two-hour monologue about how you're their best friend ever in the whole world.

Mixing alcohol with speed can lead to a lack of inhibitions, so the risks of unsafe sex have to be considered. The come-down can be bad too, with tiredness, a feeling of being generally ill and weak, combined sometimes with paranoia, depression, even hallucinations. Not recommended for anyone with high blood pressure or heart problems, and not a good mixer with poppers, coke or an E. And definitely not to be mixed with antidepressants – that combination has sometimes been fatal.

Link

www.aromadome.com/amphetamine.html

SPIT ROAST

A gloriously visual description of a sexual act which is applicable to both gay and straight couples or, to be more precise, threesomes. Basically, it requires one person to engage in anal and oral sex simultaneously, with two men providing the, er . . . input to both the recipient's mouth and arse. The jury's out as to who gleans the most enjoyment from the act but it probably comes down to whether you like being screwed, like sucking cock or like to give it rather than get it. There's scope for plenty of variation depending on the versatility and willingness of the participants but there's also a definite requirement for all three people to be very clear about who is going to do what, and to know just how far everyone wants to go. Certainly not something you'd try in the back seat of a car or at a wedding reception, unless you knew the relatives really well.

Viewpoint

'I've done it a few times and it's very good fun if you're in the right kind of mood for it. It's a really intense sensation to be sucking a bloke's cock and be getting fucked at the same time, and really good. But it's not the sort of thing that everyone would like and it's not something I'd want to do all the time. It's not like really relaxed love-type of sex; it's a really horny knocking-things-off-the-wall-type of thing and sometimes that's what you want. You have to know what you enjoy I guess and be able to be relaxed with two other people.'

Simon (student, 18), Manchester

STDS

Eww . . . Sexually Transmitted Diseases. Not the kind of subject to bring up over the dinner table, but the unpleasant nature of the subject encourages embarrassment and shame, which of course ultimately leads to yet more infections. It's a vicious circle. So what are the unmentionables which we dread? Have a stiff drink, take a deep breath and enjoy . . .

CHLAMYDIA (OR NON SPECIFIC URETHRITIS)

It usually starts with a stinging sensation when you take a pee, and can sometimes progress to a discharge from both the penis and anus (stick with it, don't puke just yet). Caused by germs and bacteria, the disease can progress to the eyes and throat. You can catch it through fucking (without a condom), rimming and sucking. The good news is that antibiotics cure it.

CRABS (PUBIC LICE)

Those sweet little friends that you just can't get rid of. The itch becomes a rash, and on closer inspection the little spots have legs. Eww! They hang out in your pubic hair and can often take a vacation in your facial hair and eyebrows. Worse still, there's no real way to avoid them as they are spread by contact rather than by sexual activity. You know the story about how your friend caught crabs from a bed or a sofa? Maybe they weren't lying . . . Thankfully a visit to your chemist will provide you with a suitable lotion that you bathe in (and you need to be pretty thorough with it), and the little visitors will be gone.

CANDIDA & BALANITIS (THRUSH)

Another rash found on the penis, anus, mouth or throat. Caused by a yeast infection (a fungus), it can be caught through close (not necessarily sexual) contact, so try not to get too close to your friends if you don't know where they've been, OK? Anti-fungal creams and pills can be obtained from a sexual-health clinic to take care of the problem.

GENITAL WARTS

Small fleshy lumps around the genital region, this little problem comes from close body contact (primarily sexual) and, yes, they're very infectious, so if your prospective partner either admits the problem or you see the signs, it might be a good idea to put your clothes back on. Treatment involves a visit to your local clinic to have the warts removed (usually they're frozen off).

GONORRHOEA

More discharge from the penis or anus (feeling ill yet?) and pain when passing water. Caused by a germ which lives in the genital areas or throat, gonorrhoea is picked up from all the usual sexual contact routes (and you thought rimming that guy was such a good idea?). But, thanks to antibiotics, it's something you can get rid of without too much trouble.

HEPATITIS B

This one's no picnic. The symptoms can sometimes be hard to find, but it can cause jaundice, dark urine, tiredness and flu-like feelings. The virus is present in all types of bodily fluid so you could pick up Hep B from almost any form of sexual contact. It can take months to recover from it, and in some cases it can even be fatal. The best advice is to seek treatment early or, better still, get a Hep B vaccination to avoid getting it in the first place.

HERPES

Small and often painful blisters they're the same as the cold sores you get round your mouth but these affect your genitals too. Discharge and the painful pee syndrome is also possible. Here's the great news – once you get it you can't ever get rid of it, although tablets and creams can suppress outbreaks. If you suspect your partner has herpes, stay well clear until any sores have completely cleared or else you're likely to get 'em too.

HIV

Potentially the most dangerous of all STDs, HIV does lead to symptoms, although they vary from person to person and can sometimes take years to develop. Swollen glands are one sign, as well as night sweats and other general infections, but there are many potential symptoms, almost all of which could be due to other illnesses. Unprotected anal sex is the primary route of infection as well as the sharing of needles in drug use. Oral sex is a potential risk but a relatively low one. Of course, there is no cure as yet, but drug combinations can effectively slow down the progression of the disease, and early detection is the key for providing effective treatment.

SCABIES

The most common STD in Britain, scabies symptoms include an itchy rash around the groin, under the arms, behind the knees, or anywhere that these nasty little mites can make their home. They also have an endearing tendency to bury themselves under your skin. Sweet. Apart from sexual contact, the sharing of bedding and clothing (dressing gowns, etc.) can spread the problem, but, as with crabs, a lotion will take care of the problem and tablets can control the itching. Brr!

SYPHILIS

Starting with sores on the penis, anus or mouth, the syphilis germ spreads through bodily fluids and can ultimately develop into mental illness, heart disease and even death. Luckily, unless it's left untreated for too long, simple antibiotics will get rid of it so that even this potentially serious disease isn't anything to worry about, providing that you do something about it.

So, if you're still not feeling like throwing up, you might at least be thinking that indiscriminate sex isn't quite so exciting as you imagined, when you consider the potential side-effects. But the lesson is simple – safe sex makes the risk of STD transmission minimal and, providing that you use your brains as well as a condom, and avoid rimming or sucking off total strangers, you'll probably avoid most of the nasty maladies described here. If, however, you're unlucky enough to catch one or two, then the local sexual-health clinic will soon provide a means to deal with the problem without any embarrassment, judgement or lecturing. There's no need to be shy either – the clinic staff have seen things that you can't even imagine, so your scabby dick isn't likely even to raise an eyebrow. And even if you think you're fit and well, an occasional check-up isn't a bad idea if you're planning to put it about a bit.

Links

www.gaylife.about.com/cs/physicalhealth

STRIPPERS

When it comes down to free entertainment in gay pubs and clubs, you probably have two options. One is a drag queen miming to a Shirley Bassey number, and the other is some fella taking his clothes off. Strippers are cheap and cheerful (actually some are pretty expensive and damned miserable but that's another story) and what could be more appropriate for a room full of horny men? You'd think it would be a match made in (gay) heaven but, in reality, strippers aren't quite as big a hit as you might have imagined.

OK, the theory is good but the reality is often pretty disappointing. It has to be said that an awful lot of strippers would probably look way sexier if they kept their clothes on, and it's also more than fair to say that the typical stripper stage act is, shall we say, less than imaginative. You know the deal – you start with a stereotypical uniform (fireman, policeman, pilot, sailor, or whatever) and you strut up and down, whipping the audience into a frenzy of indifference. Then, just as everyone is thinking about running off to buy another pint, off come the clothes and . . . oh dear, he's a little on the podgy side, but no matter, it's time for the baby lotion which (almost by tradition) has to be splashed around until pretty much everyone within thirty feet is covered. Then out comes a flag (preferably a Stars and Stripes) and off comes the underwear, tantalisingly hidden behind the flag. There then follows a bit of vaguely absurd knob waving from behind the flag (reminiscent of a cheap magician's trick) until (finally) the stripper reaches the climax of his performance and reveals . . . well, it's his penis actually, and when you've seen one you've pretty much seen 'em all. And that's it. Show's over.

Thanks to years of assumptions and false notions of what constitutes 'gay entertainment', the stripper act has become a sort of iconic cliché which barely even amuses the most drunken audience, and yet nobody seems able or willing to ask why we keep coming back for more. There's certainly nothing particularly arousing about some oil-covered penis being waved in your face while you're either trying to hold a conversation or have a drink, and there's really nothing very amusing about having baby oil splashed on your finest outfit by some overweight straight guy who imagines that you must be burning with sexual frustration and desire simply on the basis that he's male and he's naked. The really ironic performances are those where some poor lad is dragged from the audience to be ritually humiliated on stage and, as he gets his clothes pulled off, the audience is starting to wonder whether he's actually rather sexier than the stripper. It does happen.

VANILLA

Nothing to do with ice cream, vanilla is a fairly new term which describes the kind of unadventurous sex that your mum and dad might have had (or might still be having – keep that door shut). The gay scene has reached a saturation point for sexual peculiarities and fetishes, so that the plain old man-on-man or woman-on-woman stuff has actually reached a point where it's referred to as being 'vanilla'. Actually, don't believe a word of it; even though the media and the internet might make you think that everyone is hanging from chandeliers, most people are quite happy to make sex simple and uncomplicated. Vanilla's a nice flavour.

WANKING

Undoubtedly the most popular sexual activity performed by gay (and straight) men. Masturbating, wanking, jacking or jerking off, beating off, spanking the monkey, bashing the bishop, we could go on all night. Not the kind of thing that often crops up in polite conversation but everyone does it, and most people engage in this harmless pastime at least once a day (some particularly randy individuals manage six or even eight performances or more per day, begging the question as to whether they even have time to eat). Contrary to what your mother told you, there's no risk of getting hairy hands, nor will it make you go blind. In fact, wanking helps to lower blood pressure and it undoubtedly makes you feel better, so medical advice is that you may as well unzip and enjoy. When it comes to sexual contact with other men, wanking is still the most popular activity, especially when the vast majority of sexual contact between men (either gay, straight or bisexual) is in the form of the briefest encounters in toilets, clubs, dark rooms, cars, alleyways or bushes. Above all, its safe sex at it's best and it's perfectly harmless.

WATER SPORTS

Nothing to do with surfing in any way, water sports (or 'golden showers') describes the act of urinating as part of a sex act. Another of those rather unusual activities which are inevitably assigned to the supposedly decadent world of gay sex, but actually something which straight couples also indulge in. The variations on this theme are endless but basically it involves pissing on your partner, or him (or her) pissing on you. Whether you think this could be described as fun or just plain ridiculous (and pretty messy) is down to your personal preferences, but some people do find the pastime enjoyable, and at least it can be classed as completely safe sex, there being no risks involved in any contact with urine, although it's probably advisable to shower afterwards. Definitely something best confined to the bathroom rather than the bedroom.

3: Diversity

If there really is such a thing as the Gay Community, then where the hell is it? Is there some hillside somewhere that we should all be gathering on, holding hands to sing round a campfire? Nah, of course the reality of our so-called community is very different. Homosexuality is, by definition, the one thing that joins us together; we are all attracted to people of the same sex. But that's not the end of the story. That one fundamental fact which separates us from the rest of society also opens up a whole world of interests, views, activities, beliefs and lifestyles that we also share, to a greater or lesser degree. Because our view of the world is coloured by our sexuality, we tend to look at things from a slightly different angle, and it's this eccentricity which often endears us to, or isolates us from, the rest of society. But let's not be scared of our difference – we should celebrate our diversity.

ADOPTION

It's worth remembering that it's perfectly legal for either a gay man or a lesbian to adopt a child. It's something which already happens, and lots of kids have already been successfully raised by single (gay) parents or couples. The peculiar part about the law has always been that it wasn't legal for a gay couple to adopt a child, a fact which some people saw as merely silly, while others felt was downright offensive. In practice the law didn't make much day-to-day difference to the lives of the adopted children or their parents, but you can imagine the kind of confusion it still causes when you start to consider responsibilities, partnership break-ups, deaths, wills and so on. Adoption has consequently been high on the agenda of gay rights campaigners for many years, and it wasn't until May 2002 that the House of Commons finally voted in favour of a Bill to give gay couples the same adoption legal rights as heterosexual couples, despite protests from the usual range of right-wing and pro-family religious groups. MP Peter Lilley commented that 'children are not trophies and should not be tools for social engineering either for the politically correct agenda or for those of us who believe in marriage'. Fair point, but he also said that the change in the law would make it even harder for married couples to adopt a child. In fact, all of the country's adoption agencies and experts agree that the change in the law will actually make no difference to married couples who are already trying to adopt, but that it will hopefully make it much easier for countless children to be placed with parents.

So, despite the continued whining and bitching of the 'moral right' this legislation isn't really about gay rights, but about the rights of children to be placed with parents. Even so, anti-gay icon Norman Tebbit felt compelled to decline a wedding invitation from his MP friend, John Bercow, simply because he'd supported the issue of gay adoption. He replied, 'You will not be surprised to know that I believe it would now be quite wrong for my wife and I to be guests at the marriage of your daughter and Mr Bercow.'

But no matter, like it or not, the Bill went to the House of Lords in November 2002, where both protagonists and antagonists expected the assembly to throw out the proposal, as was always the accepted practice with any legislation which appeared to be overtly pro-gay. Astonishingly, the vote went in favour of the Bill, and now looks set to be introduced as legislation in the not too distant future, leaving the anti-gay campaigners with some seriously sour grapes to swallow. The ever-offensive Christian Institute managed to come up with an almost-comical 'donor card' which reads, 'In the event of my death I do not want my children to be adopted by homosexuals. Let your relatives know my wishes.' You can't help hoping that somebody publishes another card which reads, 'In the event of my death I do not want my children to be adopted by religious bigots.'

James Newton, a co-ordinator of a gay youth support programme, said that 'There is a lot of research saying that there is no detriment to children adopted by gay parents. I would like to see the evidence of the opposite.'

Stonewall's chief Angela Mason said, 'We are very pleased that Parliament has approved a reform that will help children find loving homes. The Christian Right tried to hijack this Bill and used every questionable argument and unsubstantiated claim that it could muster to distract attention from the case made by those who have a real and in-depth understanding of adoption and children.'

Most confusingly, James Davenport, the chairman of gay Conservative group Torch, said, 'Labour has put the cart before the horse by trying to introduce gay adoption before registered partnerships.' Er, actually, we'll have those too please.

Maybe the last word should be left to the delightfully loopy Family Fortress group and one of their commentators who said, with more than a hint of unintentional irony, 'Families reared by a father and mother who are married show respect and love to each other and their children represent the time-tested, most effective method of building a secure society.' Don't laugh.

Links

www.gay.com/news

Viewpoints

'We adopted a child a couple of years ago, and it was probably the best thing we ever did. Our child is brought up in just the same way as any

other kid would be. She goes to school and has friends just like anyone else. I know there's always a worry that she might get abuse from other kids if they start making a big thing out of her having two dads instead of a mum and a dad, but I really don't know if that will happen. I think kids around her age don't really question things like that anyway, but when you look at all the single-parent families, broken homes, divorces, and all the stuff that goes on, it's stupid to imagine that everyone lives in a little house with a mummy and daddy and roses round the door. Real life isn't like that very often and I think most kids know that.

We both make sure that we're involved with the school as much as possible in any case, even if it's just taking her to and from school every day, so both parents and kids know who we are, and I don't think they look at us any differently to anyone else.

It's great that the law is finally changing, because it was so unfair to children. It wasn't really about gay rights because we always had the right to adopt, although it had to be like us, with only one person as the child's parent. But that is a bad situation for the child more than anything else, because it creates all kinds of difficulties if the parent dies. Suddenly, your partner would be left with a child that he isn't even legally responsible for, and that's got to be stupid no matter how you look at it.'

Brian (office administrator, 45), Kent

ALCOHOL

A subject close to the hearts of almost every gay boy and girl. Alcohol. According to statistics, it seems that young people are drinking more alcohol, and binge-drinking is becoming more common. It's also become clear that women are drinking much more alcohol than ever before. Getting pissed is now socially acceptable. But like any drug abuse, it can get out of control, and support organisations report an increase in the numbers of people seeking help in handling their addiction to the hard stuff. Serious stuff. Better have another drink . . .

Link

www.health.org/features/lgbt/health.htm

Viewpoints

'I drink when I'm out pubbing and clubbing, but I don't drink any more than I need to get drunk enough to just be having a laugh. I don't see any point in getting so shit-faced that I can't even remember what I've done the next day. I have friends who constantly drink themselves almost to unconsciousness and I just think they're stupid wasting all that money

and getting so pissed that they can't even walk. OK, if you want to let your hair down and get smashed that's fine, but you can go way too far.'

John (unemployed, 30), Wolverhampton

'You have to get drunk to have a good time really. Most gay pubs and clubs are just so boring and predictable, they're all full of people just standing around trying to pull each other, and the music's so deafening that you can't actually talk to anyone, and it's crap music anyway, so you can't enjoy it if you're sober. But once you're pissed, the music doesn't matter – you'll dance to anything and you just relax and have a good time. It's a bit sad that so many people have to get totally wasted when they're out just in order to have fun, but I suppose that's a reflection of how bad a lot of clubs are. They all try to do the same thing – just put up some lights, switch on a smoke machine and bang out some music at top volume and everyone will be happy. It's mad.'

David (photographer, 32), Bristol

'Everyone likes a drink, especially when they're out clubbing it. My only complaint is the way that clubs in particular never try and cater for people who have got to drive. They always try and have some sort of cheap drinks offer to attract punters, but if you want non-alcoholic drinks they're always priced way too high. So it just encourages people to drink alcohol even if they're driving and I think that's really irresponsible. You'd think that they would have a bit more consideration.'

Michael (sales assistant, 25), London

APARTMENTS

A creature of the late nineties, nobody can really work out where the gay love affair with lofts and apartments came from, but it might well have come out of an Ikea catalogue. It's something about the laminate floors, the stainless steel furniture, the angled spotlights, the sheer minimalism of it all. Or maybe it's the urban style, the distinct non-family and non-convention image that makes the whole idea of a fancy gay apartment just irresistible. As if we needed any confirmation of our desires, one of the leading characters in the much-acclaimed *Queer As Folk* television drama was depicted as being the archetypal A-list queen, complete with flashy jeep, posh designer labels and, of course, a huge under-furnished apartment.

But, as you might expect, it all went horribly wrong . . . No sooner had we found yet another gay 'must-have' than the rest of society (those darned straight people) decided that they wanted a piece of the action too. Jumping on to the gay band wagon, they snapped up every available space until prices soared out of control. Even the glitzy apartments round Manchester's Canal Street were gone, consumed by a straight frenzy which paid no heed to the fact that they were buying into a gay village. Go figure. Suddenly, the gay dream of buying an apartment was so over . . .

CAMP

According to the *Oxford English Dictionary*, camp is defined as being effeminate or homosexual. Of course, anyone who really understands what camp is all about will know only too well that camp really has nothing to do with homosexuality, but sadly it seems that (straight) society thinks that it does. We all know why, of course – it's the tireless staple diet of television comedy from the likes of Graham Norton, Julian Clary and the late Larry Grayson that forges the link between gay and camp. But although the two may go hand-in-hand, they are, of course, not the same thing.

Unfortunately, the word has now become a greatly overused adjective and unless we're very careful, its true meaning will eventually be lost for ever. You can see how its definition is already blurred by watching the various 'Top Ten Camp – whatever' shows much beloved of Channel 4 and Five (it's heroically cheap television, of course – just get an uninformed script writer and a pile of old film clips). Looking at some of the 'chart' entries, you begin to wonder how any of them could even be loosely described as amusing, let alone camp.

The whole problem seems to be that the typical straight observer regards anything slightly 'poofy' as being camp. With this kind of mind-set, you can define almost anything as camp when, of course, it patently isn't. Perhaps the most notable example of straight campery is artist, motorway builder and mass-murderer Adolf Hitler, who was possibly one of the most camp humans ever. Why? Well, it wasn't because he wore pink feathers or made cheap gags about wanting a warm hand on his entrance, missus. Not at all; he was as deadly serious as anyone could be. But just look at him. He strutted around like a peacock with a salute that any lesser mortal would have been too embarrassed to try out in public. He oversaw design of the most outlandish uniforms ever, and his eye for architecture was just awe-inspiring. Check out the Munich stadium for a classic example of overstatement. But that was Hitler's whole point; he overstated everything. Not content with a soapbox to shout from, he had to have a mile-wide stadium full of jackbooted solders, stripped to the waist, of course. And even that wasn't enough – he had to invade neighbouring countries to get attention. Absolutely ludicrous, but that's the real essence of camp; it's about a jackboot not a limp wrist.

The gay connection comes from the undeniable fact that gay men have an almost radar-like ability to sniff out anything camp, as if by nature. To 'camp it up' is a gift which is only bestowed on a few, even though many think it's a universal attribute (it so isn't). Making something camp is to ridicule it, to belittle it, to show it up for what it really is, and lots of gay men are good at it. Damned good. Camp is a way of making the serious become frivolous, the bad become good. The positive aspect of camp is that it has become a tool with which gay men have become accepted or even loved by the wider public. The down side is that society then believes that all gay men are, as if by definition, camp, and anyone who doesn't fit the job description is either a threat or an irrelevance. Worse still, this notion has created a whole new generation of gay men who positively dislike all things camp (or at least claim to) and profess to be 'straight acting' (whatever that means). It's a very confusing situation; if being camp is perceived as being so awful, does this mean that it's because camp-equals-gay? And does that mean that there's a whole new generation of gay men who don't actually want to be identified as gay?

Perhaps the solution is to try and encourage analysts and commentators alike to use their adjectives more carefully. To describe Guy Pearce (in the movie *Priscilla – Queen of the Desert*) playing a screaming queen, dressed head-to-toe in sequins as being camp is just plain lazy; there's nothing particularly ludicrous about seeing a man in a frock any more. But put him on a twenty-foot stiletto shoe atop a pink-painted bus? Now that's camp. Get the point?

CATS

What is it with homos and cats? While the straight world babbles on about the dog being man's best friend (even though there are more cats in England than there are doggies), it's the ubiquitous moggy that gay men and lesbians inevitably love. With good reason, of course; cats look after themselves; they don't have to be walked and they don't bark. They also look good (they're still visually fascinating even when they're old and scabby), and they have a snotty attitude that any self-respecting queen would kill for. They've become a living, breathing fashion accessory, self-sufficient and packed with glamour and style. Always aloof and always ready to look down their noses at anyone who dares to venture into their domain. Cats truly rock.

CLOSET

To open the door or keep it closed. The age-old dilemma. Nobody really knows where this archaic phrase came from, but we've all shared the same decision-making process as to when to open that proverbial closet door and come out. Of course, much depends on your personal circumstances: your family or friends, your age, your job, or your beliefs. For some, indeed for many, coming out of the closet is a liberating experience; no longer do you have to pretend to be straight and profess to be interested in families, cars, football or Jordan's tits (OK, there's plenty of lesbians who might disagree with part of that line), and no longer do you have to avoid laughing too loudly at Graham Norton's gags. Suddenly everything is OK and you can be yourself. Wear that crop top.

But for others it can be a nightmare, with families who don't approve and kick you out, friends who turn against you and employers who will fire you just for being gay. It's easy to say that you should just pluck up the courage to come out, but life's often not that simple. It would be great if everyone could be completely honest about their sexuality (and wouldn't that be a revelation?) but that day won't be coming along for a very long time; not while there are newspapers, Church leaders, fascist activists and politicians who still think being queer is some kind of perversion. Hopefully, sooner or later, they'll all be dead. Have patience.

Viewpoints

'I decided to come out to my parents when I was eighteen, and my mum was good about it. She said that she didn't approve but that she still loved me for who I was which was OK. My dad was nasty about it though and he just wouldn't even talk about it, and he said he wanted me to leave if I was going to live like that. You just couldn't talk to him about it and I think it's pathetic that anyone can be so stupid, but I just left. I feel a bit sorry for my mum but in a way I'm glad I left 'cause I don't want to be in a house with that kind of attitude, stuck in the closet because of people like him.'

Brian (unemployed, 22), Wolverhampton

'It's a bit different for a girl and I think lots of lesbians stay in the closet, but not because they're ashamed or anything, it's just that they don't feel a need to come out. It's often easier to just go along the same way, never getting married or anything, but nobody judges you. OK, lots of girls do come out but they're more in-your-face types who do that. I told my parents when I was 22 and they were totally relaxed; in fact, I think they kinda knew anyway although they've never said so. Ideally, I'd advise everyone to never be in the closet as it just reinforces the notion that being gay or lesbian is something to hide, which is stupid.'

Lisa (student, 19), Leeds

'I never actually came out of the closet because I was never really in, I suppose. I don't know how but they just sort of assumed I was gay eventually and never actually said anything which I suppose is quite sweet, if they just didn't want to have a scene or something. I know that they know I'm gay, so I don't push the subject with them. I've nothing to be ashamed of but at the same time my parents are fairly old and I think maybe it's a lot to handle when you've been brought up in a different society. So I don't see why I should bash on about it to them.'

Mark (unemployed, 27), Lincoln

'Coming out is a big thing for some people. I don't agree with the idea that you should make people come out of the closet if they don't want to, because they might have good reasons to stay in. I know it would be better if people didn't pretend to be straight but sometimes people have to deal with their jobs or things like that, and you just have to say what people want to hear.'

Ian (student, 18), Coventry

'OK, I know some people have to stay in the closet if they want to keep their jobs or whatever but I firmly believe that there are very, very few genuine cases like that. People use things like jobs and parents as an excuse for just not telling the truth. Closet cases annoy me because they're just giving a signal to society that being gay is wrong. Celebrities are the worst offenders and I think any celebrity that comes out after years of pretending to be straight shouldn't be praised; they should be shot for being lying bastards.'

Mark (sales assistant, 22), Blackpool

CLOTHES

We like our clothes. We're supposedly recognised for our dress sense (although sometimes you wonder why) and our interest in fashion, style and innovation. It's probably true that we do have a thing about clothes, and it's also fair to say that we have some of our own unique styles which identify us with particular 'looks' within the gay scene:

MA1 JACKET

A classic piece of fruit fashion. If you haven't bought an MA1 jacket, then you're not gay. OK, a bit of an exaggeration but it's fair to say that the ubiquitous US fighter pilot jacket (from where the code name originates) has become one of our enduring favourites. Simplicity of design, combined with lots of useful pockets and a marvellous 'butch' look, make it irresistible, particularly with skinheads and other lads who like to aim for that 'bit of rough' image. Not surprisingly, the jacket's also a big hit with almost every self-respecting shaven-headed lesbian in the country.

For the folks who want to be a little bit adventurous (or at least camp it up a bit), there are some pretty fancy coloured versions of the original green issue, and of course there's the designer version for the label queens, courtesy of Schott. Best worn with a simple white T-shirt, or no shirt at all, the MA1 is possibly the gayest item of clothing you could ever hope to own. What are you waiting for?

T-SHIRTS

Every gay man's favourite fashion item, and one that lots of the ladies prefer too, the humble T-shirt continues to reign supreme. Loved not only for its simplicity and inexpensiveness (and a perfect medium to display your muscles if you have any), it also provides a marvellous space to place your favourite slogan, billboard-like, right across your chest. The fashion for slogan-emblazoned shirts raged in the 1990s and gay businesses were quick to exploit the trend with such delights as 'I'm not gay but my boyfriend is' and 'Some of my best friends are straight', plus countless other less witty and often downright offensive variations. The world was your slogan, but, like every gay-led fashion trend, we got bored with it and went back to plain white, the famous Adidas striped shoulders or the rather more daring crop-top. However, it doesn't take much imagination to realise that what goes around comes around and, just as you thought the slogan T-shirt was history, it's more than likely to be back before too long. Why wait? Set a trend.

COMBAT PANTS

The essential item for every gay boy and girl, combats now consistently out-sell denim jeans as the preferred choice for everyday wear. As usual, it was us queer folks that spotted them first, rescuing them from the army surplus shelves until they caught on and the fashion designers took over. Not only do they look funky, but they're way more useful than jeans, because they've got pockets that you can actually put things in. The variations on your basic combats are endless, but there are some rules to remember: cheap combats look cheap and cut-off combats rarely if ever look good, especially if you've got chicken legs. Camouflage combats are pretty cool but you need the US Army regulation camouflage (or a coloured version of the same pattern), and not the British version or, God forbid, something European. If somebody starts selling combats in Day-Glo orange they'll make a small fortune.

HANKIES

One that the older fellas (and some ladies) will remember. Back in the days when homosexuality wasn't legal, it was fashionable to wear a handkerchief about your person. It had nothing to do with style but everything to do with sex actually, as the colour of the hanky, or the place where you put it, told everyone else what you were, er . . . into. It was reputedly started in America as a joke but it was taken pretty seriously for many years, and the craze even took off over here. You want some examples? OK, well, a red hanky meant you were into fisting; yellow meant spit (among other things); lavender was drag; blue was oral; black was sado-masochism, and so on. The side of your body that you wore it signified whether you were the 'giver' or 'getter' so to speak, and you can just imagine the potential for confusion . . . Little wonder the hanky thing died out when the infinitely more practical internet came along. History now records that the girls dabbled with the hanky code too. Be careful what you wear, OK?

BOOTS

No, not the chemist, the footwear thing, loved by lots of gay guys and possibly even more gay girls. Doc Martens were once all the rage, then it was Caterpillar, but now the field seems to be wide open. Always good with combats, sometimes OK with jeans, but rarely a good idea with shorts, unless you've got chunky legs and a pair of big socks.

TRACKSUITS

Not reserved exclusively for estate trash, trackie bottoms are also very popular with some gay boys who are into the sporty look. It also often has something to do with the revealing nature of the trackie bottoms if you're not wearing any underwear. If you're Jewish, everyone's gonna know about it . . .

UNDERWEAR

A subject which seems to split opinion right down the middle. While some people have a thing about pants and shorts, a whole lot more just can't understand the fascination. OK, a crisp, white pair of Calvins might look pretty hot if you've got the body to carry it off, but saggy (or grubby) knickers draped under a beer gut just doesn't do anything for your image. Likewise, if you're going for boxer shorts, try to remember that they're supposed to be proper shorts (in typical American style) rather than the overgrown Y-fronts that are peddled in England. And as if the ill-advised wearing of dodgy pants wasn't bad enough, some guys still seem to think there's something erotic about jock straps. Have you people ever looked in a mirror? It's not nice. Some sensible advice on underwear? Go commando – get rid.

COMING OUT

The big moment in our gay lives. The seminal act of announcing to your parents, or the whole world, that you're a big ol' screaming queen or a shove-it-up-your-muff lezzie. No wonder it's a day that so many of us dread. But while we anticipate tears, tearing of hair and throwing of crockery, it very often turns out to be one of the biggest non-events of our lives. Parents have a remarkably good instinct for just knowing when their son or daughter is 'a bit unusual' but they just keep it to themselves, either in the hope that if they ignore it, then it'll go away, or that discretion is the best policy.

Of course, coming out doesn't always go so smoothly, and announcing your same-sex preference can sometimes be a genuine shock for some parents, and they don't always accept the announcement with a smile. There are many unfortunate cases where people have been kicked out of their homes by intolerant parents, and more than a few instances of years-long silences between parents and children, all caused by the very mention of the 'g-word'.

But thankfully such instances are increasingly rare, now that society is shifting inexorably towards acceptance, and the success of your 'outing' will probably have more to do with your presentation than the actual facts. Simply announcing megaphone-like that you're queer can be a bit much for some people, and it's often wise to prepare the path that you're about to go down. Mentioning that you 'have no problem with gay people' is a good start (and a great way to sound out your parents' reactions too), and then you can use your judgement just how far to go, and how quickly.

If you're unlucky enough to be met by disbelief, anger or a fainting spell (some parents can be so dramatic), you could always call on the services of the many support groups around the country who can offer leaflets, telephone advisers and even personal contact to explain to your parents that you're actually not a freak, but that grandchildren may not now be a viable prospect for the future. But the most important fact is that it is hardly ever as bad as you think it's going to be. And once the deed is done it is almost inevitably an exciting and liberating experience.

But what of your friends? Should you tell them first? And which ones, and when, and how? There are, of course, no simple answers and nobody can predict the reaction of a friend. Most will inevitably say 'so what?' and change the conversation, but some will undoubtedly have a problem with your newly discovered status, and the way that you handle it is your choice. But if your best friend does suddenly go all weird on you, remind yourself that it is they who have a problem, not you, and it's up to them to get their heads round it, either with or without your help. Ultimately, if somebody no longer wants to be your friend because you're gay, then why the hell would you want to be friends with someone like that anyway? Kick 'em to the kerb, girl.

Viewpoints

'I came out to my parents when I was still at school. They were brilliant actually and I made more of a deal of it that they did. I told my mum first and she told my dad, but when he mentioned it to me he just said it as a joke and didn't really say anything much, and now I just talk openly about being gay and he never objects, in fact he just makes crap jokes. My mum just did the "you just be careful whatever you do" thing which was nice. It really was so much less of a big thing than I imagined it would be.'

Richard (clerk, 26), Northampton

'Things didn't go all that well really, but I didn't expect them to. My parents aren't ever any good at things like that and it was my dad who confronted me about being gay first off, and I just admitted it because we had this big row. He said he didn't want me living there any more because it was disgusting for a son of his to be going with boys, so I just left the same day and went to stay with my mate at his parents' house. I never went back to live and it was over a year before I even visited, and even then I was just sort of polite with my dad. My mum did come and speak to

me one day and said that she loved me whatever; but that it was dad's house and he didn't approve. It was all crap, and if that's the way they want to be then whatever; I've got to get on with my life. I've got plenty of good friends who don't give a shit whether I'm gay so I just forget about it.'

David (driver, 29), London

'My parents never had any problem with the whole gay thing and I never had to make any proper coming-out announcement to them, as I'd never really made any secret about who I was with and what I thought about the subject, so they must have just assumed that I was gay as I grew older. The bizarre thing was my best friend who I spent lots of my time with; we were like brothers at one time, and I was his best man when he got married. So I didn't think being gay would worry him that much as we were so close that I thought nothing would bother him. But one day he sent me a letter saying he'd guessed I was gay and that him and his wife were big church-goers, and they didn't approve of that sort of lifestyle. It was really sanctimonious, and he said they'd pray for me and hoped I'd change my ways, like I was some sort of deviant. It just disgusted me, and I wrote back to him saying so. I said I didn't want to be prayed for because I hadn't done anything wrong, and it was his stupid fucking church that needed praying for if anyone did. I said I didn't want to speak to him again if that was how he felt, and we never have spoken ever since. Fuck him, the judgemental bastard. In a way I'm glad it happened because it opened my eyes to how he really thought about some things.'

Tim (writer, 40), Sheffield

Links

www.gayyouth.co.uk

outrage.nabumedia.com/links.asp?c=103

www.dmoz.org/Society/Gay,_Lesbian,_and_Bisexual/Youth/Advice_and_Support

DRAG

'We were born naked. Everything else is drag', or so says RuPaul, and he should know. Men dressing up as women is part of history and something which gay men have traditionally done since the beginning of time. But it's important to distinguish a drag queen (a man who dresses as a woman ostensibly for amusement) from a transvestite (a man who dresses and actually pretends to be a real woman) or a transsexual (a man undergoing or having undergone a sex-change process). Then there's a relatively rare phenomenon, the drag king (a woman who dresses as a man) . . . God this is getting complicated. The essential point is that a drag queen isn't supposed to be taken seriously. The whole point of the outfit is that it should be good, but not too good. You've got to be able to get the gag, that it's a man mimicking a woman, and we're all supposed to be in on the joke.

Why do people do it? A variety of reasons, the most obvious being that the pay can be good (there aren't many entertainment bars that don't employ a drag queen in some capacity these days) or that the attention can be fun. If you're bored with the constant battle to look like a gym bunny, forget about it – pop on a wig. But there's no doubt that drag queens are a special breed of men. It takes a certain mind-set and a certain attitude to dress like a woman but be seen to be a man. You certainly need balls for the job in more ways than one, and make no mistake – most drag queens are no pushovers (they'd probably just as happily whip off their wigs and punch you if they got angry).

Sadly, drag seems to be losing some of its fashionable status, now that the whole gay style thing has supposedly moved on into a new world of laminated floors, cocktails and networking. But tastes change and, while the drag queens find their niche as entertainment for heterosexuals (who all want their very own local Lily Savage), we can confidently expect that gay fashion will soon evolve once more, and the feisty gals – those cocks in frocks – will be back in charge.

Viewpoints

'I've been a drag queen since I was a teenager, and I still am. Don't know why I do it really, but I think it's because it's fun and I like the attention. People do treat you like a lady even though they know you're a bloke. You get people buying you drinks and they just want you to entertain them, so fuck it, you just do it, if they're buying you drinks. I think at first it was more to do with being gay, and just pushing the fact that you were different as far as you could. Dressing like a woman really freaked people out not too long ago, and it was like a power thing 'cause it puts people on the defensive.'

Michael (sales administrator, 32), Manchester

'Up to now I've never gone out in drag but I probably will one day. I don't see why lots of gay people look down on drag queens now, because they're funny and they give clubs and stuff a bit of fun that they need. It's just a laugh really and it's nothing that we ought to sneer about. I can't get my head around proper trannies though when they hang around and they want to make out that they're real women 'cause you know and they know that they still look like men, so it's just a bit weird. But with a proper drag queen, then they do make it like a send-up and it's just a piss-take, so it's good.'

Mark (unemployed, 28), London

FAG HAGS

Nobody knows why some girls have a thing about gay boys, but fag hags (women who like gay men) are as prevalent as they ever were. Maybe it's a perception of excitement ('oh I go out with gay people, you know, yes, really I do') or maybe it's because gay men tend to be rather more fun to be with than their straight counterparts. We don't talk endlessly about football and cars, and we often share interests with girls (soft furnishings, alcohol and cock) so it's probably no surprise that more than a few girls would rather spend their nights with a homo than with a hettie.

But sometimes you wonder whether these girls have some issues that they're just not dealing with. Is it because gay men are 'safe' and there's no risk of sexual contact? Or is it that they can't get a man so they consciously hang out with us homos so they know that they won't have to deal with the problem? It's hard to tell but, for whatever reason, girlies just love us to bits.

The only slightly disturbing aspect of this situation is the way that so many young gay boys have acquired themselves surgically-attached fag hags that they drag around with them everywhere they go. It's reaching epidemic proportions and frankly it's a little bit sad. Isn't the whole point of being gay that you hang out with people of the same sex at least some of the time?

FASHION

A subject close to our hearts 'cause we all like dressing up, it's as simple as that. We all know that the fashion industry is packed full of screaming queens, and becoming a fashion designer is probably only second to hairdressers in the list of stereotypical gay clichés. But thanks to the new gay thinking which requires us to abandon anything even remotely queer, we're in danger of sneering so hard at the fashion industry that it becomes a heterosexual haven. The catwalks are already full of skinny boys who look like they should be swinging handbags, but then they go and spoil the image by announcing that they 'shag birds' (for heaven's sake). As we all know, it's now gloriously fashionable to look gay and act gay, even if you've never so much as visited Ikea. Traditionally, all the great and good ideas in the world of fashion design have come from gay men, so let's hope that we don't end up at the mercy of (cough) straight designers who'll probably have us all wearing drip-dry in a few years if we're not careful.

THE FASHIONABLE FASHION ICONS

ALEXANDER MCQUEEN

'I'm not the stereotypical gay man,' says Alexander (his real name is Lee actually), but he's certainly as bizarre and outrageous as you'd expect a big fashion name to be. Picture amputees walking down the catwalk or a dress stuffed with moths, that's our boy. East End lad done good, he joined Givenchy but hated being controlled, and eventually signed a deal for his own label with Gucci. Did he really write 'I am a cunt' inside the lining of one of Prince Charles's suits?

CHRISTIAN LACROIX

You'd probably have never heard of him if it hadn't been for *Absolutely Fabulous* and Edina's obsession with all things LaCroix. Mind you, he does produce some brilliant stuff, and he's obviously not in love with himself, otherwise he wouldn't have actually popped up in the television show, would he? French flair, classy style and a totally sorted fella too.

DOLCE & GABBANA

Gay but not gay, they refuse to join the 'gay ghetto' and despite protests they won't even join Milan's Gay Pride March, because they're all about integration and the 'normality' of gay relationships. Oh well, they're huge on the fashion scene but they're obviously not quite so good at getting their heads round homosexuality. No matter, the D&G label is way too straight and mainstream these days anyway. Move on.

JEAN PAUL GAULTIER

Gay and outrageous. God love him.

VERSACE

Bad taste and hilariously camp, but what the hell, it's got a Versace label on it. But since Gianni's untimely death, the whole Versace thing just hasn't been quite so hip. Donatella just doesn't quite cut the mustard.

WAYNE HEMMINGWAY

Fashion guru with a refreshing down-to-earth style and attitude. The man behind Red or Dead, Wayne pays no respect to the haughty fashion houses – he does his own thing. Just brilliant.

Links

www.alexandermcqueen.net

www.christian-lacroix.fr

www.dolcegabbana.it

www.jeanpaulgaultier.com

www.versace.com

www.britishcouncil.org/arts/design/zuppainglese.htm

FISH NAMES

Once upon a time, long before we got swept up in a tide of straight-acting faux machismo, it was fun to be gay and girly. Almost by tradition, every gay man was referred to as 'she' or 'her' and your gay friends inevitably christened you with a suitably ludicrous girl's name – a Fish Name, if you will (fish being a commonly used Palare term for girl). The name you got often had a vague connection to your real name, so that Simon would become Simone, Mark became Marsha, Danny became Daniella and so on, but there were always glorious exceptions. It was just a bit of simple fun, a piss-take at convention but the tradition has tended to fade away, and only a few people (usually the ones with a sense of humour) maintain the tradition. These days, of course, the obsession with normality would make most gay boys shudder at the very idea; they claim that's because it's old-fashioned, but it probably has more to do with embarrassment. The truth is that most young gay men wouldn't have the balls to do it. Sad, ain't it?

GAY GENE

No, not some drag queen name, it's a much-used term describing the recent discovery (by Salk Institute researcher Simon LeVay) that significant physical differences can be found between the brains of gay and straight men. To be precise, straight men have (deep breath . . .) an enlarged third interstitial nucleus of the anterior hypothalamus. So there. Other researchers have disputed these findings, but the search for a physical distinction between heterosexuality and homosexuality continues – the search for the mythical 'gay gene'. It's all to do with the age-old nurture-or-nature question. Are we born gay because of an hereditary cause, or is it our lifestyle or upbringing that makes us this way? Nobody knows, although everyone has an opinion. Of course, you'd be hard-pressed to find any homo who believed that it was his upbringing that made him develop a liking for show tunes or Steps. We're all quite sure that we're simply made this way, and the discovery of a physical designator would be the final conclusive evidence that we're not just choosing to act all limp-wristed merely in order to get some attention.

But such a discovery might also have some rather more sinister implications; the former Chief Rabbi of Britain said that 'Homosexuality is a disability and, if people wish to have it eliminated before they have children, I do not see any moral objections to using genetic engineering to limit this particular trend.' Without getting into the question as to whether the aforementioned Rabbi ought to be sectioned or simply stoned to death, you can see how a 'gay gene' would potentially provide the means to simply wipe out homosexuality at a stroke, as if we all had some sort of disease. It could be the gay Final Solution.

GAYDAR

Three distinct definitions here; the first applies to that special 'sixth sense' that us homos seem to have, when it comes to spotting like-minded people. It's easy enough to determine that the lad wearing a pink crop-top with bleached hair and dancing wildly to a Kylie tune is gay, but sometimes there are no visual clues, and yet . . . well, you just know somehow, don't ya? It's something to do with the way you dress or the way you walk, your expression, your eye contact . . . just a certain indefinable quality which shouts 'homo' to those in the know. The really scary thing is that you can often sense it in blokes who say they're not gay too. Hmm . . .

Then there's definition number two, which applied to a long-gone gadget which presumably originated in Japan, which was like a sort of personal radar device you carried around on your key chain or in your pocket. Aimed at us gay folk, the deal was that if you (and therefore your gizmo) came within range of someone else who was carrying one, you'd start beeping or flashing or whatever, and hey presto – you've made a new friend. Nice idea, but when the guy starts beeping a few feet away and you turn round to find that it's your brother . . . well, you can imagine all kinds of scenarios where the last thing you'd want is an indiscriminate gay beacon. Needless to say, the gadget just never caught on.

And finally, there's Gaydar definition number three or, to be more precise, Gaydar.co.uk, the much-used, much-loved and much-maligned website patronised by (or so it seems) every gay man in the country, plus more than a few others around the world. While other gay web spaces offer all kinds of information and news, Gaydar has remained faithful to just one aim – communication between gay people through a variety of profiles, photo galleries and virtual chat rooms.

The concept of live on-screen chat first took off on a rival site (Gay.com) but when the latter company disastrously decided to overhaul and modernise its chat rooms, the punters left in droves (chiefly because nobody had a clue how the new site actually worked) and Gaydar became the place to be (although the tide seems to be gradually turning back towards Gay.com now – queens are so fickle).

So what happens on Gaydar? You write yourself a profile, telling the world (or at least the rest of Gaydar-land) what your interests are, whether you're looking for friends, sex, a relationship or just a chat, what kind of people you like, whatever you like in fact. You stick on a few photographs (if you have any) and away you go. Your profile is read by thousands (eventually) and anyone who likes what they see will contact you. Or you can contact them. Then there's the chat rooms, the virtual meeting places for people who want to talk. Armed with your profile link, you enter the virtual chat rooms where you can chat to whoever else happens to be signed in. There's a list of rooms for all kinds of interests (bisexuals, truckers, students, muscle, and these are just the obvious ones) and you can talk about anything you like, but you won't be surprised to know what the main topic is. While a few brave souls heroically try to steer conversation towards television or hobbies or just the weather conditions, somebody will inevitably chime in with a message such as 'anyone up for some no-strings fun' or 'virgin ass needs fucking tonite' or 'teen boy wants to suck cock now'. You name it and somebody will have asked for it, and you have to be prepared to be totally unshockable if you plan on spending any time in a Gaydar room.

There's also the opportunity to exchange private messages between people, and the conversations can only be limited by your imagination. It's fair to say that if you want to have a sensible conversation with another human being you can certainly do that, but make no mistake – Gaydar is all about cock. Or arse, judging by some of the more graphic photographs which hit you in the face when you least expect it.

OK, it has to be said that if you don't want to feast on filth you don't have to be logged on to Gaydar – you could just switch off, but at the same time you have to wonder why so much of the photography which is readily accessible is harder than the hardest pornography. When somebody sends you a message saying 'hello' and you click on his profile, you don't necessarily want to see a top-quality colour photograph of an anal sphincter. Likewise, the receipt of gratuitous pictures of some stranger's penis can either be regarded as hilarious or offensive, depending on your mood. You just have to wonder what kind of intelligence the sender has – maybe he just plans on sending his dick along for a date while he stays home and watches television.

Love it or hate it, Gaydar has a compulsive appeal and, even when you're totally jaded by the endless requests for anonymous shags, or enquiries asking 'what are you wearing?', you tell yourself that you've had enough, and you switch off, you know that the next day you'll be back for more. You can't help it. But one question remains unanswered: where are all the lesbians? The final word comes from the satirical pen of Adrian Pitt:

> To those folk who like their cock shots and their ass shots and no more
>
> To those folk who've done the quiz and show their damn 'straight-acting' score
>
> To those folk whose pictures are blurry and produced five years ago
>
> To those folk who put up porn and make us think it's *them* on show
>
> To those folk who say they're 'lads' when pushing forty years of age
>
> To those folk who claim they're into brown and blue and red and beige
>
> To those folk who think they're 'sane' and follow that with 'I'm sorted'
>
> To those folk who say 'no timewasters' you'll soon have that one thwarted

To those folk who think monogamy is a wood they use for tables
To those folk with legs akimbo, out their arse electric cables
To those folk with sexual consonants - tt, ff and cp
To those folk in 'happy' relationships yet looking for 'number three'
To those folk who claim 'good looking', but who says - Aunty Mary?
To those folk who flaunt their 'butchness' are they man, mouse or fairy?
To those folk who state 'defined' but what's *their* dictionary's definition?
To those folk you *know* will ask for sex - the art of premonition
To those folk who aren't spontaneous and steadfastly 'top' or 'bottom'
To those folk you know you've messaged, a reply is sadly forgotten
To those folk I say It's Gaydar – a weird and wacky lot
Still, you've kept me entertained and what an insight this man's got
I've seen things that made me tremble; I've seen things that made me chortle
I've seen things I thought weren't possible from a homosexual mortal
But however much I knock it in my sad old cynical way
The world of profile hits and dangly bits is definitely here to stay.

Link

www.gaydar.co.uk

GAY.COM

Having been around slightly longer than Gaydar, Gay.com is an American giant with a number of national sites around the world, including the UK. The size and international status of Gay.com gives the site a much broader base, with a huge news and lifestyle reference magazine, combined with chat rooms for all parts of the globe although, not surprisingly, most of the chat goes on in the American rooms. Not too long ago Gay.com completely revised their chat system and the homos stayed away in droves, having been confused by the new operation and the sudden lack of people to chat to. But things have now picked up again and Gay.com chat is as lively as ever. In overall terms, Gay.com is probably the best gay website, combining information, entertainment and chat in just the right proportions.

Link

www.gay.com

INTERNET

If you want to identify a key development in the history of gay lifestyles, nothing, but nothing, has been more significant than the arrival of computers and the world-wide web. Pink hands embraced the technology and clung on hard, and there's absolutely no sign of us ever letting go. It's not hard to understand why – the internet enabled gay people to talk directly to each other without any fuss and without the approval or even the knowledge of wider society. It completely reinvented the way that gay people communicate with each other.

OK, it's fair to say that the internet was primarily always going to be a very obvious opportunity for lots of people to make a very fast buck, selling pornography to gay and straight people all around the world. But in doing so, it also helped to shake up our own pornography laws which (all in the name of protection, you understand) managed to discriminate shamelessly against gay people. No surprises there then.

Thankfully, the very existence of the internet illustrated that it was no longer possible to claim that we needed protection from any sort of image. What was the point when you could press a few keys and find images of anything ranging from group sex to bestiality? It gave our film censors a well-deserved kick up the butt and at long last we're able to purchase porn videos which show guys with, gasp, erections! It's a small victory but an important one in terms of equality, serving to emphasise in broad terms that we do exist and that, yes, we do actually have sex too (judging by older videos you'd be forgiven for thinking that gay men never did anything more exciting than kiss).

But the internet gave us so much more than smut, even if it was rather more realistic smut. Apart from a handful of very worthy (but slightly dull) online magazines (such as Rainbownetwork and Queercompany) it was the arrival of Gay.com and Gaydar.co.uk that really shook up the gay community. The chat room was born! What a great idea – you type in your name and you press a key and, hey presto, you're talking to a virtual room full of gay people. Nobody watching you and nobody to judge you. A fantastic concept, and it was one which gay people really liked in a big way. For the first time it was possible for gay people to talk directly to each other without having to think about the consequences, the views of their peers or their parents, or the opinions of society. You could say what you wanted to say in real time. Not that many people had any desire to discuss politics or television – the chat room was, and still is, all about sex.

It didn't take much imagination to realise that a real-time chat room would give people a means with which to bypass the time-consuming personal ads in magazines and the expensive telephone chat lines. If you wanted to actually meet another homo, the internet allowed you to do it cheaply and quickly. Even more attractive was the facility for exchanging photographs so that you could actually see (often in rather more detail than you actually wanted) the guy or girl that you were talking to. No more blind dates – you could now arrange the whole thing on your computer screen down to the smallest intimate detail.

The system worked well and it is still by far the easiest and most popular way for gay men in particular, to meet other gay men (oddly, the girls don't seem to have embraced the technology quite so warmly). The chat room is a true reflection of the no-strings world of wham-bam meaningless sex which society has always imagined gay lifestyle to be all about, either rightly or wrongly. But should we criticise? It's easy to frown upon popular sites like Gaydar, as if it's some kind of virtual meat market for men whose lives rarely extend beyond their dicks. But there's nothing wrong with that – it's not as if anyone is forced to log on to Gaydar or wherever and, given that lots of gay guys will almost inevitably be looking for sex with other guys, it means that the net simply provides an effective means of achieving what was always happening anyway, albeit more discreetly. So let's not get too snotty about it, OK?

Maybe the only really sad aspect of sites like Gaydar is the attitude of some of the people that use it. You don't need to spend too long in a chat room to see a pattern of activity emerge, and you have to question the motives, manners, good sense or even the sanity of some of the people that you can encounter. High on the list of sad but vaguely amusing activity is the sending of unsolicited instant messages, which, when opened, reveal a picture of some guy's penis. Sweet. There's usually some chat-up line attached which tends to be something like 'so u fancy it then?' or something equally romantic, and the notion seems to be that you're expected to gratefully accept the invitation. Whether anyone ever does is open to question, but you can't help wondering what kind of individual thinks it's entirely normal to arrange a date on the basis of his penis shape or size.

It can get a whole lot more graphic than that, of course, especially if you venture into chat rooms with titles like 'Masters and Servants' or whatever. There's no point in getting too obsessed by the patently bizarre nature of some people's sexual preferences, but at the same time it's slightly scary to see what some people will happily do, all in the name of good sex. Truly frightening is the growing number of people who are looking for unprotected sex, almost as if the Aids crisis had never happened, but it's also fascinating to talk to individuals and find out that good ol' plain vanilla sex just isn't quite as common as you might imagine. In fact, the more you investigate and communicate you find that almost any kind of activity is somebody's idea of a turn-on. The list is seemingly endless, from watersports (and we don't mean surfboarding), fisting, nipple torture and breath control to scat (no, really), public humiliation, and even the odd vampire.

Nothing is taboo, and the temptation is to reel in disgust, but what's the point? It's not as if Gaydar invented sexual perversions; it's just that, thanks to the internet, you now have a window on the world and you can really see what goes on between the sheets, and even though some of the revelations might be a tad stomach-churning, it's undoubtedly fascinating.

For most people, however, the internet is simply an effective way to meet someone without having to go through the tedium of endless chat-up lines or even so much as a drink. Maybe it is a shame that such a useful communication tool can't be used for something more constructive than setting up a shag, but you can't knock success. There's no doubt that if you're bored, lonely or just plain horny, the world-wide web provides a fast solution.

Viewpoints

'I used Gay.com for about a year until they changed their chat room site and everybody stopped using it, because it was too confusing. Everyone seemed to start using Gaydar, so I went on there. I've got a free internet connection so I can log into the internet any time without it costing me anything, and I tend to leave my computer connected while I'm at home, so that people can send me a message if it's a mate or if it's someone who has seen my profile and likes what they see. I only really look for mates on there though 'cause I'm not really looking for sex, but I don't make any rules about it as such. It depends who you're talking to. Gaydar isn't as good as it used to be though, and there's less people using the chat rooms now. You tend to see the same names day after day, which is a bit boring, and nobody seems to want to talk about anything much in the chat rooms now. Most people are just sending private messages to each other, whereas they used to talk much more about television, politics, clubs and stuff like that. I suppose it's got a bit tired, so maybe a different site will come along that everyone will want to use.'

Mark (student, 18), Stoke

'I've met lots of people through the internet, mostly for sex really. It's way better than using phone lines because it's free and you can also swap photos of each other so that you know who you're gonna meet, and you can decide whether you fancy 'em or not. I met people after talking on phone lines and they're always completely different to how they describe themselves, but with a photo you know what to expect. Some people use old photos though, and when you meet them, they don't look much like their photos, so it's not like it's fool-proof. It's a good way to meet people though, if you're just looking for sex without wanting a boyfriend or anything like that. You can say what you want, and what you like doing and stuff, which is good. Quite a few people are getting webcams now too, so you don't have to just go on what their picture looks like. You can connect and see them live which is even better, then you know precisely what they look like and stuff.'

Brian (unemployed, 21), Doncaster

'The thing that really pisses me off with things like Gaydar are the ones who think they're drop-dead gorgeous because they're nineteen or whatever. I mean, lots of 'em are, but you get lots of these prissy little student types that come on, and they start giving you attitude if you speak to them, as if you're bound to be wanting to get into their pants. Then you look at their photos and it's some total minger, and you wonder what the hell they're on about. They just think that because they're under twenty-one or whatever, they're fantastic, and they're so not. They just look like complete tossers. I really hate that kind of attitude. I mean, if somebody contacts you and they fancy you, and you don't fancy them, then, OK, you can just say you're not my type thanks, but lots of these people just get so nasty as if you're not even worthy of being in the chat room with them 'cause you're forty or whatever, and that you can't be attractive to anyone if you're over twenty-five. It's such crap, and when they do that they make themselves look really sad which is funny, I guess.'

James (student, 19), Manchester

'I hate people that send you messages that just ask you your age and, when you reply, if they don't like the reply they just click off without even saying goodbye. It's so rude. Or you send somebody a message that you fancy and you wait for them to look at your profile and your photos and then they just disappear. If they don't like you that's fine, but you'd think they could have the manners to say no thanks or at least have a conversation with you. It's so bad the way some people use chat rooms like that. It encourages people to be really rude.'

Ian (unemployed, 27), Liverpool

'Places like Gaydar aren't as good as they used to be, but I've met some great people off there. I have mates all over the country now and, if I want to go some place, I can go and stay with them and go clubbing and things like that. It's made it so easy to meet people that you either share interests with or that you fancy or whatever. You get people that talk to you and you exchange email addresses or whatever and they say they want to keep in touch, but they never do. But some people are good and you become friends, so it's worth talking to people. It's much easier than standing in some club trying to shout to each other, or trying to start a conversation with a stranger.'

Michael (unemployed, 27), Grimsby

'I really hate some of the people in chat rooms. You get loads of vile old blokes that send you messages and when you read their profiles they're like fifty or sixty and they just want sex. I mean, it's OK if they do go with other men and do sex, but it's insulting that they think I'd want to have sex with them, if you get me? You sometimes feel like being kinda polite and just saying no thank you, but some days you think, for fuck's sake, do

I look desperate or something? And guys that send you a photo to like chat you up, and when you open it it's some close-up picture of their arse. What the fuck is that all about? The ones I really hate are the blokes that you know are making it all up. You look at their profile and photos, and you can tell they've just taken the photo from some porn site and it's supposed to be them. And the ones that say they're virgins, or straight guys that want to try gay sex. You know it's such crap and they're just making it up, and it's probably some fat 60-year-old bloke having some wank fantasy.'

Jody (sales assistant, 22), Birmingham

'I guess it depends what your view is about internet stuff and what you want from it. If you don't want to actually meet someone because you're too lazy or too choosy, then you can have cyber sex, or you can get someone to phone you and do phone sex, or you can combine the two things sometimes. You can talk to lads about their fantasies if you want, but lots of people have webcams now, so you can just talk face-to-face with your camera and watch each other strip or wank or whatever you want to do, and that's excellent if it's someone that looks sexy. It's like totally safe sex 'cause you're not even meeting anyone, and it's way easier than going and meeting someone, wasting money and time when you just want to get your rocks off. Lots of people think it's really sad 'cause you could be actually meeting someone but sometimes you just don't want to bother, and it's not affecting anyone else, so I don't think it's anyone else's business. It can be a bit addictive though and sometimes you lose your sense of time because you get so into it. You think you'll just talk to some guys for maybe half an hour and next thing you know you've been there all day, and that's really scary sometimes. So you can get carried away but after a while it gets a bit boring.'

Steve (unemployed, 28), Bristol

'There are good points and bad points with the internet. There are some web pages like Rainbow network which are good for news and things like that, but they're not all that interesting once you've looked through them. Most of the sites are just for porn and, even if you want to look at them, you find that most of them want you to give credit card details and pay as soon as you start looking into them, so they're mostly rubbish. So there's only really chat sites and some of them are OK, but for most of the time there's not much chatting going on because people send private messages to each other. I've got a boyfriend and I don't go looking for sex or anything, but I'm quite attractive, I think, and it's definitely an ego boost when you get people sending you messages saying that they think you're really nice and stuff. You can't deny that, it does make you feel better sometimes. I know people will say that you're just being judged on your looks and that's true, but it's also a bit dishonest to say that you don't like people saying that you look good or that they fancy you. I admit

it's not very nice for someone who isn't good looking but that's like saying you should just not use chat rooms because it's unfair to some people, and that's stupid.'

John (student, 20), Leeds

WEB SLANG

Of course, the internet is full of abbreviations and acronyms, and gay sites have their own special vocabulary. Here's our brutally honest (and slightly cynical) web slang dictionary:

WLTM	Would like to meet
ASL	Age, sex and location (from people too lazy to read a profile)
ISO	Is seeking only
Average Build	Fat
Stocky Build	Fat
Chubby Build	Fat
Rugby Build	Fat
Slim Build	Either slim or possibly anorexic
Muscular Build	Sometimes muscular but more likely an optimistic fatty
Defined Build	Average build
Athletic Build	Skinny
Swimmer's Build	Skinny
Age Unimportant	Old
Practise Safer Sex – Sometimes	Possibly mentally unstable and best avoided
Practise Safer Sex – Always	Sane and possibly quite normal (imagine. . .)
Practise Safer Sex – Never	Don't even go there
Passive	Likes being shagged
Active	Likes shagging or pretends to be butch
GSOH	Good sense of humour (often a necessity)
Seeking Fun Times	Wants sex
No-strings Sex	Definitely a one-night stand

Seeking Chat	Likes one-handed typing . . .
Seeking Relationship	Looking for a boyfriend – potential stalker
Outgoing	Loud and slightly embarrassing
Straight Acting	Closet case or has unresolved issues
Camp	A no-nonsense queen, up for a laugh
Monogamous	Sleeps around behind his boyfriend's back
Open Relationship	Sleeps around with his boyfriend's consent
Non Scene	Hates clubs – probably old and/or ugly or shy
Exhibitionist	Likes dancing topless
BRB	Be right back (reading your profile to see if you're worth a shag)
LOL	Laugh out loud
ROFL	Roll on floor laughing (when they've over-used LOL)
Boi	Eminem wannabe
Well Endowed	Thinks he has a large penis
Average Endowed	Has a large penis
Straight	Bisexual
Bisexual	Gay
Virgin	Fantasy expert
First-timer	Fantasy expert
Role Play	Dresses up (probably in rubber)
Watersports	Likes taking a leak but not in the toilet
Scat	Likes taking a dump but not in the toilet
FF	Fist fucking – not for the faint-hearted
BB	Bareback sex (without a condom) – psycho best avoided
Voyeur	Wants to watch you perform
Curious	Closet case fantasy expert
Versatile	Easily pleased

MAN NOT INCLUDED

The ultimate designer lesbian experience? When you've furnished the house and you've bought all the clothes, it'll come as no surprise (at least to more cynical readers) that even babies can be purchased from the internet, albeit in a slightly indirect way. Just can't get hold of that pesky sperm? No problem; now there's the perfect place to pick up that missing piece of the equation without having to even so much as see a man.

Links

www.mannotincluded.com

www.boldopinion.com/men.htm

MARDI GRAS

Where did it all go wrong? Not so long ago, the highlight of our gay year was the annual trip to London, where every self-respecting faggot and dyke from around the country all gathered together for a long and loud march through the streets of the capital. The march lasted for hours and the crowds of happy, cheering (or whistling) people stretched for miles. There was even time to sit down, eat your lunch or go shopping and still come back to rejoin the march 'cause it would still be going. There were just so many people it was staggering. Then, when the march was over, everybody made their way to a park for an afternoon of drinking, partying, talking and cruising, with entertainment from a whole galaxy of top-notch stars. When the evening ended, the fireworks erupted and we either set off home or hit the club scene in the city. It was a great day and everyone just loved it.

But that was then . . . A few years on, and the whole Gay Pride thing has lost much of its appeal. The big march isn't quite so big any more and every year the crowd gets gradually smaller as the downward spiral of indifference creates even greater apathy for each successive year. The many thousands of people who still take part will tell you that they still enjoy it, and they'll tell you that it serves an important purpose by keeping the gay community firmly in the media's (and therefore the government's and the public's) eye.

But while the marchers don't need any encouragement, it's a whole lot harder to persuade many others to get out of bed. Their argument is simple: there's nothing to march for, so why make a fuss? It's a valid viewpoint but, of course, it's fatally flawed because it ignores the lessons of history. If we don't remain visible then we cease to exist. That's the way the modern world works and, if we are to keep the momentum of change moving in our favour, we need to keep reminding the papers, the television and the government that we're still here.

But political aspirations just aren't enough to persuade the vast majority of Britain's queer population to get off their backsides and join the march. This fact has been realised by the event organisers, and they've wisely concluded that the march should become more of a parade, combining political visibility with the entertainment, glamour and fun of parades like Sydney's. Nice idea, but somehow it just doesn't seem to have worked (at least not yet). While the Australians effortlessly create a breathtaking spectacle of costume, dance and music, we still settle for a handful of dykes on top of a London bus, followed by six shivering go-go dancers on a flatbed truck. It's vaguely embarrassing and slightly insulting that Britain, with such a huge population of openly gay people, can't create a parade which is any better than a local school fête. Little wonder that most good-time queens simply fall out of bed and head straight for the park party, bypassing the march entirely.

But even the party has lost its appeal. The once-popular piss-up became boring. Stage acts degenerated into a meagre line-up of D-list boy bands and has-beens; the drink prices (and queues) got bigger; the food prices went through the proverbial roof, and the crowds of happy gay men and lesbians slowly began to merge into a mix of prams, tracksuits and children on fathers' shoulders. The great gay day had become a family freak show.

The final blow was when the 2002 event was staged at Hackney Marshes, and the crowds just stayed away. And who could blame them? Fundamentally, many people objected to the notion that our big day of visibility should be shoved into such an insignificant part of the capital, and many others simply felt the effort of getting there, combined with the admission cost, just made the whole exercise distinctly unappealing. Likewise, lots of people simply felt that the whole event had become one huge commercial sell-out, catering for anyone and everyone who was stupid enough to part with hefty amounts of cash to simply stand in a field and get drunk. It was no surprise that Purple in the Park (a gay dance and music festival) proved to be the big hit of the year, and Mardi Gras was largely ignored. But what a shame that Mardi Gras has become such a joke. It could have been wonderful and maybe (just maybe) it will be one day.

MARDI GRAS: POINTS TO PONDER

① It's the best opportunity for an annual get-together, to have fun and meet as many gay people as you could ever want to. A festival of alcohol and debauchery, whohoo!

② Our big opportunity to make ourselves visible to the rest of society. We have the chance to show the newspapers and television that we are here, that we're perfectly normal (well, maybe), fun-loving people, and we expect to be treated with equality. If the media sees us, then it follows that the government is reminded that we're not going away. And that's always a good thing.

③ We have the opportunity to stage a truly world-class parade with thousands of marchers, thousands of glammed-up revellers, hundreds of costumes, dozens of floats and a party atmosphere which could buzz through central London all afternoon. If Sydney can do it so well (it's even televised, it's so good), then why can't we? There are more gay people here and we have the same resources. So what's the problem? And where have the famous faces gone that used to be at the front of the march? Barbara Windsor dressed in pink in an open-top car – that was the way to go.

④ The Mardi Gras party could be a great event if it was organised properly. The venue is important and everyone agrees that ultimately it should be in Hyde Park. We've heard way too many feeble arguments about how there are 'special laws' preventing drinking or this or that, but who cares? Change the damned laws then, it's a park for heaven's sake. Wasn't Ken Livingstone going to push this matter for us?

⑤ Let's move the march to the afternoon. You know what queens are like; they've all been out on the piss the night before and they can't be bothered to get up on a Saturday morning just for a march. Let's make things a little easier by starting the march at three, maybe. And it's time that we started getting the numbers back up to the levels we had just a few years ago. Let's not lose the momentum. All those student groups and local gay and lesbian support groups – get yourselves a coach hired and fill it.

⑥ Time to modernise. We should ditch the fat guys in leather thongs (sorry, we love you, but you guys are the number-one excuse for people staying away from the march 'cause you're a little bit embarrassing) and we should abandon the OutRage! placards. We can make a political point without getting into the old-fashioned banner-waving stuff, can't we? It's time to put our message across with a little more subtlety. Let's make the Pride March a must-see parade so that the media wants to be there. When we've got them with us, we can give them our message. Waving a placard is just so Countryside Alliance. Eww.

⑦ The big post-march party has got to change. If it's going to cost some serious dosh to get through the gates, then we expect something in return for our money. Where have all the celebrities gone? Years ago we had Lily Savage, Boy George, Erasure, Pet Shop Boys, Steps, Alison Moyet, Sparks (no, really), Julian Clary, Kylie Minogue and all manner of big-name people up there on stage performing for us. Now we're left with a line-up of third-rate has-beens and wannabes, and even compere Graham Norton's heroic enthusiasm can't disguise the fact that we're being sold short. All those stars down in Hyde Park performing for the Prince's Trust – why can't they support us? The time is long overdue for organisers to remind these celebs that we're a very significant part of their fan base.

⑧ If the big names won't come, then let's downsize the event accordingly. We don't even need a park really. We've got Soho and it's already seriously gay, so why not open it up for an evening of post-march revelry? Yes, the police will whine and bitch, but ultimately it's our choice, and if we want to take over the streets, then we will. Right on.

⑨ Where has all the gay media support gone for Mardi Gras? Considering that it's the biggest event in our gay calendar, it's treated with indifference in the magazines. A couple of pages here and there, and a few more after the event. Big deal. Why aren't they promoting the big day properly? Coverage of the march is even more shameful. It either fails to be mentioned at all or it's included as a paragraph, almost as an afterthought. Have all the magazine muppets forgotten what the whole day is all about? They should be explaining the whole point of the march, and helping to make it into a world-class parade, instead of banging on about how many dance tents there will be in some park. Big deal, who cares?

⑩ Will somebody please remind every gay boy and girl across the country that Mardi Gras used to be fun! It was a fantastic day that everybody loved. It can be again; in fact it could be bigger and better than ever before. If only we could get away from political in-fighting, commercial interests, apathy, indifference and this new wave of self-hating anti-gay and anti-festival thinking. Can't we allow ourselves to have any fun?

Viewpoints

'I must have gone to every Pride March for about the past ten years now, and I do enjoy it every time, although I do think it's lost much of its fun over the past couple of years or so. Most of all me and my boyfriend go because it's just a good laugh. It's a really good event to take part in, and you get to see thousands of other gay people, all marching through the middle of London, winding up and upsetting all the miserable straight homophobic people. That gives you a great feeling of belonging, like you know you're with all these other people who are the same as you. It's quite good for cruising other lads too, as everyone's out to have a good time and everyone's really friendly. You get lots of good-looking lads who take their tops off or just wear skimpy shorts and whatever, which makes it even better, so it's like a free show.

I think it's all to do with visibility really, and although it's mostly a fun event, it does still have a serious purpose too. OK, it's not like years ago

when they were campaigning for gay rights and stuff 'cause we've come a long way since then and there isn't all that much left to fight for. But I think it's true that gay people and lesbians are still treated like we are in some way inferior to the rest of the world, and there's always this kind of attitude that we're just being tolerated instead of being accepted for who we are. I don't know if that will ever change, but big marches like the one in London do help to keep us visible, and show the world that we are here and that there's an awful lot of us.

You get other gay people moaning that it's bad for our image because there are drag queens and old fat guys in leather and stuff like that, all showing off in public. But I just don't agree with that kind of attitude. I think that there are all kinds of gay people just like there are all kinds of straight people, so they have a right to be in the march showing that they have a right to be treated the same as anyone else. It's like some sort of gay fascism this idea that the march should be scrapped or just restricted to people that look and act straight. That's such a negative view and I really hate it. I think it's time that we got some self-respect and just showed the whole world who we are, love us or hate us, but treat us the same as anyone else. You could say that all the dancers in the Notting Hill Carnival should all wear white make-up and formal suits with that kind of argument, it's just ridiculous.

The biggest complaint I have about the march is that it's not organised or advertised as well as it ought to be, and I think it's this problem that has stopped a lot of people from taking part. I remember the first march I went on was absolutely huge. I'd not been out as a gay man for very long and, even though I wasn't naive about anything, it was astonishing to see so many other gay people. I always remember looking up Park Lane and just seeing thousands of heads from one end of the road and out of sight in the other direction; it just went on for miles and I thought, wow, I'm definitely not alone, we've taken over the capital here. But now it's probably only about a tenth of that size and it's still huge, but what a shame that it's not like it used to be.

I think it's got smaller because people don't think there's any reason to march any more which is pretty short-sighted. I think there's always going to be good reason to have a big parade and just show everyone that there are so many of us and that we expect to be treated like the rest of society. I think that if we stop having marches or gatherings, the media and then the politicians will start to think that we've disappeared, and then it will be impossible to make any progress for whatever rights we might still be fighting for. Also, I think a big march is a great way to show young people especially that they're not alone, and that we're a big part of society. I can't think of a better way for anyone to come to terms with being gay than to stand in a crowd of ten or twenty thousand other gay people and realise that you're not a one-off weirdo at all.

And most of all, the march is fun and it could be even more fun if lots more people took part and dressed up, and just went for a laugh instead of getting all stuck-up about being seen in public or, worse still, being more interested in running straight to a park to get drunk.'

Simon (student, 19), Watford

'I think the whole Pride and Mardi Gras thing has become such a load of crap. And that's a real shame because it was our biggest chance to do something good. I don't want any of this bollocks about integration and so on 'cause I don't believe it. We're not integrated with society and we probably never will be, or at least not for a very long time. So why don't all these fuckwits who want to be straight just go and shag girls and get over themselves? If you have sex with a guy then you're gay, so you might as well forget about snivelling over being normal or straight acting or whatever stupid label you want to hide behind.

It's no good saying we're treated equally because we just aren't. You know the reality of the situation, and the law doesn't treat gay people equally and we're still treated like some kind of second-class group of perverts, while the black community is treated with complete equality and respect. That's probably because black people have stood up for themselves and stopped the rest of the country thinking that they can treat them as if they're inferior to everyone else. But the so-called gay community? Nope, we can't ever do that 'cause there's so many tossers out there who want to pretend they're straight but that they just have sex with other men. It makes me puke. You're gay, for Christ's sake!

I think that's the main reason why the Pride March has shrunk and that we've got into this obsession with the park festivals crap. There are just so many people that avoid the march because they're frightened of being seen with skinheads or prissy camp queens or people in drag or whatever. They think that they've got to hide away in straight pubs, in their designer clothes and with some sad fag hag girl hung on their arm so that they look like all the other boring grey straight people they hang out with. I say fuck 'em all; the rest of us, the real queers that don't have issues in our heads to deal with, should all get out on the march and do whatever we like, just have a good time and show the people and the politicians that we're real and that there's lots of us, so that they can't treat us like some obscure self-interest group whenever they're not fishing for votes.

The mindless pop concerts in the parks just make the problem worse because you get everyone saying that they'll stay in bed until lunchtime, and save their energy to go straight to a park and watch some shit boy band or some other past-it pop singer trying to get some credibility back by appearing at a gay event. I mean, there's nothing wrong with having a knees-up in a park, but it's so typical of gay people that most of 'em can't

even be arsed to go on a march first, and that was supposed to be the main purpose of the whole day at one time.Tragically, all it comes down to now is having a good time, and most people just want to go straight to a park, get pissed, get shagged and fall over. It's mindless crap but you can't slag people off for doing it because I go too, but what really pisses me off is the way that they can't have some self-respect and motivation to march through London first and show a bit of unity with other gay people.

I think that in lots of ways gay people are self-loathing and they can't bear to remind themselves of who or what they are, so marching through London would be too much to handle. It's really sad 'cause at the end of the day, the march could be really fantastic, like the Sydney Mardi Gras, with floats, dancers and lots of television coverage. But here you get three flat-top trucks with a few scabby lads dancing to Kylie, and a couple of open-top buses with six fat dykes stood on the top deck. It's slightly embarrassing really and I don't know how you go about making it better.

We certainly have more than enough people out there, but actually getting everyone to come to London on a Saturday morning, and dress up or make a parade float? Well, it's not going to happen unless some big businesses start paying for it and start providing some kind of incentive, I guess. I think that if organisers could get sponsors to pay for floats, like they do in the Lord Mayor's Parade and stuff, then we could make it a great event again, and maybe move it to the afternoon or something, but then everyone would be terrified that they'd miss the event in the park. I guess the real truth is that the whole park concert event is poison, and we ought to get rid of it, and replace it with something else before the whole day just disappears up its own arse.'

John (nurse, 30), Swindon

'We've always gone to the park concerts at Mardi Gras, as it's a great place to meet friends and meet new people too. There's lots of community stuff where you can find out about other groups and things like that, and of course it's good fun to just do the fairground and the dance tents and things like that. But it has got a bit old now, and it would be great to do something new in the future. The Hackney Marshes day this year was really bad and it just didn't have any atmosphere, and it was in such a stupid place to have to get to.

But the organisers seem to be blaming the fall in attendance on the location, and I don't think it had anything to do with that really. I just think people are getting bored with the same old thing year after year. The stage acts are really naff now, especially when you look at the people they used to get. They were real stars at the time but now all you get are endless wannabe boy bands and crappy people who want to get pop credibility by being seen at a gay concert. It stinks, and you wish that

they'd just have real stars, or people that really are part of the gay community, or at least support us, not hangers-on who just want to use us as a career move. Maybe they just can't get big names any more, but if that's the case then, OK, stuff the people who don't want to appear; we'll know who supports us and who doesn't. It's no good just trying to fill a stage by getting crap straight pop bands, I'd rather not have a stage if that's all they can get. Now that there's things like Purple in the Park, you've already got a day to do the big party thing anyway, so I don't think the big Mardi Gras events will ever be as good as they used to be.

Perhaps the way to go is to close off Soho and all that area and have a big street party on the Saturday afternoon. That way we wouldn't have to go off to some obscure park, and you wouldn't have to pay for dance tents or any of that stuff, as it would already be there. You could just have a stage some place for real gay or gay-friendly acts and just have a big party until late at night. Or else I guess the only thing worth doing would be to get Hyde Park, and not just a little bit of it, but a big event. If they can have the Prince's Trust thing there, I don't see why we can't have our party there too. They say it's because of laws and so on, but the way I see it, anyone that comes up with a real reason why we can't have it there, when they can have the Prince's Trust thing and so on, is being homophobic, it's as simple as that. If they can have other events there, why can't we, unless you're excluding us because we're gays and lesbians?'

Michael (unemployed, 20), London

MARRIAGE

While we might be happy to leave all the wedding bullshit to the breeders, we shouldn't dismiss the whole marriage thing completely. Getting hitched can make financial sense and it can make life so much easier for long-term relationships. As the law presently stands, a gay couple can't legally be each other's next-of-kin, even though they might register themselves as such whenever required to do so. And while you might be able to turn up at a hospital and expect to see your partner if he's ill, the same hospital could (if they so wished) refuse you entry. Worse still, if you share a house and your partner dies, you have no right to inherit the property. There are all kinds of nasty little twists in the law which discriminate shamelessly against gay couples. But the law is going to be changed, at long last, and before too long a gay couple will have the same legal rights as a married (straight) couple. But in order to be recognised as such, we might well have to register our status with a local authority. In effect, it's going to be like getting married without the wedding. Have we sold out? Have we fallen in with convention in order to be assimilated into society? Maybe, but let's be positive; we will at least be treated fairly and properly, and that's got to be a good thing.

Viewpoints

'The whole gay marriage thing is complicated, and it depends on your own feelings. I wouldn't want to be married even if I could be, because I think marriage is all about straight people's values and religion. It's got nothing to do with the way I feel about my life, my partner or my religious views. I think we should be treated in the same way as any other couple though, so if we have to register as a partnership then that's OK. It's worth doing in order to ensure that we have the law on our side for the future. I also think it helps to send out a signal to the rest of the public that gay couples do actually exist, and we're not all just running around having one-night stands.'

Brian (office administrator, 29), Exeter

'I don't think I'd ever sign any sort of partnership thing even if I was in a long-term relationship and it helped with inheritance rights and so on. The way I see things, two people of the same sex can share their lives together, but they don't have to make any agreements with society to do that. We spend too much time getting wrapped up in what society expects of us, and that's just crap. I don't think the change in the law will give us many rights that we don't have now in any case. Frankly I don't give a fuck what the government wants to do for us, or more likely for themselves; they're just pandering to voters as usual.'

Becky (student, 18), Leeds

MOBO

That's Music Of Black Origin to you and me. Just in case you've been burying your head in the sand for more than a few years, you might like to note that it's become traditional for black singers to do the anti-gay thing, as if it's really cool to hate faggots 'cause black guys are all straight, blah, blah . . . This institutionalised hatred reached a peak in October 2002 at the Mobo Awards ceremony in London, where OutRage! campaigners staged a protest, and were met by physical and verbal abuse from black teenagers. Amongst some of the more endearing chants were 'kill the batty boys' and 'kill chi chi men' (apparently 'chi chi' is a Jamaican term for gay). How sweet.

Some of the award nominations went to singers who have almost made a career out of their anti-gay lyrics and the time was long overdue for somebody to stand up and make a stand against such blatant incitement to hatred and violence. Not surprisingly it was Peter Tatchell who was at the forefront, later commenting that he urged 'black community leaders to speak out against artists who incite homophobic hatred and violence. It is appalling for members of one minority to attack members of another minority. We should stand together united against all forms of prejudice and discrimination.'

Of course, we could all do our bit by steering well clear of the whole black reggae genre. There's nothing clever about songs which babble on about shagging birds and killing gay men, it's just plain offensive. And if you think about it, the music's pretty crap too.

MR GAY UK

Who would have ever thought it? The love that (once) dared not speak its name now parades down a catwalk in a pair of Calvin Klein underpants courtesy of the annual Mr Gay UK competition, a national all-male beauty pageant exclusively for gay contestants. Oscar Wilde is probably spinning in his grave at the very thought. It started quietly and innocently as a joke, a tongue-in-cheek gay version of the spectacularly pointless Miss World competition, eventually becoming embraced as a countrywide phenomenon with heats staged at pubs and clubs all around the UK. Not surprisingly, the opportunity to ogle half-naked lads at your local gay club became quite an event, and the competition grew in popularity, the grand final even reaching the nation's television screens (all right it was only Channel Five) for a couple of years.

But then the joke wore a little thin, and we started questioning the motives of both the entrants and the organisers, and more importantly, the way in which the competition was becoming familiar to a distinctly non-gay audience.

It's easy to understand the mind-set of the brave (or are they mad?) people who enter the competition every year; there's an opportunity to win a few bob just for getting up on stage and whipping your clothes off and, if you're really lucky, you stand a chance of winning even more cash in the final, plus the prospect of a whole year to be adored and worshipped as the crowned champion of all things gay – the sexiest and best-looking gay guy in the country. All it takes is nerves of steel and a (fairly) trim waistline, plus a bit of encouragement either from your mates or a few bottles of beer.

That's the theory, of course, but you can't help but wonder whether that's the way it really is. We're constantly told by most of the contestants that they entered 'for a laugh' and that they just found themselves up on stage because they were drunk, and that they 'never expected to win the heat'. OK, well, maybe that's the truth but when you look at the way that so many of the contestants have dressed up, pumped up and preened themselves, it starts to look as if they were on a serious mission to win. And what kind of guy makes a conscious decision to try and win a male beauty competition? Certainly not the kind of guy that you're likely to meet down your local pub.

Of course, the competition also sends out some very negative signals to the gay community as a whole. Simply by being billed as a 'Mr Gay UK' event (rather than a simple 'beauty pageant') it reinforces the notion that we should all strive to achieve the same attributes as the competition entrants, and that as gay men we should try our very best to be slim, handsome and preferably under thirty. If by some horrible fate we don't fit into these categories we are by definition of no significance to the competition and, therefore, the wider gay community. Ask the organisers and in their defence they'll tell you that there are no rules as such for entering, and even a fat forty-year-old is welcome to jump on stage (can you imagine?) but we all know that it's just not going to happen. We're unconsciously expected to conform to the accepted norms and it's all about white pants and boots and faux sexuality. It's almost as big a cliché as the actual competition.

But even if we shrug our collective shoulders and regard the event as just a laugh, of no great significance other than a chance to gawp at some flesh, we still have to look at the other signals that such a competition sends out, not just to gay men, but to society at large. You can't appoint someone as Mr Gay UK without implying that he is in some way a representative of British gay people as a whole, especially when he is wheeled out to be interviewed on television or radio, or expected to pop up in a chat show. Whether we like it or not, he's going to be seen as our spokesman, our shining example to the rest of the (straight) world. All well and good but just look at what's happened year after year. Have our crowned beauties wowed the public? Have they stood up for our rights and explained our lifestyle, our ambitions and our hopes? Nope, they've stripped down to a pair of pants. Cheers, thanks for nothing.

The latest heir to the throne is Rob Conn, a ruggedly handsome 26-year-old from Plymouth with good looks, an impressively toned body and, astonishingly, a surprising amount of grey matter between his ears. Unlike some of the winners from past years, Rob sounds like he might actually have the intelligence to match his looks, but what can we expect from him? Will he be preparing written notes for the House of Lords? Will he be appearing on the BBC's *Question Time*? The national papers? Writing a book? Nope, the pinnacle of his year will probably be a two-minute slot on *Trisha*, minus his clothes.

To be fair, it's not going to be Rob's fault. He's a pretty face attached to pectorals, abs and arms, and that's all the Gay UK competition has ever been, or probably ever will be, about. But what a waste of a golden opportunity. Unlike anyone else, he has the potential to become what his title implies that he already is – except that he isn't. If only his managers would steer him away from the endless round of appearances at gay pubs and clubs into the mainstream media where he can do what he ought to be doing – telling the rest of the world what we're all about and ensuring that we have a voice which makes sense and doesn't come from the mouth of some left-wing vegetarian lesbian (no offence to the aforementioned is intended, of course). Is Rob Conn doomed to be nothing more than a pair of tits? Let's hope not.

A true cynic would conclude that the Mr Gay UK competition has nothing to do with the gay community and everything to do with advertising potential for the event organiser (you'll not be surprised to see that images of the eventual winner become a major part of the same company's chat line and porn video sales pitch), in which case somebody should be asking how a company can effectively hijack the title from the community it represents.

But if we're going to resign ourselves to an annual parade of self-obsessed scabby kids in underpants, perhaps we could be forgiven for wanting something more from the competition than a smiling face that whips his shirt off on demand at a club near you. Wouldn't it be great if the next competition was a little more demanding? Instead of just coaxing the contestants out of their clothes, we could also look for someone who can string a sentence together. And if intelligence (and maybe even a personality too) is also a requirement of the eventual winner, maybe his assets could be used to give us back something more useful than a couple of tedious interviews in the gay press, telling us whether he has a boyfriend and whether he's 'out' to his parents. Like we care. Mr Gay UK has the potential to give the ever-hungry national media a pretty face with a viewpoint – a rare and useful asset which we should use to our advantage. On the other hand, do you think Rob would fancy a shag?

Links

www.mrgayuk.co.uk

www.dnamag.com/_dont-miss/mr_gay_uk.asp

NAMES

As a community, we're pretty good with names, seeing as we've been called just about anything and everything imaginable until we've become immune to the whole name-calling thing. But while the bigots still think they can insult us with a mere name (and usually very unimaginative ones), what are we supposed to call ourselves? The jury is still firmly out on this one, and even the government can't get its act together, having recently decided that the word 'gay' might now be perceived as being slightly offensive to some if used in any of their discussion documents. Certainly it has become part of schoolground vocabulary as a term for 'naff', but whether that's a good reason to abandon the word is open to question.

But if 'gay' is so last year, what are the alternatives? For starters 'faggot' has made a big comeback now that more than a few people have realised that this once-insulting term is perfectly acceptable if used by a, er . . . faggot, but obviously not a word to be thrown around by anyone else (bit like 'nigger' in fact, which is fine if you're black, but otherwise unacceptable). But if the f-word is too strong for your palette, take heart and consider that 'queer' is also fashionable once again, or 'homo' if you prefer; just don't try 'poof' if you want to keep a straight face. And the girls? It looks like you still have a choice between 'lezzie' or 'dyke' unless somebody comes up with something more colourful.

PALARE

You know those stuck-up types who claim that they're not gay, they just happen to sleep with men? They whine about how the gay scene is so, er . . . gay, and how their lives are so commendably straight and wonderful, and how their lives owe absolutely nothing to gay culture? Well, here's something which might amuse you. Stop to consider our everyday vocabulary and some of the words which we carelessly use, without any idea as to where they came from. You might be surprised to learn that quite a few have their origins in some darker corners of the 1960s, when British society still refused to accept that gay people existed, and regarded same-sex acts as perversions to be punished by law.

Not surprisingly, gay people really did stick together like glue, even developing their own rather strange and wonderful language which enabled them to communicate without fear of drawing any unwanted attention from straight people. Whether this gay vocabulary (which became known as Palare) was intentionally created or whether a few keywords became adopted almost unconsciously is unclear, but by the late 1960s Palare (or at least selected parts of this subversive language) had become an accepted part of gay life, and had started to infiltrate mainstream society.

Undoubtedly, it was the BBC radio series *Round the Horne* which was responsible for the transition of gay slang into widespread use, thanks to the endless series of hilarious sketches read by Kenneth Williams and Hugh Paddick, better known as the infamous Julian and Sandy. Their comical overuse of Palare enabled words such as butch, drag, dizzy, slap and naff to become part of everyday language, and although some analysts claim that Palare also effectively stole words from other cultures (cockney and gypsy slang and even Latin, amongst other sources), it was *Round the Horne* which cemented them into mainstream British culture.

Sadly, Palare has almost completely died out within the gay community, and only the odd word will occasionally pop up in conversations between older people who still recognise the value of words which can be both colourful and descriptive, and reflect something of our past which anyone with a sense of history would be eager to hold on to.

Unfortunately, a media-fuelled overeagerness to 'integrate' has encouraged younger generations to compulsively abandon anything which can be identified as gay, and Palare has become another victim of our anodyne gay community, dumped in favour of designer labels and manufactured pop music. What a waste, and what an insult to our past.

Link

www.chris-d.net/polari

PALARE – SOME KEY WORDS	
Batts	shoes
Basket	a man's bulge (lunch box)
Barney	fight
Bijou	small
Bona	good
Bevvie	drink (beverage)
Carsey	toilet
Camp	effeminate or ludicrously overdone
Chicken	young boy
Cottage	public toilet
Cottaging	looking for or having sex in a public toilet
Dish	good-looking man or woman
Dizzy	scatterbrained
Dolly-palome	good-looking girl
Drag	women's or outrageous clothing
Eek	face
Fish	woman
Fruit	gay man
Glossies	magazines
Lallies	legs
Latty	house or flat
Luppers	fingers
Mince	walk effeminately
Mish	mouth
Naff	bad or boring

Ogles	eyes
Omi	man
Omi-palome	butch woman or gay man
Onk	nose
Orbs	eyes
Plates	feet
Palome	woman
Pots	teeth
Riah	hair
Riah-shusher	hairdresser
Scarper	to run away
Sharpy	policeman
Slap	make-up
Trade	sexual partner
Troll	walk about
Varda	look at
Willets	breasts

PDA (PUBLIC DISPLAYS OF AFFECTION)

That's kissing and holding hands to you and me. It's a controversial subject as everyone has a different view, often depending upon their background, where they live, who they socialise with and how 'out' they happen to be. In principle, we might all expect to be able to express affection in public without any fear of causing a fuss, but you know what it's like; it doesn't take much to cause a sensation. It's fine for a boy and girl to virtually fuck on the tube, but two guys or two girls? No, that just wouldn't be right and proper. Indeed, it's unusual to see two homos even holding hands anywhere other than in the gayest of places, and yet we should be able to do all the things that straight people do, without having to look over our proverbial shoulders.

But guess what? We can – we just need to have the balls to do it. OK, it's probably not a good idea to snog your boyfriend on a football terrace, but next time you're in the supermarket and you see the yukky straight couples hand in hand as if they're the only people to have ever been in love – give 'em a taste of the queer alternative. You can hold hands and you can kiss. Theoretically it could be construed as being illegal (yes, another bit of anti-gay repression) but your local bobby isn't exactly waiting with binoculars to bang you up, especially now that the law on such matters is soon to be changed (and about time too). So start a trend. Raise some eyebrows.

Viewpoints

'Personally I'd be a bit embarrassed to hold my boyfriend's hand in public, as people would be looking at you and it would feel silly. I know we should be the same as anyone else, but I just don't think it's an acceptable thing for lots of people. I'd also be worried that someone might recognise me and beat me up. I know people that have been attacked in the past, and they've been sure that it's because they've seen them acting gay, and it's got them into trouble. You have to be careful.'

Nick (student, 19), Manchester

'The whole thing seems so trivial, as if holding hands is some major crime, but it really does spook people if it's not in the middle of Soho or wherever. Me and my boyfriend don't go around kissing and touching in public a lot because we're not that sort of people, but when you see the way people can be so offended, it just makes me want to do it in order to confront them. You want to stop and say "what's your fucking problem?" or something. I remember just briefly holding hands as a laugh walking down Oxford Street once, and people were actually kissing their teeth and tutting. That just made us want to do it even more, so we ended up camping it up hand-in-hand walking down the street. People can be so bigoted and make so much out of nothing, just because it's two blokes.'

Mark (student, 21), London.

PERSONAL WEB PAGES

While you're ogling the talent in the Gay.com or Gaydar profiles, you might also care to consider the huge number of private web pages ('home pages') which are available on the internet, created by individuals who want to offer the viewer something a little more interesting than a plain old profile sheet and a mug shot. Some of the sites can be just plain awful (imagine a whole page about some fella's interest in trainspotting), but most of the sassy gay boys on the internet know what you're looking for, and they usually oblige with a tasty range of sexy photographs, and some of the sites even surprise you with intelligent comment too (no, really – some homos actually have brains too).

Some of these home pages are like miniature websites, but most have a nice, amateurish feel and it's often very interesting to take a peek into the lives of some of the people lurking out there in cyber space.

On the other hand, some sites seem to do little more than pay homage to people's egos (check out Chrisgeary.co.uk for an obnoxious festival of self-obsession). They're a good way to spend an afternoon (or a day, or a week), and a refreshing change from the more commercial sites on offer.

PIERCINGS

It started off with earrings and just got a little bit out of control. Next it was your nose, then your tongue, then your nipples, your navel and then your dick (if you have one). Piercing fans have never really advocated the notion that less is more, and what started off as a fashion (stolen mercilessly from the sado-masochism scene that had been into piercings for years and years, of course) became just that little bit too common. And you know what happens when everybody starts following a fashion? Yep, it's suddenly just not fashionable any more. Time to take the metalwork out, folks, the future is flesh.

PINK POUND

A sweet phrase coined by advertising executives back in the 1990s when it was suddenly realised that gay men and women (single, with no commitments) had a higher disposable income than the rest of society. Of course, it was something of a generalisation, as you're just as likely to meet a fellow homo in the dole queue, but there was (and is) some truth in the belief that there is a fairly big pool of gay people out there with plenty of money to spend. Consequently, a great deal of business effort is now made to attract the interest (and money) of gay men, and it's no coincidence that lifestyle magazines and television adverts have become havens for gratuitously naked male bodies. You think it's just for women?

The result has been a gradual shift in consumerism, driven by advertising. Straight guys who would have winced at the idea of using anything other than a bar of soap will now happily use moisturisers, aftershave (rather than Brut) and hair products. Even a cursory look through a typical clothing store will show just how 'gay' the straight man's wardrobe has become. Look at the huge surge in the popularity of loft apartments. It's all thanks to the Pink Pound.

By contrast, the Pink Pound epithet has also been applied to gay business, catering specifically for gay consumerism. Possibly the worst examples of gay ghetto mentality, there are gay-run taxis, funeral directors, florists, designers, printers, decorators, plumbers, photographers, in fact just about anything you could care to imagine. The customer service and value for money is the same but the business is gay.

It might sound slightly absurd to employ the services of any business just because it's gay but, on the other hand, there's much to be said for taking a (small) stand against the ravages of mainstream consumerism, all driven to extract the maximum amount of money from our gay pockets. Instead of surrendering to the onslaught, how about putting your money back into another gay pocket? It might seem a little petty but, if you've got the choice, it might be worth choosing gay. Who knows, it might help to convince mainstream (straight) businesses that by proverbially painting your product pink you don't necessarily make it any better.

THE PINK TRIANGLE

Its history dates back to the Second World War, when gay men were forced to wear a pink triangle (point faced down) to identify themselves in Hitler's concentration camps (lesbians were obliged to wear a similar mark, but in black). As if this discrimination-within-discrimination wasn't bad enough, the triangle then served as a means of identification for post-war liberating forces, who then sent the same victims directly to jail. While most Jewish (and other) camp survivors were ultimately compensated, the gay men (and their families) were conveniently overlooked.

Not surprisingly, the pink triangle is perhaps the most poignant and political gay symbol that we have, but it has largely disappeared from widespread use. Why? Well, it's probably got more than a little to do with the red Aids ribbon which, almost by definition, became a 'gay badge' and one which was perceived to be more politically correct than the old pink triangle.

But now that the Aids crisis has effectively been hijacked by heterosexuals, the red ribbon no longer carries the same gay connotations that it did a few years ago, so will the pink triangle come back? Let's hope so, if only to display some respect to our forebears who learned much harder lessons about discrimination than we ever will.

THE PINKIE RING

Famously fashioned by the terminally straight Prince Charles, the wearing of a pinkie ring was used to signify that you were gay back in the 1950s and 1960s. The practice died out when earrings took over, and we got into all that business about wearing one earring on your left lobe . . . or was it your right? Or both? It all got hopelessly out of hand and died out completely when everyone suddenly realised that we could just stand up and say, 'I'm gay.' So much easier, don't you think?

THE RAINBOW FLAG

It came from San Francisco as an internationally accepted symbol of gay, lesbian, transgender, transvestite, drag queen, bisexual . . . we could go on all day. What exactly does the rainbow flag stand for? It stands for cop-out. It's become a convenient way to indicate gay support, while not overtly saying so to the straight folks. You know the sort of thing – the flag gets stuck outside a pub when it wants to be gay, and then it goes inside again when the straight people are in the majority. Or else it becomes a convenient lapel badge to say 'hey, I support gay rights' to gay people, while it says 'I embrace all beliefs and lifestyle choices' to everyone else. It's all things to all people, and as such it stinks. If you or your business really support gay rights and gay people, then go get a pink triangle – it tells everyone what you stand for, and it even uses less paint. Ditch the flag, for heaven's sake.

RAINBOW NETWORK

Although the internet has given us a variety of exciting modes of communication and entertainment, there are surprisingly few websites devoted to gay interests. Many were created but just as many have eventually fallen victim to indifference, lack of interest or lack of cash. The surviving sites are by definition pretty strong and very popular, and Rainbow is one of the best, as described by a company spokesman: 'Rainbow Network was launched in September 1999 and has grown exponentially to establish itself as one of the UK's most successful consumer sites. Over the years since its launch, it has come to depend a great deal on its 600,000 users for the direction, tone and "voice" of its content. Aiming to provide an informative but light-hearted look at gay lifestyle, the site has sections such as Entertainment, Fun, Classifieds, Shopping, Travel, Men's Room and Dyke's Domain, as well as news and health for the more serious minded. Because of the breadth of the gay target audience, the content of the site has grown beyond all expectation over the years to provide areas of interest to every aspect of the users' lives. To differentiate itself from the standard gay and lesbian sites, it chose early on to concentrate on content rather than chat or personals, although its Flirt! and Personals sections provide a welcome relief to those overwhelmed by some of the more hardcore offerings available.

Above all, we try to encourage user interaction across the site; to that end eighteen-year-old bar boys seem to have taken over the scene areas; lesbians seem to have control of the forums; theatre queens have taken over a large part of the entertainment areas, although there still is a good crossover between the different zones. Also hugely popular are the myriad competitions that run on the site, offering VIP access to nightclubs, free DVDs and CDs, books, toys and a host of other freebies.

The result is one of the deepest gay sites around, with over 70,000 pages of content, demonstrating the varied and eclectic interests of gay men and lesbians in the UK. With over 600,000 users generating five million-plus page views a month, it seems a safe bet that we must be doing something right at least some of the time.'

Link

www.rainbownetwork.com

SHOPPING

They say that shopping and fucking are what gay boys (and more than a few girls) are all about, and it's probably true that, while a few straight-acting (or at least strait-laced) homos like to pretend that they hate the very idea, most of us would happily spend most of our lives mincing round shopping malls with a credit card (oh, if only . . .). But what are the places to be for the about-town merchandise mary?

1 IKEA

Still the king (or is it princess?) of gay shopping, Ikea (or 'Eye-queer') maintains its status as the all-powerful shrine to gay taste. Endless avenues of pretty things, combining furniture with furnishings, fabulous little tableaux (don't you just want to settle into one of those faux lounges?), lighting, foliage, flooring, you name it, they have it all, and always with that mix of good taste without the pretence. The aisles are littered with homos, switching their glances between the fancy furniture and the equally desirable fellas doing the shopping. Tragically, the whole Ikea experience is slowly becoming a 'family' experience, and the stores are best avoided at weekends when the entourage of screaming kids slightly spoils the atmosphere.

2 LUSH

Who would have thought it? A gay oasis in a high street of dreary straightness. Lush finally gave the nation's shopping queens the store that they'd always wanted, selling gorgeous, slightly overpriced goodies which are all ultimately useless (mostly designed to be washed down the plughole in fact). It's a recipe for gay success, and little wonder that every Lush store is always alive with mincing homos, sniffing their way through the merchandise while keeping an eye on the talent. Undoubtedly the must-have gift for any gay occasion, Lush addiction is the way to go.

3 SAFEWAY

Supermarkets have never been rated as gay spaces, although in America the major supermarkets have traditionally been recognised as good places for cruising and meeting other gay people. Maybe it's British reserve but there doesn't seem to be much dating going on round our shopping aisles, at least not yet anyway. However, Safeway (which is an American import, of course) has started to buck the trend, and most of their stores seem to have attracted a steady trickle of cruisy gay boys who seem to be looking for more than fresh lettuce. The new late or all-night opening hours seem to have helped things along (3 a.m. can be a fascinating time to go shopping) and it may be that Safeway is the way to go if you're bored with the Sainsbury's Jamie Oliver mockney fan club (and who isn't?). Let's pray that when the takeovers are finished, the supermarket survives.

4 WATERSTONE'S

Bookshops are undoubtedly a dying breed in Britain, but the Waterstone's chain seems to be maintaining its high-street success. Combining tasteful surroundings (in-store coffee shops seem to be the latest attraction) with good products, Waterstone's has always had a special queer quality, often expressed through the disproportionately large photography and art sections, and a reliable range of gay books. Most stores even sell copies of *Gay Times* and stock local free gay news sheets and *Pink Paper*. How cool is that?

Links

www.ikea.com

www.lush.co.uk

www.waterstones.co.uk

SKINHEADS

One of those 'looks' which has endured in gay circles for years, and it looks like it's here to stay. In direct contrast to the slightly fay appearance of crop-tops, cut-off trousers and spiky bleached hair, the skinhead look is pure neo-nazi. To do it properly, we're talking about a completely shaved head, skin-tight jeans, Doc Martens, braces, a checked shirt and an MA1 jacket, combined with a scowl which would scatter a crowd from a hundred yards. Essentially a carbon copy of the right-wing fascist thug look, there are quite a few gay men who actively support right-wing racist politics which go with the 'uniform', although exactly how they deal with the strident homophobia that goes with it is hard to imagine.

On the other hand, there are many more men (and quite a few dykes) who simply like the 'look' and use the skinhead outfit as little more than drag, either as a sort of ironic comment on its fascist overtones or simply because they think it looks sexy.

For those who are less concerned with the complete image makeover, the skinhead hairstyle remains hugely popular, ranging from shaved heads through to severe buzz-cuts, and into all kinds of variations with hair-clippered designs, colour dye and so on. The Doc Martens are often replaced by Caterpillar boots (or other more mainstream items) and the checked shirt is exchanged for a simple T-shirt. This slightly less in-your-face skinhead look has become common amongst both straight and gay people, and stretches across a huge age span, ranging from students (with a commendably rebellious streak) through to fifty-somethings, who have learned that receding hair is best shaved off rather than simply rearranged.

Links

www.skinheads.diversity.org.uk

STRAIGHT ACTING

A relatively new phrase in our gay vocabulary, and one which has become pretty common inside internet chat rooms. What does it mean? Well, it's usually found in personal profiles – the all-about-me bit where you can find out all the fascinating details you want to know about the guy you're chatting up in the chat room. You look for the bit where he describes himself and, hey presto, he says, 'I'm very straight acting'.

Apart from the fact that the phrase is hopelessly over used, you have to wonder how anyone could seriously describe themselves as such. Clearly, if you're a gay man (or woman for that matter), then presumably you act gay, at least when you're naked with someone between the sheets. Having sex with someone of the same gender is, by definition, a gay act. Any other time you could be described as normal, or camp, or effeminate, outrageous, boring, whatever you like, but straight acting? Does that mean you pretend to be straight? And if so, then why?

On the other hand, does it mean you ramble on about football scores and how you'd like to give Melinda Messenger a good seeing-to (OK, some of you girls might but that's not the point)? Worse still, what does the whole 'acting' bit mean? That your life is an act? Worth thinking about if you want to give yourself a headache.

TATTOOS

So popular a couple of years ago, the country is now crammed full of gay boys and girls who wish they'd learned the meaning of the term 'moderation' before it was too late. A little would have gone a long way but like the piercing fad which came before it, tattoos literally just grew and grew. Don't those wavy armband things just look so stupid now? The future of tattoos? Er . . . less is more?

TRUCKERS

They're up there with the firemen, those sexy truck drivers that whizz up and down the motorways, mysteriously stripped to the waist even when the sun's not shining. Nobody's quite worked out why gay men (and women) often have a thing about truck drivers, but maybe it's something to do with their reputation for no-strings sex while the wife's tucked up at home, a few hundred miles away.

Particularly interesting is the surprising revelation that the view isn't all one-way, as a Liverpool trucker comments, 'You just can't imagine the number of guys I see driving along, having a wank. They think nobody can see them because their car door blocks the view but when you're high up in a truck's cab, you can see everything. It's just unreal.' Who knew? And what is it with Eddie Stobart and this uniform and tie thing? Since when has anybody wanted to see a trucker wearing a tie?

SANDALS

What the world needs now is love, sweet love . . . Don't laugh; that was the song they played over the now-infamous television advert that holiday travel company Sandals slapped on to our television screens not so long ago. Trouble was, the small print in their television and print media hid some slightly disturbing restrictions like 'mixed couples only' and 'couples over 18 (one male, one female) are welcome'. Go figure.

Not surprisingly, when the homos spotted the offending text they were outraged, and the complaints started flowing in. Unrepentant, Sandals took no notice, but Barclaycard, who were advertising their online banking service through a prize draw with Sandals, decided to get out.

Barclaycard's Chief Executive said, 'I fully understand how some of the prize arrangements have caused offence and really regret the mistake which led to the situation. We will not be working in future with any suppliers who do not meet our high standards on these important issues.'

A spokeswoman for Sandals added that 'We presume that we will not be working with them in the future.' You bet you won't, honey, and excuse us while we all go get ourselves a Barclaycard . . .

Link

www.sandals.com

4: Scene and seen

Although sexuality may be the defining subject which connects us in mind and spirit, it is the gay pub and club scene which ultimately brings us together. Just about every town in the country has at least one bar where gay men and lesbians can get together and socialise, safe and content in the knowledge that most of the people they're drinking with are all pretty much on the same wavelength. Of course, the bigger cities like London, Manchester and Birmingham have so many gay pubs and clubs that they've effectively created their own gay 'villages' complete with gay taxi firms, food outlets and businesses, and if you're in the right part of town you can (if you want to) immerse yourself in a glitzy gay world of hand-holding, kissing, cruising and campery, without having to look over your shoulder to see who's watching.

But while this kind of environment was a welcome haven of safety back in the days when homosexuality was a taboo, there's a younger generation of gay people who just can't understand what the gay scene is all about. Their viewpoint is that a gay village is effectively a gay ghetto, where you're cut off from the rest of society, cornered into an alleyway of mutual mistrust. They say (quite understandably) that you don't have to go to gay clubs to be gay, and you can be open about your sexuality anywhere, and just be yourself. Why hide away in segregated ghettos when the whole world is at your feet? It's an interesting viewpoint but a slightly specious one, built on the assumption that the whole of Britain is the same as Soho. It's very easy to be openly gay if you're in the right place and with the right people, but you don't have to look too far to see places where the very mention of homosexuality could get you beaten, or worse. Even in our supposedly glittering new world of acceptance and assimilation, it's misleading to suggest that any homo could mince into every straight club and be entirely comfortable, unless he (or she) is a master of camouflage or self-deception.

The truth is that while society is feeding on the amusement of celebrities like Graham Norton and Lily Savage, gay is seen to be acceptable, chiefly because it's amusing and oh-so avant-garde. But what about when fashions change, as they always inevitably do? Where will we go if we've abandoned our gay clubs or allowed gay spaces to fill with hen parties and fag hags? The trend has already begun, and the clubs which stay gay are slowly losing customers, while the rest of the clubs are increasingly welcoming straight people into the new wave of 'mixed' clubbing (to make up the numbers and pay the bills). Let's hope and pray that being gay remains fashionable because, if mainstream tastes eventually change, we might find that we have nowhere to go. What will we do, go back into the closet? Let's do the Time Warp again.

Let's look at the movers and shakers on the gay scene.

ATTITUDE

Launched in 1994, *Attitude* was the first British mainstream lifestyle magazine to be aimed directly at gay men. That in itself was something of an achievement, bearing in mind that up until that year, the only commercially available magazine for gay readers was *Gay Times* – a very worthy and informative publication but hardly the stuff of coffee-table entertainment. *Attitude* was without doubt the proverbial breath of fresh air, instantly destroying the notion that gay readers were only interested in gay sex, straight sex and sex. Indeed, a few years later the then editor commented that they didn't 'cover things just because they're gay'. Nice sentiments indeed, but like any seemingly innovative idea, this straight-magazine-for-gay-readers concept has possibly been stretched beyond its credible limit, and *Attitude* has started to become a victim of its own dogma.

Nearly a decade on, it has to be said that *Attitude* is becoming predictable and slightly tired, changing very little from month to month. Its mainstream appeal has certainly been a useful tool in attracting some very big names (the sainted David Beckham has to be mentioned in this context) but, when a magazine becomes so 'straight' in both style and content that you could easily pick it up and, shall we say, rather miss the point, it's hardly surprising that even the biggest star is willing to dabble in this artificially sterile world of anodyne non-gayness. Indeed, this let's-not-be-too-gay trick is used with almost every celebrity that the magazine has featured – the usual publicity waffle with a couple of cheeky 'so do you mind being fancied by gay men?' questions thrown in for effect. All rather pointless really, seeing as every celebrity automatically professes to embrace the gay community when they're getting some good publicity. You start to wonder what the point of it all is, when you might as well read the same stuff in *Hello!* magazine.

There are, of course, some delicious exceptions (Graham Norton, Julian Clary, Boy George, Divine David and many more), and some good features written by talented writers, discussing some genuinely interesting topics. But the 'straight-acting' tone does eventually start to leave an unpleasant taste in your mouth, especially when readers' letters are consistently used to bang home the (questionable) fact that we (supposedly) appreciate that we're reading such a commendably non-gay magazine. Indeed, *Attitude* regularly avoids even mentioning the 'g' word, choosing the curious euphemism 'mox' whenever possible (although nobody in the known universe ever uses this word apart from the magazine's staff). Maybe the masquerade has gone on just that little bit too long. We are homosexuals, let's not forget.

But it would be unfair to criticise *Attitude* too much, when the magazine has achieved something remarkable – finding a place within the nation's mainstream magazines, a good few inches down from the dreaded top shelf, in a position where even the most homophobic shopper can read it and weep. Maybe now it's secure in that place, it can afford to be just that little bit more, er . . . mox?

AXM

Take a copy of *Attitude*, rip out the good bits and you've pretty much got yourself a copy of *Axm*. No, the letters don't actually stand for anything (it started off as *Axiom* . . . don't ask), and the magazine doesn't seem to stand for much either. Taking all of *Attitude*'s bad points and none of the good ones, *Axm* gives you that warm feeling of déjà vu every time you read it, that is, of course, if you could even be bothered to try. Your newsagent is crammed full of magazines, but try and find a decent gay publication, if you will . . .

BLACKPOOL

Everything you've heard about Blackpool is true. It's a vulgar mix of candy floss, fish and chips, screaming kids and donkey shit, combined with endless miles of amusement arcades, seriously tacky gift shops and more trashy people than you ever imagined could co-exist on one planet. It also rains a lot. So why is Blackpool so great? Well, it's all to do with your mind-set, and whether you know what you want. If you're looking for relaxation, try the countryside. If you're looking for sophistication, then try a few art galleries or museums. But Blackpool's about fun, pure and simple. And best of all, it's unashamedly gay. Unlike Brighton, which has developed into a sort of London-on-Sea, Blackpool has retained its true holiday resort identity, with a crowd of people who are just looking for cheap fun and entertainment, and the gay scene is just part of the landscape that nobody seems to notice, unless you happen to be gay, of course. Littered with pubs and clubs all catering for queer tastes, Blackpool is probably the number-one destination for anyone looking for a totally outrageous girlie weekend.

Apart from the famous attractions (the Tower, the Pleasure Beach, the ancient tramcars and the miles of illuminations), there's the nationally famous Funny Girls showbar to check out. Funny Girls is primarily part of Blackpool's straight entertainment but, when you consider that the entertainment consists of drag queens performing show tunes, you can't be surprised that about half of the audience (and the place is always packed to capacity) is gay. But make no mistake – Funny Girls is more than just some bloke in a frock miming to a Shirley Bassey song – this is stage performance at its best. You will be impressed, and Funny Girls has become a sort of semi-traditional starting point to a holiday gay night out in Blackpool.

Next morning, you can recover in one of the countless greasy cafes, or hide under the sheets in a gay guesthouse (there are quite a few). But if the sun's out, just sit on the promenade and enjoy the shirtless, trackie-bottomed rough lads, pushing their prams, while their fat wives lumber along behind. So very Blackpool.

Link

www.astabgay.com/Blackpool_gay_Clubs.htm

BOOKS

Homos seem to enjoy a strange love/hate relationship with books catering specifically for gay tastes. It's fair to say that there are plenty to be found, even if they're not readily available on the front shelves at your local bookstore, but they are out there . . . somewhere. Sadly, gay publishing is perceived as being a non-commercial specialist trade, so almost every gay self-help, politics, guide, history or biography book is usually doomed to be tucked away in obscure mail order lists or the Amazon catalogue. Accessibility has always been a problem when it comes to gay books, but things have improved slightly, now that shops like Prowler Soho have come along, with space devoted to gay books. Likewise, the Waterstone's chain has adopted a commendable gay-friendly identity and, even if their shelves are still woefully short on gay-themed titles, they do at least make an effort to cater for our interests, and in some cases even stock free gay magazines as an added bonus. Pretty cool, eh?

LEIGH BOWERY

Some people almost defy description. Born appropriately in a town called Sunshine (in Australia), Bowery moved to England in 1980 and became a leading light in the London club scene of the 1980s. More than just your typical gay-boy-about-town, and so much more than your average drag queen, Leigh was a true performance artist as he recalled, 'Initially the scene seemed to be the best place to get in touch with people whose work I was interested in. Then I found the whole process of going to clubs and getting drunk and dressed up very exciting, and spent five or six years doing that exclusively.'

In 1985 he opened his own club (Taboo) just off Leicester Square, and a true legend was born. The bitchiness spewing from his lips was nothing compared to the shocking imagery of his mind-bending outfits which went way beyond the realms of pure drag, and into a world of drug-induced fantasy. Boy George famously referred to Leigh as 'modern art on legs'.

Bowery did it all and, in the finest traditions of performance artists, nothing was sacred. His years of clubland life merged into a series of multi-media performances (multi media was often underestimating things slightly – his act could include blood, spit or even – if you were particularly lucky – the contents of an enema bag), and although largely unknown outside the confines of London's more colourful venues, Leigh Bowery left his mark on the gay community, delivering a brand of outrageousness that still lives on with us today in a few places where conventionality, boy bands and acting straight hasn't destroyed every remaining bit of our souls.

Perversely, he married his friend and collaborator of ten years, Nicola Bateman, just a few months before his untimely death on New Year's Eve 1994. She and all of his friends only learned of Bowery's HIV-positive status shortly before he died. He once said that his only regret was 'having unsafe sex with 1,000 men'.

Leigh Bowery lived it large; his imagery is still to be found if you know where to look, and his legacy of larger-than-life costume and wild partying is still with us – just. Maybe a whole lot of fun died with him.

Links

www.leighbowery.kit.net

www.geocities.com.leighbowery

BOY GEORGE

There are celebrities and then there's Boy George. There are gay men and then there's Boy George. How do you categorise somebody who just doesn't fit into any pigeonhole? If any one celebrity deserved a special place in a gay book, then Boy George inevitably has to take that position. We can look at all kinds of gay rights campaigns and all sorts of fancy initiatives or policies in order to identify the ways in which gay life in Britain has changed so drastically, but make no mistake – the seminal moment in our modern gay history was in February 1982 when George Alan O'Dowd walked on to the BBC *Top of the Pops* stage and sang. In drag.

First appearing on the punk scene, George O'Dowd was already something of a celebrity even before he made his first record. A classic case of the right person being in the right place at just the right time, George was out there in the middle of the New Romantic clubland with outrageous make-up, big hair and drag to die for. After a few unsuccessful attempts at recording, he became the lead singer of Culture Club and suddenly his singing career took off.

But, of course, George was always rather more than just his voice. Twenty years on it's difficult to imagine just what a shock to the nation's sensibilities he was. Men only did drag in pantomimes, not on *Top of the Pops*, but here was a towering six-foot-plus fella looking more camp than Blackpool. Lipstick, for heaven's sake?

As if to hammer home this assault on middle-class England, Culture Club became hugely successful, but while teenage girls were happily dressing up in Culture Club drag, Boy George was carefully avoiding saying anything much about his sexuality. In retrospect it was hard to imagine that anyone ever thought that he was straight but George did attract the attentions of many pro-gay activist groups who felt that, with the benefit of his celebrity status, he should have come out of the closet and told the world what he was all about. In contrast, George coyly made his infamous remark that he'd rather have a cup of tea than have sex.

More recently, George has defended his position by claiming that he was a victim of his record company's wishes, and that coming out would have been commercial suicide. But, of course, the reality of the situation was rather murkier and, while there's always going to be some debate as to whether George should have 'come out' right from the start of his career, it would have been a seriously short-sighted observer who couldn't see that, even with his mouth firmly shut, Boy George was as gay and as camp as it could possibly get. Rather than being Fleet Street's gift he was their worst nightmare – a gay man that the public loved. Whatever the truth, Boy George remained on the fence, but in more recent years he's more than compensated for his early ambiguity. Out of the closet, he's locked the door firmly behind him.

Sadly, Culture Club fell victim to a combination of disasters which were all waiting to happen. George developed an abusive and often volatile relationship with the group's drummer John Moss and became close friends with Marilyn, an outrageous and glamorous club scene drag queen who developed a love/hate relationship with George, ultimately ending in a court case surrounding George and his friend's heroin abuse. Marilyn also did much to mould George's lifestyle and personality and it's questionable as to whether George's in-your-face attitude and flamboyant personality would ever have been as strong or as magical, had it not been for Marilyn's influence. It was a messy affair which effectively destroyed both Culture Club and Boy George's career, and the brief one-hit career which Marilyn achieved ('Calling Your Name' was a chart success).

But George bounced back and even though the days of Culture Club's huge success were over, he managed to find a place back in the charts as a solo artist. He also wrote his autobiography *Take It Like a Man*, a surprisingly frank look at his life and career which was widely acclaimed by critics, encouraging George to turn more of his attention to literary matters. Becoming a columnist in the *Sunday Express* (and who would have ever imagined that?), he has also made some remarkably honest comments recently about the ineffectiveness of gay politics and the integration-obsessed gay club scene. Not surprisingly, his views haven't exactly been embraced by much of the gay community even though much of what he's said is undoubtedly true – it's just that a lot of people didn't want to hear it, especially from Boy George. Hugely popular as a guest DJ, and with both a recording label (More Protein) and a hugely successful musical (*Taboo*) under his belt, Boy George is even more in-your-face than he ever was.

Discussion of Culture Club's pop influence would be to miss the point slightly. Boy George was always bigger than the group, and his influence on the way that British people perceive gay men and lesbians shouldn't be underestimated just because George was a mere singer. He didn't have to make any eloquent speeches or any grand public gestures. He just was, and is. And whatever you might think of him, you've got to admire him and be thankful for just that simple, delicious fact.

Links

www.boy.george.net

www.boy-george.net

BOYZ

Since the 1980s the UK's gay pubs and clubs have been lavishly furnished with a steady diet of free-issue newsletters and magazines. Some are good; some are just plain vile, but *Boyz* has reigned supreme as the survivor which has earned a place in our collective gay history. Launched in 1991, *Boyz* was new and exciting when it first hit the streets. Professionally produced, the paper's emphasis was far away from the usual menu of politics and news, and aimed squarely at the kind of subjects that really interested the gay men that frequented the bars and clubs where the paper was distributed. This publication was (and still is) all about cock.

Not surprisingly, *Boyz* was a huge success and over the next few years the paper was developed and transformed into a fully fledged glossy magazine, still produced for free, but with all the trappings of a mainstream commercial publication, attracting some big names from the world of pop music and television celebrity to its pages. The emphasis was still on sex, however, and the down-to-earth style of the words and images made the paper a must-read for every scene queen across the country, even if more than a few readers quietly tucked their copies under their beds at night. Whether the preoccupation with sex went a little too far is open to question (the full-page nude picture in each issue was always a major love/hate subject), but even the most prudish of readers couldn't help taking a peek at the more risqué parts of the paper. Well, you had to . . .

Tragically, a combination of cost factors eventually forced the publishers to kill off the national circulation of the paper, and *Boyz* is now restricted to outlets in London and the South. Not surprisingly, more than a few people north of Watford feel a little bit insulted that so much of the country is now effectively excluded from what was once a well-liked national magazine, and the once-great *Boyz* is now gone, devoured in a seemingly endless series of uninspiring advert-chasing free-issue comics which neither inform nor entertain. Maybe one day the real *Boyz* will return. For everyone.

BRIGHTON

They like to call it London-on-Sea, as if that's a good thing, but whether the idea of transposing all of London's colourful population to the coast is really such a nice thought is maybe not worth dwelling on. The whole point of Brighton, at least as far as us homos are concerned, is that it's unashamedly gay; it's not far from London and it's a seaside resort. Brighton has lots of pubs and bars catering almost exclusively for gay customers, and a decent supply of queer nightclubs to dance away the evenings. With easy and (fairly) regular train connections directly to the heart of London, you can see why so many gay boys and girls make Brighton their weekend destination choice or their permanent home.

Particularly popular are the annual Brighton Pride celebrations which, although substantially smaller than London's efforts, are arguably a whole lot more fun, with a parade of costumes and floats that our beloved capital hasn't even got close to matching (and how sad is that?) plus a (free) concert and gathering in the town's main park. Don't expect to find anywhere to stay in Brighton during the Pride weekend though, as every hotel and guesthouse (including all the straight ones) is almost guaranteed to be full, so be prepared for a night-long clubbing experience, or a kip on the beach.

The downside to Brighton is that it's just too damned popular. The affluent 'beautiful people' up in London have decided that Brighton is now the place to be (now that the gay boys and girls have made it fabulous, of course) and they've snapped up every available property for miles. Consequently, if you fall in love with Brighton, you're doomed to have a hard time finding anywhere affordable to live which is any bigger than a garden shed. Let's be patient and wait until these hetties-with-cash learn that Brighton was only fabulous and desirable until they started moving in. However, when they're gone . . .

Link

www.gaytoz.com/barsbrighton.asp

TYLER BRULE

The much-admired Tyler was born in Canada back in 1969, and worked in Australian television before arriving in the UK in 1989. His freelance writing work eventually led to his creation of the great icon of style magazines *Wallpaper** in 1996. *Wallpaper** is everything that a glossy should be – a triumph of presentation over content, a delicious cavalcade of imagery unencumbered by thought or discussion. It's the ultimate designer collection of nice things. Tyler (who is, unsurprisingly, gay) sold *Wallpaper** to Time Inc. in 1997 for more than a million, but he continued to oversee its success, and by 2001 it had a monthly circulation of more than 134,000. More than a third of the readership are estimated to be gay. Imagine.

Link

www.wallpaper.com

CANAL STREET

Once upon a time there was a derelict part of Manchester's city centre which had been neglected since the days of canal transportation ended. The warehouses were either empty or in desperate need of repair, and the only people to frequent the area were workers, drunks or gay men and women visiting the handful of pubs which had sprung up in the area. The rest, as they say, is history. Manchester's 'gay village' was born and more pubs opened, followed by clubs, cafes, restaurants, taxi firms, even a barber's shop. The warehouses became apartments; Canal Street was refurbished and everything was beautiful. Then along came television, and the 1999 hit series *Queer As Folk*.

While we all delighted at the mainstream popularity of a television series which essentially portrayed gay lifestyles as being fantastically glamorous (at least by straight standards), the heterosexual viewers were looking at things slightly differently. Seeing Canal Street (where *Queer As Folk* was located) on their television screens convinced more than a few people that they were missing out on something fabulous. Suddenly, the usual diet of straight nightclubs and bars didn't seem quite so appealing, particularly to girls who could see a glittering world of shiny dance music, decorated by fit-bodied, half-naked guys who were never going to start slobbering over them asking for a shag. Overnight, Canal Street became the place to be.

It was probably entirely predictable, and business along Canal Street boomed. The pubs and clubs were full and the burger bars were serving up food into the small hours every night. How wonderful that the gay scene was so popular, so glamorous, so desirable. But, of course, like a cold, wet Monday morning along the same street, the gloss eventually wore off. The straight guys got bored and eventually realised that even the most glitzy club wasn't quite so fantastic if you couldn't actually pull any birds, and guys kept looking at you.

The girls, however, liked what they saw. Not only were the pubs and clubs inevitably busy and lively, they were also full of gay boys, many of whom were either impossibly cute or outrageously funny. The clubs were funky and most of the lads danced with their shirts off. Better still, the guys didn't want to chase you around all night trying to get laid. It was the ultimate safe space.

All very good, of course, but three years on the girls are still there and they're not going away. In fact, things have got a whole lot worse and Canal Street is now top of the list for a girlie night out in Manchester. The hen night has become Canal Street's collective nightmare for all of the street's gay venues. It's not that anyone objects to straight girls frequenting gay pubs and clubs, but the hen night girlies are methodically destroying the very gay scene that they supposedly want to enjoy. Crowds of screaming, giggling, staggering girls just aren't very funny, especially when they think it outrageously funny to repeatedly ask 'are you a faggot then' or pinch your bum as if you're some cheap tart.

Even worse is the notion that every gay man is a sort of local Julian Clary, ready to deliver a half-hour stand-up camp comedy routine free of charge and without a stage. Some of those girls look seriously disappointed if you can't summon up at least a dozen cock jokes on demand.

The basic truth is that gay people go to gay pubs to be with other gay people. If they wanted to be with straight people, they'd go to straight pubs and clubs. It's as simple as that. It might be a ghetto mentality, but it's what people want, even though there are plenty of ill-informed 'right-on' people (usually only a few months out of university) that will tell you we don't. It might seem unfair and it might seem rude, but the girls just ain't welcome down Canal Street, even though the pubs can sometimes seem (understandably) reluctant to turn away their business.

Ironically, one of Manchester's oldest gay pubs (the New Union) actively caters for straight audiences with a steady stream of drag acts and dancers on their stage, providing the usual brand of outrageous entertainment that isn't actually outrageous to anyone unless they're distinctly straight. But when even the people on stage are confirmed heterosexuals performing pseudo-sexual male-female dance routines, you begin to wonder what the point of it all really is.

As if the girls aren't enough to worry about, they do still attract some male attention from the kind of people that would otherwise stay well clear of gay places like Canal Street. Consequently, what is still regarded as one of the safest places in Manchester is now prone to random muggings and attacks, so much so that a panic button (linked to the police) is now installed in the centre of the village. If the girls went, then so would the remaining straight men. Even queer-bashers wouldn't bother to make a special trip if there was nothing to see.

As for the future, who can predict what will happen to the once-happy Canal Street. Every gay paper has written an obituary for Manchester's gay village but it still survives, even though a sunny weekend afternoon would make you think you were in a theme park, judging by the crowds of pram-pushing families which drift down Canal Street to look at the homos or simply embrace the glamour and avant-gardeness of being amongst gay people ('yes, we even spoke to one of them'). You can't help praying that the novelty will die off and the leech-like fancy bars and restaurants on the edge of the village (where the straight folk can safely meet and pretend to be oh-so fashionable without actually having to touch the homosexuals) will go bust, as they rightly deserve to. Maybe then Canal Street can be given back to the people that created it and, by definition, deserve to have it all to themselves.

Viewpoints

'I can't fucking stand the way the straight people come in and think it's like some sort of free entertainment. You can see it on their faces. You get groups and they'll literally just stand there and point and laugh at someone 'cause he looks camp or he's in drag or something, and they don't even realise how insulting it is. I mean, if we went into a straight club in a group and started pointing and laughing at people they'd be disgusted, but it's OK to do it to us. I wish they'd just fuck off back to their own clubs and pubs, and if we all stopped being so polite and nice to them then they'd get the message that they're so not welcome.'

Sam (decorator, 38), Manchester

'Well, a lot of the gay pubs and clubs round Canal Street are pretty careful now about what people they let in, and they won't even let hen parties in at all. I know it's a bit unfair and it's like segregation or something, but what can you do? It's unfair to have gangs of girls rolling about all over the place when you've gone there to be with gay people. I've had girls pinch my backside and ask if I want a shag and all kinds of stuff. One group even asked me to get my knob out as if I'm just some stage act for them or something. It's really not fair to use gay places like that.'

Jamie (student, 19), Manchester

'I think that if things don't change, gay clubs will move away from the Canal Street area completely. It's already happening to a degree and if it's just going to be full of straight people then there's no point in just sticking to this area. You may as well open a place anywhere in Manchester. I hope it doesn't happen but you have to expect it. All over the country you get rundown places that gay people take over when nobody wants them, and they make them nice, and eventually they become so attractive that straight people want to be there too and they end up taking over again. Then the gay people just move away and

reinvent themselves somewhere else. It's like a sort of vicious circle and I think that's what will happen here.'

Jane (student, 18), Manchester

'Worst of all is in the summer when it's good weather, especially on a weekend when people come down here to drink and sit outside on the canal. You get guys sunbathing and you meet your mates and it's all good fun with lads to cruise and eye up and so on. But now, ever since **Queer As** ***fucking*** **Folk,** ***you also get groups of straight people and families all trudging up and down 'cause they think it's really trendy to come down here so they can tell their friends they've been in the gay village, like they've been so outrageous or something. So all the tables and chairs get full of families, and then there's new bars and restaurants keep opening which are so clearly aimed at straight people, so they come down and fill the place up, just so they can get off on this perceived thrill of being in the gay village, like it's really exciting now it's been on television. But they don't actually want anything to do with us; they just take our space. They're all nice to your face and I think they do genuinely believe you're great 'cause you're gay and so interesting and colourful. But actually it's a bit sad when you think about it, because they're treating you as if you're some kind of amusement attraction, not people, and you sometimes want to tell 'em to just get a life.'***

Mike (social worker, 34), Manchester

Links

www.outuk.com/outgoing/uk/manchester

www.gaytoz.com/barsmanchester.asp

CLUBS

Where would we be without gay clubs? How could we even exist? Would we exist? It's an interesting question (when you've had a few pints), and one which leads you to all kinds of possible conclusions. It's easy to dismiss the club scene as frivolous and ultimately irrelevant, but that would be to ignore history. It's worth remembering that the very beginnings of gay rights were in the Stonewall riots in New York, where the blossoming gay club scene was almost beaten out of existence by the police force, until that fateful day when the drag queens just wouldn't take any more. Our present-day relationship with the rest of society and indeed much of our accepted identity comes directly from Stonewall and therefore comes from nightclubs. So let's not be too dismissive of the scene, OK? It's what made us, er . . . us.

Of course, clubs have done much more than create our identity. It's the clubs where all forms of music have been explored and developed, and where the gay scene has repeatedly found a style and made it internationally popular. Boy George came from the gay clubs, and boy bands came from the gay clubs (Take That famously moulded their career performing almost exclusively for gay boys). Drug culture, fashion and body image all ultimately come from the same source and the whole notion of meeting, dating and shagging other people is driven by the gay club scene. No matter whether you love clubs or hate them, you can't escape their influence.

But what of the present day? The whole club thing just seems to be stagnating. There's nothing new, nothing exciting and certainly nothing original. We've been listening to the same music for years. Originality has gone. We're trapped in a weekly cycle of predictable dance music and techno house babble, played at ear-splitting volume so that the slightest chance of conversation is destroyed. Image is everything and communication is nothing. Worse still, the images are old.

Even scarier is the fact that the very concept of gay clubbing is under threat as more and more 'mixed' clubs appear. The definition of a mixed club (according to the organisers) is a venue where both gay and straight people can socialise in harmony or, in other words, it's a typical run-of-the-mill straight club which you can find down any street. If you want to dance with gay and straight people you really can do that anywhere. The whole point of a gay club was that it was for gay people (otherwise it's not a gay club, is it?).

But we seem to be missing the whole point. If we're to open our club doors to everyone, then there's absolutely no reason to be there in the first place, and we might as well head off down the high street with all the other Tracys and Sharons to the nearest place where the drinks are cheap. Wasn't the whole concept of a gay club that it was for gay men and women, so that we knew who we were, and who we were dancing with?

Gay clubs were places where we could be ourselves, without having to keep one eye open for disapproval or a broken bottle. It was a place where you could eye up another guy and be confident that, even if he didn't fancy you, he didn't actually fancy the opposite sex. Follow this new trend to its fatal conclusion and the gay clubs will all disappear, and we'll have encouraged history to turn itself back to the 1960s. We will have collectively herded ourselves back into the closet, unable to be too gay again for risk of upsetting the rest of the crowd. Not only will we have danced our way out of the gay ghetto – we will have danced our way out of existence.

What a relief, then, that some club venues have identified the danger and are now making that all-important move to exclude straight people from gay clubs. It's a move which has long been overdue. Selfish or not, they're our clubs, and we have a right to keep them.

Viewpoints

'The bitching and back-biting really gets me down the most on the gay scene. It's so pathetic most of the time. There is a lot of needless shit-stirring about people, although I won't say any names and it's the same everywhere in any case. The main reason for it all is just jealousy. My real name is Aaron, although I call myself Jay-Lo Boi. I don't label myself as gay because I'm bisexual which means I find women sexually arousing too, so I'm half and half at the moment, which is the case for a lot of lesbian, gay and bisexual people I think, both young and old. As for coming out, it's something that I'm not ready to do just yet.

The first time I went to a gay club it was really good because the people were friendly and it was a very nice place really. A lot of men fancied me too, which was a bonus. I went there with about seven friends who were local guys from my area and they were all gay or bisexual as well. We originally met each other using that fabulous thing called the internet, through other people in my area where I live in London. We were quite a big group and most of the guys had already been out clubbing before. Now I love going out and meeting lots of cute guys and most of the clubs are big and beautiful, especially when they've just been refurbished. They're pure class.

I think sex is better with boys because they know what they're doing. You have to understand that boys know what they want off someone of the same sex and, of course, they can think and feel the same sort of emotions. Girls know what they're doing too but not as well as boys because a boy would know what we both want.

I don't want to get married at all. I can't imagine myself ever getting married in fact but I'd like to have a child at some point, although not for a long time yet. It's hard for me to think about a bisexual guy categorising myself as gay because, when you're bisexual like me, I can say during the week that I can be attracted to girls living around my area. But then I would go out at the weekend and see a boy and think he's well fit. I realised I was bisexual when I started thinking of guys as being attractive and nice looking. When men fancy me it gives me a boost of confidence and stuff like that.

I haven't come out to my family at all. They probably know but they sort of don't at the same time. I think they have an inclination that they might know but they won't say anything to me, and I feel OK about it. I'm an only child so they must know it would be hard for me to come out properly because I'm the only person who would give them a grandchild in the family. I sometimes feel pressure on myself to be the main breadwinner and carry on my family name, and like I say I do want a child at some point in my life. But I don't use my sexuality as a cover or anything. I'm openly bisexual to most people. I like both sexes.

There's quite a big drugs influence in the bars and clubs. People will always try and get other people into drugs. If someone asks if I want drugs I tell them to fuck off normally but it depends if one of my friends wants to have drugs or something, because then they can have it if they want, but I'm not really into it. I sort of miss the highs though. I've been introduced to charlie or coke, which is cocaine, and pills like ecstasy, and weed, poppers, well, everything really. I have taken pills before and, of course, they're not very healthy for you. I feel like shit after taking them because they give you such a strong headache, sickness, or pure rage and hallucinations. I used to get so tired so I stopped taking them now. I've been a good boy lately. They were bad for me because they were using up so much energy that my body just didn't have.

I've been going clubbing for two and a half years now. I go during the weekdays and weekends. I love my favourite club which is Heaven in London. I go on a Monday, Wednesday and Saturday. It's a sociable place to go to with good music and a real laugh to go with your mates. If I'm looking for a fella, then I look for a guy who is like me really. Someone decent and compatible. I had a relationship for a while but my last boyfriend was a cunt because he treated me bad, but then again he could treat me nice as well, depending on what mood he was in. A thing called hormones, I guess. Generally the verbal abuse I got was whenever he wanted to get his anger out at me. He treated me nice too though by getting me presents, taking me out for dinner and cinema and stuff like that.

Some clubs and bars are made for older people, but places like the Ku Bar are made more for younger people under twenty-five years old. I do believe it has to be like this because like when you go to an older type bar you sort of know it is older because of the dirty pervy old men who sit at the bar and line the stairs like vampires, and the music they play is old and outdated. Places like the Ku Bar and the G.A.Y. bar play more lively upbeat music that us younger people want to dance to.

My best night out so far was probably when my friend Kandi and I went out to Heaven and had a proper good time. I was really drunk and stuff and I started climbing up lampposts and Kandi did as well and we were singing all the way up the street (Laughs). Dusty 'O is a really good DJ. She's a tranny. She plays bubblegum-type pop music, which is like a sort of hardcore pop music.

I love every Jennifer Lopez songs 'cause she is just pretty. She's like me; she's good looking. Jennifer Lopez is my idol because she's an actress, singer and a feminine figure along with Britney Spears and that's good for gay people. She's a diva. Will Young is cool too because when he came out he was honest and open and everyone accepted him.'

Aaron interviewed by Craig Paul Johnson

'I'm a total clubbing addict. I'm out on the piss every weekend and sometimes the odd night during the week too when I get the chance. Yes, I do drugs too but nothing serious, just Es or K or stuff like that so that the night is really good. I love dressing up, going out and just having a laugh. I don't really go to pick up anyone although that has happened sometimes, of course, but only by accident really, if I've just got interested in someone or they've liked me. It's all about fun though, and if I end up going home with someone then that's just an added bonus to me'.

Will (customer care, 20), Brighton

'There is much more mixed clubbing now, and I think that it's just because the clubs can't afford to be gay-only any more. Lots of people have stopped going just in gay clubs because there's so much more choice with straight places, and you just get bored with the same thing every time in a gay place. The straight places are often cheaper and better decorated, because the owners seem to put more investment and effort into making the places exciting and entertaining, or at least pleasant to be in, so you can't blame people. It is a shame though because as a girl I feel happier in a place where you know most of the other girls are the same as you. I mean, it doesn't matter if you're in a mixed crowd but it's just better when you're in a gay place or a girls-only event, because you can be totally yourself then'.

Katie (paramedic, 26), Leeds

'It's really depressing the way that the club scene has got so dull. It's still OK in London I suppose and maybe Manchester is still fairly alive, but in every other place the gay clubs just seem to have got into a rut, and they're always the same, with the same décor, the same music and style and the same old faces week in and week out. Where has all the effort gone like it used to be back in the eighties? You don't see people dressed up in drag or in mad outfits hardly ever now, and you don't even see that many of the club staff dressing up or anything, and they just seem totally disinterested.

It's got so bad that most places you hardly even get lads taking their tops off now, as if it's like some kind of wedding party and you've got to behave yourself and be all prim and proper. I thought we were all much more up for a good time than that, but everyone's just got really uptight and boring. There's no sense of fun now, and I think there should be more effort to make clubs more entertaining with more choice and madness like it used to be, so that everyone can just get wild and have lots of fun, and want to keep going back for more. We need places like Taboo again, but all over the country though.'

Colin (fireman, 38), London

'I went to gay clubs a fair bit when I first came out, and it was OK, but there's no real attraction for me when I have lots of straight friends. I can

go out with them and go to straight clubs that are always full and everybody seems more party-minded. The gay clubs I went to, and most of the ones I still go to occasionally, are just really dull now and seem to attract just lots of ugly blokes who are trying to pick up for sex. They all try and play the same house or trance-type music even at the start of the night as if they're really cutting edge or in Ibiza or something, but it's just sad when the place is half empty and everything looks like it's been painted with a yard brush in an afternoon.'

Paul (driver, 23), Leeds

'Don't get me wrong, I wish gay clubs would get their act together again 'cause I hate the way they're either never very busy, or they're just slowly filling up with straight people. If I wanted to spend the night with straight people I'd go to a fucking straight club, you know what I mean? I think lots of the clubs just don't give a shit any more, they're just after your cash that's all. I mean, you could go into Heaven in London and you'll have the place looking funky and clean, and you'll have good-looking lads behind the bars, you know, all really happening. Then you go in some naff gay club and it's dirty and falling apart; the bar staff are fat women or something, and they're playing some mindless fucking techno to about ten scruffy guys who look like they're about sixty, and it's so loud that your eardrums are bleeding, when they ought to just slap some Kylie or Madonna on, or some fucking Steps, and just get everyone to get over themselves and get dancing. Just have some fun'.

Brian (unemployed, 21), Newcastle

Links

www.outuk.com

www.gayguide.co.uk

www.gaytoz.com

DAILY MAIL

Oh bless, our beloved *Daily Mail* newspaper, the Hate Mail as it is so fondly known. What is their problem? You can't pick up a copy of the *Mail* without finding some story about homosexuality. They're positively obsessed by the subject, almost to the point where you wonder if it's a sort of psychosis, and they're shouting way too loud about a subject when they don't even know why. It's pretty clear that they just don't like faggots. OK, we get the message, but then we don't like the *Mail* much either. A paper that relies on the balanced and reasoned viewpoints of columnists like Norman Tebbit has got to be a little suspect. But take heart: nobody takes the *Daily Mail* seriously, and the more that they hammer on with their hatred, the more ridiculous and out of touch they become. It's tempting to say that we should just make a point of never buying such a contemptible old rag, but that would be counterproductive. By all means buy a copy, and keep yourself up to date with the latest trends of thought amongst the ever-diminishing community of Bible-bashing right-wing, family-value morons that feast on such garbage. It's always nice to know what the stupid people are thinking, isn't it?

DIVA

Sister publication to *Gay Times* (produced by the same company), *Diva* is aimed squarely at lesbians, with the same style and attitude as its bigger brother (or is that sister?). There has always been great debate as to whether there would ever be a market big enough to support a commercial lesbian magazine, bearing in mind that any major publication has to rely on a huge amount of advertising support, and most of the gay scene caters for gay men rather than women. But *Diva* has shown that there is enough revenue out there and that there are plenty of readers waiting to buy each copy. Great stuff, but you can't help wondering why, if *Gay Times* is aimed at both male and female readers, there's no men-only equivalent to *Diva*?

DIVINE

Big in every sense of the word, Harris Glenn Millstead was larger than life. Close friend of bizarre film-maker John Waters, Divine appeared in all of his early films and his (or her) mix of bad taste, bad attitude and sheer outrageousness made him a huge hit with gay fans. With hit recordings of 'You Think You're A Man' and 'Walk Like A Man' under his sizeable belt, Divine even made it to the BBC *Top of the Pops* studio, causing more than a little uproar in the papers the next day (fat drag queens are still surprisingly rare on primetime television). Appearing in a club riding an elephant or sailing down the Thames on a barge, Divine was simply divine. He died prematurely at the age of just 42 due to heart failure in 1989. What a waste.

Link

www.outuk.com/content/features/divine

DIVINE DAVID

Stagger into any decent-sized gay pub and you're likely to find a staple diet of nightly entertainment on offer, usually in the form of a grubby stripper, or some fella in a frock with a stage name almost as ludicrous as his stage act. Some are better than others, and some of the big-name drag/entertainment acts really are (no, honestly) quite good. A few are very good. And then there was The Divine David. How do you describe a phenomenon like The Divine David? Certainly no run-of-the-mill drag queen (although his stage clothes were never the kind of thing you'd find many men wearing in public), he was essentially a performance artist, but to categorise him with such a title would be like calling a tiger a cat. He was something unique and rather disturbing with an agenda of bad taste, combined with a style and wit which left most half-drunk audiences wondering what the hell was going on.

Born appropriately in sunny Blackpool back in 1962, David Hoyle moved almost seamlessly from the counter of a Bhs store to the pubs of Blackpool and beyond, appearing as a character called Paul Monery-Vaine (Pulmonary vein – get it?) tasked with tedious nightly renditions of 'Hey Big Spender' and other such delights.

But David set his sights on the bright lights of London, packing his make-up case and heading south to embrace the 1980s world of sex, drugs and New Romanticism, which all came to an abrupt end in a hospital ward where he was treated for acute hepatitis, and also treated to the bad attitude of a doctor, telling him how 'his sort' disgusted him. Suitably disgusted with both the doctor and London, David returned north to Manchester, reappearing in pubs and clubs as a new incarnation – The Divine David.

And so, a phenomenon was born. Looking unnervingly like Liza Minelli after a serious car crash, his on-stage persona was friendly with a hint of menace. Reaching out to his audiences with his familiar talk of how 'each und every one of us is beau-tee-full', much of his overenunciated on-stage style was drawn from 1920s German expressionism and the kind of slightly scary flamboyance which you find in the more surreal parts of the movie *Cabaret*.

But David was much more than a pastiche; his stage act intentionally revealed a fervent contempt and dislike for the commercialism and banality of the modern gay scene, and the beliefs and attitudes which we have unconsciously adopted. Armed with barely disguised hatred (which he insisted on calling passion) David managed to target his subject so directly that it sometimes hurt. 'Do you like the way I'm dressed? Isn't it beautiful? I'm hoping to meet a neo-nazi and get fucked by his nazi cock so that I can feel really gay, and live with myself in the morning.'

The essential part of his on-stage antics was to highlight how the gay scene embraces everything that is superficial while excluding all that is perceived to be ugly, political, intelligent or mundane. He constantly ridiculed body fascism, our obsession with sex and loud music (at the expense of conversation) ageism, consumerism, in fact just about everything that the typical modern gay disco bunny holds dear. He probably had a point too, but as ever the music was too loud for most people to hear what he was saying.

Deservedly, his unique talents resulted in a breathtaking series of attention-grabbing short programmes for Channel 4 (*The Divine David Presents*), followed by a rather less inspiring series of shows with his seriously unusual on-stage partner Jay Cloth (The Divine David Heals).

Tragically, just as David's career was heading for major recognition, it all came to an end a couple of years ago when David Hoyle publicly killed off his creation in the ludicrous surroundings of Streatham Ice Rink. The show was over, and The Divine David abruptly disappeared from the scene.

The rotting corpse of The Divine David rising from the dead is an image which many people would be overjoyed to see, but it's unlikely that he'll ever be resurrected, as David Hoyle has never been the kind of artist who would subscribe to such mainstream notions. The very fact that The Divine David was becoming so popular was probably the character's death warrant, and we have probably seen the last of this particularly colourful and bizarre creature. May he rest in peace with his much-quoted epitaph etched in our hearts: 'We've had seamless disco house music for ten years now. I'm just a little bit bored. I feel that it's time to move on and change the fucking record.'

DNA

The supreme antidote to the drip-feed of gay media sameness, *DNA* magazine is always a delight to read (well, 'read' might be overestimating things slightly). Produced on mega-cheap newsprint (and available freely at gay pubs and clubs) with a layout akin to a school project newspaper, you might be excused for dismissing *DNA* as rubbish. But that would be to miss the whole point; it is rubbish and intentionally so, a sort of gay *Sunday Sport* which can (very occasionally) make you think, but much more easily make you laugh. And at the end of the day, maybe that's all we want from a magazine. Now, if only they could manage to distribute the magazine to the whole country . . .

EARLS COURT

Once known as Kangaroo Alley (because of the many Australians who used to live there), Earls Court has also long been a traditional part of British gay life, and through the seventies and eighties it was effectively the centre of London's gay scene, until Soho gradually grew in significance and took over. It is still home to a few gay pubs and hotels, shops, lots of escorts and more, and although the area is a little grubby and seedy, it's more than a little gay, even though the main action has moved further down the tube line. Good for the odd drink, sex (especially the paid-for variety), a friendly hotel and a sense of (gay) history.

JAY EFF

The world is full of talented photographers, but relatively few have devoted their career almost exclusively to men, and most of these have been women. Jay Eff, however, who moved to London from Germany in 1985, is a shining exception with a portfolio of attention-grabbing images showing the male form with a style and flair all his own. No simple portrait shots here – he gives his subject a personality and a character. OK, his models are usually buffed and relatively young, but even if he could be accused of promoting the typical gay stereotype, he does it exceptionally well. His pictures have consistently appeared in all manner of gay magazines, posters and promotional flyers. He's the best.

Link

www.jayeff.net

FABLE

Produced in 2001 by Queercompany (who later went bust, as if by an act of divine judgement), *Fable* was a shining example of everything bad. Shamelessly published in order to attract advertising revenue which couldn't be gleaned from their website, the magazine was supposedly geared towards the up-market end of Britain's gay readership. Unfortunately, the journalists who embarked on this supreme act of folly seemed to have confused the term 'up-market' with 'up-oneself' and *Fable* was a glittering presentation of glossy garbage. The style of writing made the act of actually reading the magazine something akin to water torture – you tended to lose your will to live before the final paragraph came into sight. Hardly surprising that, after the appearance of a second heroically bad edition, *Fable* disappeared and Queercompany deservedly went with it (although it has recently reappeared under new ownership). Apparently a spokesman said that the magazine had enjoyed positive feedback from customers but that 'it's an incredibly tough advertising market'. If you say so, or maybe it was just an incredibly bad magazine.

FREE MAGAZINES

Since the 1980s, every gay pub and club has stocked a huge variety of free publications, ranging from advertising flyers through to photocopied community newsletters. Quality and usefulness has ranged from good to just plain awful, and while most of the more substantial publications have been created largely through the publisher's appetite for advertising revenue ('hey, let's churn out a magazine and grab some cash from a few clubs') or through a frustrated desire to be a writer ('can't get my work published, so sod it, I'll print it myself'), some of the many products have served a useful purpose – keeping everyone informed about events, venues, views and news.

As you might expect, most of the newsletter-style magazines have a pretty short lifespan; the editor either gets bored or moves on to a more lucrative job, or the publisher realises that the advertising revenue isn't as great as expected. But some of the magazines survive and flourish, most notably the much-respected *Pink Paper* and the more controversial (well, you either love it or hate it) *Boyz*. Sadly, only the aforementioned *Pink* now manages to find its way into venues right across the country, while poor ol' *Boyz* is now confined to London and surrounding areas.

There are a few other magazines that have hung around rather longer than you might have expected, such as *NoW* (no, not an illegal copy of the commercial magazine of the same name – it originally stood for 'North of Watford', although you'd be hard-pressed to notice any geographic bias in it, among the gratuitous pictures of boys in pants); *Shout* (a cheap-looking northern newsletter which, despite being as imaginative as dishwater, does sometimes actually contain some useful venue information); *QX* magazine (entertaining but poorly presented, and entirely sex-obsessed); and *Manzone*, a relatively new comic, which furnishes the reader with nothing more edifying than, er . . . cock.

It's a pity that all of these rags (plus a whole lot more which don't even bear comment) can't combine their mediocre offerings and produce just one national publication which informs, amuses and entertains, instead of leaving you either just plain bored, or with a compulsive desire to wash your hands.

GAY TIMES

Now established as the leading national commercial gay publication, *Gay Times* owes its origins to the merger of a handful of news and porn publications (beginning with *Him Exclusive* back in 1976), and ending with the first copies of the modern *Gay Times* appearing on newsagents' shelves in 1995. Essentially a no-nonsense news magazine concerned primarily with politics, the publication also delves into broader lifestyle features, book and video reviews, television and movie news, and some scene coverage. It is unquestionably a 'serious' magazine, with little interest in the more frivolous aspects of gay life, and that's a major point in its favour – heaven knows every other magazine couldn't possibly be more lightweight – but it's also fair to say that *Gay Times* has never exactly been the most entertaining of reads (it was the sort of title that you read because you had to, not because you wanted to).

But the magazine did undergo a facelift not too long ago, and with the in-your-face attitude of its current editor Vicky Powell (ironic to note that it ultimately needed a lesbian's guidance to give the magazine some balls), *Gay Times* does now have a much brighter and modern appearance, and isn't afraid to have a view, rather than just report facts.

It's a shame that so much of the magazine is devoted to endless advertising (flick the pages too hard and you can miss the actual editorial sections completely) but if that's the price we pay to get a magazine on the newsagents' shelves, it's probably worth it. Let's hope that *Gay Times* keeps it's new-found voice and starts to take a rather harder look at some of the bastions of our supposedly great gay community.

JULIA GRANT

Julia hit the nation's television screens with a three-part documentary tracing her story from her days as a man, through a long and difficult fight to be given a sex-change operation, to a new life as a woman on the Manchester gay scene. Famous for just being Julia, she was a no-nonsense supporter of all things gay, masterminding the creation of Manchester's Hollywood Showbar and the Legends night club, and many other queer enterprises. More recently she became a major supporter and organiser of Manchester's Mardi Gras (or Gayfest, or whatever) but after things inexplicably went sour in 2002, Julia suddenly disappeared without a word of explanation. All kinds of rumours have circulated about lost money, lies, intrigue and dark deals, but nobody knows what really happened, other than the fact that Julia's gone, and it doesn't look like she's coming back. No matter what your view of Julia was, she was undoubtedly a bigger supporter of all things gay than . . . well, than most gay people actually, which is a bit of a twist when you think about it. Only Julia would climb on the Hollywood Showbar stage and welcome everyone to the establishment, before asking if there were any straight people in there, adding the words 'if there are, then fuck off' and then proceeding to walk round the joint collaring anyone who wasn't gay. How refreshing. How Julia.

MANCHESTER

They say it always rains in Manchester, but on a warm, sunny summer afternoon, down on the tree- and cafe-lined Canal Street, you have to wonder whether Manchester is the victim of way too many urban myths. Apart from the fact that the city's weather is much the same as anywhere else in the country, Manchester's gay scene has also been constantly written off, almost since the days when it first formed. The London glitterati like to think that the gay scene ends somewhere just beyond Leicester

Square, and that nothing, but nothing, could possibly be worth seeing, if it isn't on a tube line.

Of course, the boys and girls in and around Manchester see things slightly differently; they've never quite worked out what the obsession with London really is, when there's a thriving selection of gay bars and clubs, businesses, support groups and community associations all firmly attached to Manchester. Life does exist beyond the M25 and Manchester's doing just fine, thank you very much. It is, in essence, the second-biggest gay scene outside the capital. But with success comes fame (thanks to the *Queer as Folk* television series), and with fame comes popularity, and Manchester's 'gay village' (aka Canal Street) has become a victim of its own attractiveness. When a television show portrays a place as being a non-stop frenzy of fun, drugs, alcohol and partying, it's little wonder that everybody, both gay and straight, wants a piece of the action.

While the homos already knew how fabulous the gay village was, it was basically our own little secret – but *Queer as Folk* blew the whistle. The result has been that the gay village is no longer gay. It's just another part of Manchester's growing social diversity. But don't imagine for a minute that the faggots and the dykes have all packed up their rainbow bags and gone home. Canal Street (and a few other parts of the city) is still ours, even if we do have to sometimes share it with pushchairs and hen nights. We know that the breeders will eventually latch on to the next best thing that they've so spectacularly failed to create for themselves, and they'll leave Canal Street to the people that made it so good in the first place. We can wait.

Links

www.outuk.com/outgoing/uk/manchester

www.gaytoz.com/barsmanchester.asp

MARILYN

Doomed to be forever famous as Boy George's evil surrogate sister, Marilyn (aka Peter Robinson) was a big player on the London gay club scene during the 1980s. With stunning good looks, a beautiful wardrobe and a body to die for, Boy George was almost cast as the Ugly Sister, but of course it was George's talent and personality that eventually shone through, ultimately leaving Marilyn with only one real claim to fame, the 1983 hit 'Calling Your Name'. For some time the pair were inseparable, and Marilyn's care-free, in-your-face attitude certainly influenced Boy George's life, even if he's now loath to admit it all too often.

Thanks to a mixture of fame, drugs and money, their friendship became a love/hate battle, and today they rarely seem to have a good word for each other, even though they probably actually still quite like each other (you know how queens are).

While George is still firmly in the public eye, Marilyn has slipped into our gay history, although he has made some occasional reappearances, notably at Sound on Sunday. Wouldn't it be great if he made a comeback?

DUSTY O

Although pretty big (and getting bigger) on the London gay scene, this particular drag diva hails from Birmingham, but she moved to London after splitting with her boyfriend (wouldn't you just know) and slowly infiltrated the club scene, becoming friends with all the well-known names of the era, notably Leigh Bowery and Boy George. More recently, Miss Dusty has embarked upon a successful career as a DJ and there aren't many nights when you can't find her spinning a disc in some glitzy gay venue or other. Most notably, Miss Dusty O hosts and DJs at Sound On Sunday – a popular dance venue just off Leicester Square, but you'll also find her popping up in all manner of queer television shows, videos, magazine features, and maybe on a single or two before too long. Not just another wig on the scene, Dusty is a lively link with the great club days of the eighties, but with a carefully lined eye on the future.

Link

www.dustyo.com

PINK PAPER

Founded back in 1987, the *Pink Paper* is a free-issue publication, aimed squarely at readers with an interest in news, politics and community issues, rather than the usual gay scene ephemera. Initially styled as a 'proper' broadsheet-style newspaper, the publication was revamped during 1998, becoming a 'news magazine' (in standard journal size) with an editorial content dumbed down to match the new format. Things deteriorated further when the magazine was withdrawn from free-availability and launched as a commercial title, amid claims that the *Pink Paper* was heroically dragging itself out of the ghastly gay ghetto (although the *Independent* reported that it had more to do with ten years of losses).

Embarrassingly, it quickly jumped back into the same ghetto when the disappointing sales figures came in. Worse was to come when sister publication *Boyz* became a London-only title, and the *Pink Paper* attempted to take on some of the *Boyz* nationwide scene coverage, as if a handful of pages tucked into the back of the *Pink* could miraculously replace a full-sized magazine.

Although still the most accessible free-issue gay publication (even book stores and libraries often have copies), the modern *Pink Paper* is a mere shadow of its former self, trying to be simultaneously entertaining, advertiser-friendly, user-friendly, scene-related and news-orientated. Not surprisingly it fails to achieve any aim very successfully. And now the journal's editor appears to have become a television media darling, available for embarrassingly unconvincing talking-head appearances on our (the gay community's) behalf. Wouldn't it be great if he devoted his time to his day job, and the old *Pink Paper* newspaper came back?

REFRESH

Presumably encouraged by the astonishing lack of gay media (and the loss of both *Fluid* and the still-born *Fable* magazine) on the newsagents' shelves, a new glossy came along during 2002. Entitled *Refresh* and billed as the 'essential new read for gay men' the new magazine turned out to be a thoroughly unrefreshing, non-essential old read which looks alarmingly like a watered-down version of *Attitude*, with a few completely irrelevant property and motoring features thrown in for good measure. Oh dear – the same moody and inescapably pointless fashion pages, plus gloriously insulting features on apartments for multi-millionaires (always a good read while you're standing in the dole queue), quirky features written by, ahem, straight women (go figure), a bit of movie blurb and . . . that's about it really. Oh well, based on this kind of logic, maybe if another magazine is launched and it's called 'Same ol' Garbage' it might be worth looking into.

LILY SAVAGE

The Blonde Bombsite, Lily's is a classic tale of the drag queen wot done good. Brought up in Birkenhead, Paul O'Grady did the gay pub circuit both in the north and nationwide, dressed as his alter ego – the big, brash, loud-mouthed slag with a liking for men and kleptomania. But, unlike so many other drag acts that stay comfortably within the clubs and pubs, Lily aimed for bigger things and, after making the gradual transition to mainstream stage performances, Lily finally made it to television and the nation loved her. It was a perfect example of being in the right place at the right time; a few years previously and the viewing masses would have undoubtedly been unable to stomach a man in a frock, making cheap gags about sex; the public were used to the more comfortable 'safe' images of Danny LaRue and Hinge and Bracket. But Lily hit the screens at just the right time, and success followed success, hosting *The Big Breakfast* on Channel Four, *Blankety Blank* on ITV, appearing on stage in the musical version of the TV cult series *Prisoner Cell Block H*, and playing a starring role in the West End hit *Annie*.

Sadly, it hasn't been a completely comfortable ride to the top for Paul O'Grady. His heavy workload contributed to bouts of severe depression, and during 2002 he found himself in hospital after having suffered a heart attack. But Paul bounced back, and his most recent incarnation has been in another West End success, *Chitty Chitty Bang Bang.*

Paul's deserved success has certainly placed him far beyond the confines of the pub stages where he used to perform, and more than a few (gay) people have complained that, despite being so big on the gay scene for so long, he doesn't give much attention to gay politics or events now that he's made his way up the celebrity ladder. Paul's only response has been that nobody ought to blame him for wanting to be successful, and he's probably got a good point. There's no doubt that Lily Savage was always very much part of the gay scene, and now that she's moved on to better things (although Paul makes regular hints that he might hang up his wig for good before too long), we ought to be content to just remember the good old days when Lily opened her filthy mouth just for us, long before 'family entertainment' beckoned. Let's wish Paul well. You go, girl!

Links

www.geocities.com/lilysavage_uk

TRANNIES

Although the term 'gay' is generally accepted to refer to both homosexual men and women, it's worth noting that the gay scene also embraces lots of other people who don't neatly fit into the 'gay' category. Most notably, the gay scene has traditionally included 'trannies' or, to be more precise, transvestites (guys or girls who like dressing up in the clothing of the opposite sex) and transsexuals (men or women with the physical appearance of the opposite sex, or having undergone a sex-change operation). It's interesting to note that most transvestites are men, and they're almost always straight. Likewise, a transsexual is almost always attracted to an opposite gender, so you can see how fluid and flexible the term 'tranny' can be.

You can't make any assumptions about a guy who looks like a woman. He could be a guy dressed in women's clothing or he could be a guy who has become a woman. Or he could be a very convincing drag queen. He might be attracted to men or women, or both. It's enough to give you a headache.

But whatever the confusion, we've all been linked for a long time. Sexual ambiguity doesn't necessarily mean homosexuality, or vice versa. Confused?

Viewpoints

'In ten years time I'm one hundred and ten per cent sure that I will not regret having had the operation. It'll be like I'm all bird, with pure breasts and I'll be totally fit. All my life I've wanted to be a woman. I was just born with it and I think that the way I am now is better than the way I was when I was male because I think life's ultimately all about women and girls. The earliest memory I can remember is wishing I were a girl when I was only four years old. I didn't wake up one morning though and just think, right I'm going to be a woman. I had a normal and secure childhood. No real traumas really, so there was nothing that could ever have been described as a cause for my feelings.

I'm employed as a beautician at the moment, and generally I keep fit at the gym; I eat healthy foods and enjoy dancing. My week involves going out, getting bibbed by men in cars, chatting to builders, going out with my friend Aaron and sticking my fingers up at Aaron mostly! I like to style myself against beautiful celebrities like Christina Aguilera and Jordan, but sometimes Jordan isn't that respectable so I like Christina more because she's more attractive. It sometimes takes me two hours to doll myself up for a night on the town, so I guess you can say I make an effort.

I came out to my mum when I was fifteen, but not just as a gay boy. I told her I wanted to be a girl. From the time I told my mum and all the week after, I just couldn't face seeing my mum. My exact words to her were "mum, I want to be a girl" and she was really shocked because she said that she had always known about this, like it was some sort of destiny or something. My nan and aunty were shocked because they just thought I was gay.

I've considered having a boob job and have taken hormone tablets, much to the amazement of my best friend Aaron. I had to go to the doctors twice, visit a psychiatrist and then a gynaecologist. They knew straight away what I was all about. Physically I am fine; I've got quite big boobs actually. They'll be bigger in about a year's time. I feel very feminine and attractive. I'm a woman twenty-four-seven. I got prescribed the drugs the first time I ever went to the doctors and you're supposed to go there twice.

I lived as a woman for two years, and I had to eat, sleep, work and play as a woman. I've been dressing up as a woman for three years now. I've felt truly like a woman for four years. I'm happy with myself too, and I don't want any children or to adopt them or anything like that. When you have the operation, you're in hospital for two weeks and they do the boobs before, but it depends on whether you're taking hormones or not. In my case I've got to take one pill a day. I don't think I'll be happy with my size and I will probably have another breast enlargement to be a thirty-six double-D and then about four months after that I'll go into hospital and have the penis taken away and they'll make it into a vagina. The side-effects are supposed to be vomiting, period pains and stomach cramps and I will be in hospital for a maximum of three weeks so I'm told. It's worth it at the end of the day because I want to be a complete woman. I just won't feel complete until I have all my male parts taken away.

I haven't even spoken properly about all this to my family yet. I don't know how other people think of me really. I mean, if I'm with a boy and they approach me and I tell them I'm a man, they can just sorta see fire and I get scared, like the other day when I was in a bar and a guy was dancing with me, but when someone told him I was actually a man he got really upset and just walked off.

Four years ago everyone in my estate used to think I was queer and I didn't like it. I'm a pretty seventeen-year-old girl now thankfully. My family is very supportive now and my friends love it. My best friend Aaron just loves it. He says, 'She's my mate' and he loves me and I'm a star. Good looking too!

In the long term I guess I am looking for a relationship with a straight man. It's very easy to pull a straight man. I just flutter my eyelids and they fall for me. I never tell them that I used to be a guy, but I'd always tell the person I care about though. I would describe myself as bubbly, friendly, quite bitchy sometimes, and a bit of a slag because of the way I dress; which is kinda slaggy. My best feature is my beautiful body, don't you think?'

Kandi, interviewed by Craig Paul Johnson

Links

www.intercomtrust.org.uk/listings/outlinks.htm

www.tzone.members.easyspace.com

www.gay-links.co.uk/links/genderissues.html

TRANSFORMER

Burnel Penhaul was better known to the gay scene as Transformer, a drag queen and performance artist in a league all his own. Big on the London scene (twice crowned as the Alternative Miss World), Transformer took costume into a whole new dimension, creating an endless series of jaw-dropping outfits which were more akin to three-dimensional art than mere costume. Transformer also famously entered politics briefly, when he stood against Neil Hamilton in the last general election as Miss Moneypenny (vowing to 'put the tat back into Tatton'). His annual appearances in the London Pride March were always anticipated and enjoyed by everyone, both participants and spectators alike. Tragically, he died in August 2002. We miss him.

ALAN TURING

Not a name which crops up very often in gay circles, but it would do if we had any brains or an appreciation of history (and you know what they say about history repeating itself). Alan Turing's work on mathematics laid the foundations for modern computer technology (and where would all you internet queens be without that?) and, with a chilling accuracy, he predicted back in 1950 that within fifty years a person typing questions at a computer terminal wouldn't be able to tell if it was a person or computer providing the answers (you know how you sometimes wonder when you read those Gaydar messages . . .).

He also just happened to be the genius who helped break the Nazi Enigma code during World War Two, but, his magnificent achievements aside, it was his sexuality which ultimately ruined his life. He was arrested in 1952 for having sex with a nineteen-year-old man, and he spent a year on probation but only on condition that he received oestrogen injections in an effort to control his sex drive. Not surprisingly, the hormones didn't change him; he merely grew breasts.

He died in 1954 after eating an apple laced with cyanide and, although his mother claimed his death was an accident (he often left potentially lethal chemicals in unmarked containers, although the notion of cyanide being left in a sugar bowl seems a bit unlikely), the coroner recorded that his death was an act of suicide.

A commemorative statue to Alan now sits in Manchester's Sackville Park, although most of the queers who walk past it probably haven't even got a clue what it's there for, if they've even noticed it at all (it's not wearing a crop top or a bomber jacket, for heavens sake). Oh, and if you use an Apple Mac computer, have you noticed that rainbow-coloured apple emblem with a bite taken out of it?

Link

www.turing.org.uk/turing

VIAGRA

The wonder drug which put the life back into more than a few sex lives. Undoubtedly successful, the little blue pills reportedly sort out around 70 per cent of erectile dysfunction problems (that's getting and keeping a stiffy to you and me). So, they do work, at least for most people, but they're not a miracle cure. Health advice is to go to a doctor if you think you may need Viagra, and not to buy it off the street. Why? Well, erectile dysfunction could be a symptom of a more serious disease (such as diabetes) so avoiding a visit to the doctor isn't necessarily a good idea, and, of course, Viagra shouldn't be combined with some other drugs, so it's wise to know what you're getting yourself into, before you start.

Viagra has become part of the recreational drug scene (although any perfectly healthy male isn't likely to see any benefits from taking Viagra other than psychological ones), and doctors are keen to point out that the drug should never be combined with poppers – the results can (and have been) fatal. It's also worth remembering that Viagra is not an aphrodisiac – it won't make you feel sexy; it simply helps to maintain arousal . . . getting aroused is down to you, baby.

Link

www.viagra.com

5: Fame

It might come as something of a shock to some particularly stupid people but, just like everyone else, gay boys and gay girls watch television, go to the movies and read the papers. There are celebrities that we love and celebrities that we hate, and a whole lot more that we just couldn't care less about. There are people who are famous for just being famous and there are even a few people who have earned themselves the dubious distinction of the 'infamous' epithet. But while we might stare blankly at a whole galaxy of glittering stars, there are some who have a special place in our gay hearts and minds. They're there for a whole variety of reasons, and not necessarily because they're gay; in fact most of our favourite celebs are terminally straight, but then nobody's perfect.

MARC ALMOND

Singer, songwriter, performer and one half (the other being Dave Ball) of the much-loved duo Soft Cell, Marc Almond brought us the timeless new romantic version of 'Tainted Love', followed by other gay favourites such as 'Say Hello Wave Goodbye'. Ironically, however, Marc's music career has always been slightly overshadowed (at least in gay circles) by his youthful days of partying on the gay scene, which landed him with a now famous urban legend which (without going into too much detail) involved lots of men, sex, a hospital and a stomach pump. Needless to say, Marc has always strenuously denied that there was any truth in it, and the story will probably fade into history, but it's probably to Marc's credit that he did at least seem to be the kind of guy that might just be colourful enough to actually do that sort of thing . . . imagine the same story being pasted on to Will Young?

After reinventing himself as a solo performer, Marc's career continued with a series of successful albums and more hit singles including a superb duet with sixties crooner Gene Pitney ('Something's Got a Hold of My Heart') and the truly quirky 'The Days of Pearly Spencer'. Much-acclaimed concert appearances continue, and his talents also extend to yet more new and diverse albums, and books too.

Link

www.marcalmond.co.uk

JOAN ARMATRADING

Born in 1950, on the island of St Kitts, Joan is now the proud owner of an MBE, although she's not the kind of celebrity you're ever likely to see flashing a gong around in public. Joan's a media-shy girl, which has only added to rumours that she might be gay, but if she is, then she's keeping it all to herself. But no matter, she gave us classics like 'Me Myself I', 'Drop the Pilot' and the timeless 'Love and Affection'. Nuff said.

Link

www.joanarmatrading.com

BEA ARTHUR

Bernice Frankel Beatrice Arthur, or Bea Arthur to you and me, she is forever Dorothy – the po-faced woman with the voice of a man, taking the put-downs and delivering the bitchy one-liners in the much-loved *Golden Girls*. Although she's regarded as a television comedy actress over here in the UK, Bea is probably just as well known in the USA as an acclaimed stage actress, having spent much of her career treading the boards on Broadway, and having dabbled less consistently with the odd movie or two. But it was her dead-pan delivery in the sitcom *Maude* which first brought her to our television screens, only to return in the *Golden Girls*.

Interestingly, both series were eventually cancelled when Bea decided to leave them – indication that both shows couldn't have survived without her. A true professional, she left both series when they were at their peak of success, and moved on to other projects. Still acting, and also having created a one-woman show, Bea ought to be back on television if there was any justice – if ever there was such an animal as a female drag queen, Bea's the girl.

Link

www.lgt2.com/bea

ROSEANNE BARR

The sitcom queen with a bite. Who said comedy had to be easy or comfortable? Roseanne took a sideways swipe at America, comedy and television and the public loved it. Find an institution and Rosie would kick its doors down. What a shame that she ended up doing chat shows.

Link

www.carseywerner.net/roseanne_eng.htm

SHIRLEY BASSEY

Hardly needing any introduction, Shirley Bassey has been the favourite of drag queen impersonators since the 1960s. Famous for her rich, booming voice, Bond movie classics and a taste for clothes that only Elton John could ever hope to match, Shirley has everything necessary to earn herself the status of a gay icon; two husbands (one killed himself), three children (one jumped off a bridge and another had a drugs problem), huge wealth, an extremely humble upbringing (Tiger Bay in Cardiff) and a pretty funky recording made with the Propellerheads (which Graham Norton even used as his Channel 4 theme tune). All pretty spectacular, so it's little wonder that every self-respecting drag queen has a Bassey number in their repertoire, although it's probably fair to say that her popularity with drag acts has more to do with the outlandish costumes and easy-to-imitate voice than any true gay credentials. What a pity then (how can we put this?) that Shirley doesn't exactly seem to be the most gay-friendly celebrity ever. Don't expect to see this diva at your next Pride March.

Link

www.basseyonline.com

SANDRA BERNHARD

The queen of dead-pan put-downs, born in Michigan back in 1955, Sandra Bernhard began her stand-up comic career at the age of only nineteen after moving to Hollywood where she quickly got herself regular gigs at the local comedy clubs. After her proverbial big break on the *Richard Pryor Show* she went back to the club circuit before later making movies, a theatre debut and even some singing.

She's a funny girl with a dark, satirical edge all of her own. Notorious as a friend of Roseanne (and a long-time star in her comedy series, playing, as you might have guessed, a sarcastic, satirical lesbian with attitude), Sandra was better known as a close buddy (or at least a former buddy, depending on what mood the two bitches are in) of our Mrs Ritchie, even appearing in her much-acclaimed docu-soap-movie *Truth or Dare*. Whether the two gals ever actually did the wild thing together, we'll probably never know; they either just wanted to tease us with the very idea, or now they've decided they'd rather not talk about it, but while Madonna has adopted the role of struggling mother, Sandra has maintained her status as a lesbian that isn't a lesbian – a woman without a category, playing straight girl and dyke both on and off screen, and she defiantly refuses to categorise her sexuality whenever it's challenged. Most notably, she made a point of telling the world that her new-born daughter wasn't conceived artificially, but by a good old-fashioned shag. How's that for style? Most recently she's been back in the UK and found her way (as if by gay magic) on to Graham Norton's television show, where she looked like she'd found a new friend for life. She'll doubtless be back soon.

Link

www.sandra-bernhard.com

KATHY BURKE

Slobbering with Harry Enfield, glamming it with Eddy and Patsy or camping it up with James Dreyfus, she's brilliant.

Link

www.blue.uk.com/kathy

PETE BURNS

It all started in a club called Eric's on the site of the old Cavern club in Liverpool. Pete Burns ran a clothing shop nearby and spent most of his time in the club socialising and watching the performers. The manager eventually bribed Pete (with promises of free drinks and a guest list) to form his own band (he also threatened to bar him from entry unless he did it), and The Mystery Girls were born, singing cover versions of chart songs until the band members got bored and Burns went back to his clothes shop. But, as the Liverpool scene exploded into life, Burns couldn't stay out of the limelight, and he formed another group (Nightmares in Wax) which enjoyed some notable success, performing around the country and recording sessions for John Peel. When Culture Club appeared, the record companies went on a predictable manhunt for the next Boy George, and Pete Burns was an ideal and obvious candidate, with a similar outspoken attitude and a passion for drag outfits which were even more outrageous than Boy George's. CBS eventually persuaded Burns to sign a recording deal and, in doing so, they created Dead or Alive, together with a successful album and a fairly successful single, 'That's The Way I Like It'.

Sadly, CBS didn't really know how to market someone like Pete Burns; they wanted Boy George but they'd got something rather sharper and harder. He wasn't the kind of smiling face you could slot into children's television and both the record company's and Burns's enthusiasm began to fade. Then along came an unknown team of producers called Stock, Aitken and Waterman and, well, you know the rest of the story . . . 'You Spin Me Round (Like a Record)' was a huge hit and catapulted Dead or Alive into stardom. But, despite the mega-popularity of their first chart hit, Burns never enjoyed his relationship with The Hit Factory any more than he did with CBS, and eventually the band disappeared from the pop scene after having had only one major (and a few minor) chart successes.

Dead or Alive didn't just die, however – they found success in Japan, where they still play and where they're still popular. Whether they ever return to the British charts is a hard one to call. Maybe they will – Pete Burns, with his deliciously oversized lips, evidently still has plenty to say.

Link

www.deadoralive.net

TRACY CHAPMAN

A sort of follow-on to Joan Armatrading, Tracy Chapman has the same kind of style and voice, but hasn't achieved quite as much acclaimed success. But like Joan, she's not a particularly high-profile media darling, and she likes to keep persistent rumours about lesbian relationships conspicuously unanswered. The gals love her.

Link

www.geocities.com/about_tracy_chapman

CHER

A bit of an understatement to say that she's been around for a long time, but it's only in more recent years that Cheryline Sarkasion (yes, honestly) has earned herself the status of a true gay icon. From a humble background (born in the Californian desert) through a rocky career, she's been a survivor, rightly earning herself a niche as an A-list international celebrity, with movies, television shows and countless music hits to her credit. But despite all the glamour and glitz, she still found time to get on to the Astoria stage and sing for the assembled screaming queens at G.A.Y. Gawd bless her. More recently her music has been geared towards the disco crowds but she's done it all, ranging from ballads, country-esque and rock. Never taking herself too seriously (how could you with wigs like that?), it's rumoured that she's thinking of retiring, at least from the music industry. But we'll see . . .

Link

www.cher.com

JULIAN CLARY

The bad boy of gay comedy, Julian has consistently teetered on that narrow line between the cuddly, acceptable face of homosexuality and that slightly confrontational in-your-face kind of attitude that grannies, mothers with delicate sensibilities and the *Daily Mail* just can't handle. Born in Teddington in 1959, Julian made his television debut as the delightfully bizarre Joan Collins Fan Club on a Channel 4 cabaret show in 1988. Complete with sidekick Fanny the Wonder Dog, Julian was a breath of fresh comedy air in a nation that was still recovering from a diet of Jimmy Tarbuck, Bernard Manning and Ken Dodd. It was a distinctly gay aspect of a new wave of comedy genius.

Julian's act often went beyond the bounds of even the most risqué tastes, culminating in his now infamous appearance at the British Comedy Awards in 1993, where he threw in a joke about having just fisted the Chancellor of the Exchequer (leading to the punchline 'talk about a red box'). The audience were in fits of laughter and, despite a viewing audience of three million, only twelve people thought the joke was sufficiently offensive to make a complaint. But the next day the media (yawn) had a new hobby-horse, and Julian was their hate figure *du jour*, calling for him to be banned from television (they'd have probably called for a hanging if it had been legal).

Julian retreated to Australia but eventually returned to the UK when all the fuss had died down to resume his television career. Most recently he appeared on stage, playing the part of Leigh Bowery in Boy George's acclaimed *Taboo*, and hopefully he'll be back on our screens soon, ritually upsetting the papers and making the rest of us smile.

Link

www.julianclary.net

JOAN COLLINS

She's done more movies than you could probably count. Joan's a true mega-star across the world, and deservedly so because she's good – she can act. Already famous for her starring role in *The Stud*, Joan's real celebrity success was the television super-soap *Dynasty*, which she headlined for eight years. The great thing about *Dynasty* and Joan in particular was that the whole show was (either unintentionally or by design) a send-up, a camper-than-camp joke which we were expected to pretend to take seriously, even though we all knew the whole show was just plain ludicrous. Joan was a major part of the conspiracy, playing her part with just that little extra bit of over-the-top style that gave you just a little hint that she knew we were laughing. And it's that knack of not taking herself too seriously that has endeared her to us gay boys. She's a big movie star but she can still listen to some weirdo wanking on a phone line (in Graham Norton's studio, of course – where else?) and find the whole thing hilarious. Or she can sit back and let Leonard Rossiter splash Cinzano over her for the sake of an advert. That's class.

Link

www.joancollins.net

NOEL COWARD

Born way back in 1899, Noel Pierce Coward is probably one of the nation's most celebrated stars who had a well-known liking for fellas. In fact, he had his first fling with another boy at the tender age of 13 (with fellow actor Philip Tonge) but later formed a long friendship with actress and author Esme Wynee, and spent much of his time with her, occasionally exchanging clothes and parading through London in their cross-gender drag – pretty radical stuff for the early 1900s. His climb through the class-conscious social set (Noel was from a very humble background) began thanks to a youthful friendship with Philip Streatfield – an established and well-to-do artist with a notorious liking for young boys . . .

An accomplished author, composer, screenwriter and actor, Noel Coward became internationally famous. Perhaps best known for his comical song 'Mad Dogs and Englishmen' (which he added to his London review performances in 1932), his hugely successful movie career included classics such as *Blithe Spirit*, *In Which We Serve* and *Brief Encounter*. In 1966 he wrote and starred in a West End production of three one-act plays, one of which traced the story of an ageing author, living as a closeted homosexual. Not the kind of subject that theatreland expected from Coward in the mid-sixties.

After suffering memory lapses, he decided to retire from acting and he received a knighthood in 1970. He died in 1973 at his home in Jamaica, where he was later buried in a simple grave. Coward was the epitome of style and wit – a sort of latter-day Oscar Wilde, if you will, with the same attraction to the same sex. Always able to conjure up a witty one-liner, even as a young man he always had the perfect line for any occasion. Arriving at a party in a dinner suit, he found to his horror that the guests were all dressed casually, but defiantly announced, 'Now, I don't want anybody to be embarrassed.' Such a queen.

Link

www.noelcoward.net

QUENTIN CRISP

Most people achieve celebrity status through a combination of hard work and talent, or at least through sheer determination. Few people become famous for simply being themselves, but Quentin Crisp did just that. Often described as one of the stately homos of England, Crisp earned his fame after the release of the 1972 movie *The Naked Civil Servant*, based on his autobiography published some years previously. Quentin was, as he would readily admit, nothing special. He had no great talents or abilities as such, but above all else he was himself, and made no secret of the fact that he was gay. That might not seem like something to boast about, unless you're a twenty-something gay man in 1920s England. You've got to accept that Crisp was someone exceptional. At a time when being openly gay would inevitably lead to imprisonment at best, Quentin Crisp remained resolutely true to himself and refused to lock himself into the closet. It earned him a series of beatings but also earned him the respect of almost everybody who ever had the pleasure of meeting him.

After becoming a successful writer, he finally left his filthy one-room Chelsea flat at the age of 72, to move to New York where he was embraced by the city's eclectic community and where, at long last, he finally felt at home. Despite his comfortable financial situation he remained defiantly squalid, once commenting that when it came to avoiding cleaning it was largely a case of 'never losing your nerve'. Latterly, he made appearances in a variety of movies and plays, even popping up in a Levi's advert.

He died in 1999 and the world is unquestionably the worse for his departure. Never a fan of the gay scene or gay politics, Quentin Crisp never even professed to be proud of his sexuality, but at the same time he never, ever apologised for it. He was who he was. He had guts.

Link

www.crisperanto.org

DALEKS

Who would have ever thought it? The nation's most well-known and well-loved aliens turned out to be a bunch of raving queens. We should have spotted the signs all along – the minimalist décor in their spaceship, the delicious colour schemes they applied to themselves (fancy just being able to get a repaint when you got bored – what a concept), their capacity for exterminating anyone who . . . well, anyone who just got in the way really, and their fabulous bad attitude. It was all there if we'd looked more closely. But it was Victor Lewis-Smith and his bizarre television series *TV Offal* which introduced us to the Daleks in a whole new light, complete with bitchy one-liners, handbags and too much time spent round a public toilet (well, they couldn't be going in there to take a leak, could they? I mean, how?). Brilliant stuff, which changed the way we thought about these screamers from Skaro. Nasty Queens *par excellence.*

Link

www.bbc.co.uk/cult/doctorwho/alien/daleks.htm

ELLEN DeGENERES

The funniest person in America in 1982, or so the awards circuit claimed, Ellen earned her fame as the lead actress in the eponymously titled sitcom *Ellen*, and hit the headlines big-time when her character came out as being gay. Even more sensational was the revelation that not only was the character gay, but so was the actress who played her, and Ellen even made the cover of *Time* magazine with the historic subtitle 'Yep – I'm gay' – talk about coming out in style.

But the joke soon wore thin and, while we were treated to guest appearances by the likes of KD Lang and Chastity Bono, the lesbian-fest started to sound like a one-trick pony, summed up so eloquently by Elton John when he said, 'We know you're a lesbian. Shut up! Be funny!' Even Chastity Bono later commented that she thought the show was too gay and, after Ellen made an appearance on the cover of *Entertainment Weekly* (with the subtitle 'Yep – She's too gay'), the show was cancelled after five series.

Ellen famously hooked up with actress Anne Heche in 1997, and later appeared hand in hand at the Whitehouse. They broke up in 2000. Lesbians, tsk . . .

Link

www.ellen-degeneres.com

DIANA, PRINCESS OF WALES

When the Princess of Wales died, the whole country mourned. Rightly so because, no matter whether you supported the monarchy or not, there's no doubt that Diana was an international celebrity and, by all accounts, a good woman. But was she also a 'gay icon', as we're so often told? And if she is, then why?

OK, first off, Diana's track record is pretty robust in terms of the countless worthy causes she supported. In particular, she was keen to destroy lots of myths which surrounded Aids at a time when the very mention of the word was enough to send people scurrying into dark corners in case they were infected. Aids was the Gay Plague and it was what we deserved, or so we were told. The real facts weren't important, but Diana paid no attention to the tabloids and gave Aids sufferers her support and, most importantly, her time and presence. In an era when the idea of even a B-list celebrity being seen with an Aids sufferer was absurd, Diana made it her business to visit hospital wards and (gulp) even touch the victims. It was unheard of. But her message slowly got through and society changed for the better.

But what else did Diana do? Well, not much really, apart from doing her very best to look good, wear lots of very expensive clothes and have a couple of kids. All very nice but hardly the stuff of gay-icon status. A more cynical eye could conclude that her Aids support comprised of nothing more than good public relations – popping into a hospital to shake hands with a few patients and, hey presto, she has another headline photograph to beat the other Royals over their heads with. Worse still, when she did take her afore-mentioned children to meet some Aids sufferers, she told them that they had cancer, presumably in order to avoid having to tell them about all that nasty, squishy gay sex stuff. Not exactly right-on gay activism, is it?

Yes, she was a very good friend of Miss Versace, Dame Elton, George Michael, even Michael Barrymore it seems, but whether that makes someone a gay icon or just a plain ol' fag hag is open to question.

So when we subtract all of the great and wonderful things that Diana was supposed to have actually done to earn our love, there's not that much to get excited about. So should we cast off her memory? Maybe not, because even the most hard-faced cynic would readily admit that she was evidently a very warm and friendly person who genuinely did have lots of affection for gay people and didn't have any qualms about the whole world knowing so. That in itself is enough to afford her more than a little respect ('cause it's not like she had to make a point of hanging around with old queens), but as for being a gay icon? Well, was she ever? Probably not, but some clueless (and straight) hack probably decided that she was, and the whole myth just snowballed. A tragic loss to the nation indeed, but the death of a great gay icon? Nah.

Link

www.theworkcontinues.org

BRIAN DOWLING

He famously won series two of *Big Brother* and, yes, he's gay and he said so. Good on him for that. We all marvelled at the very idea of a screaming queen actually getting voted as the winner, and wondered what would happen to such a funny, cheeky and likeable fella like Brian. Tragically, he's been consumed by the stifling world of Saturday morning children's television. As if Brian wasn't already the cuddly, acceptable face of homosexuality, he's now been de-sexed to become the latest in a long line of eunuchs doomed to a career of contrived happiness and fake blandness, all in the name of children's entertainment. Don't expect Brian to be talking about gay employment rights on *Question Time*. Take the money and run, Brian.

Link

www.briandowling.net

ERASURE

Still very much in business although their days in the charts seem to be long gone, Erasure created a whole genre of chart-topping hits, ranging from 'Sometimes' to 'Chains of Love', although it's 'A Little Respect' which is the song that has become their queer anthem. You've only got to hear Andy Bell utter, 'I try to discover . . .'

Andy was one of the UK's first openly gay pop stars, and his taste for the slightly more camp things in life led to some serious on-stage outfits and antics. Not the sort of thing that would even raise an eyebrow now, but at the time it was pretty unusual to say the least. Great talent which deserves more success.

Link

www.erasure.com

DAME EDNA EVERAGE

The most unusual kind of drag queen. A straight guy in a big frock, but Barry Humphries knows all the lines and gets the joke just as much as we do. Camp comedy combined with biting satire. Possibly Australia's finest export.

Link

www.dame-edna.com

RUPERT EVERETT

British born and bred, Rupert's now big in Hollywood, although he has often commented that he'd probably be bigger if it wasn't for the fact that he's gay. With a string of theatre and movie appearances as long as your arm, you might agree that it's a little odd that so many achievements have resulted in only mere stardom rather than superstardom, but that's the nature of the movie business – it's still not a place for homos, at least not the ones that actually say they're gay. But no matter, our Rupert's got bags of talent, good looks and he's also very good mates with Madonna, so it doesn't get any better than that, does it?

Link

www.moviething.com/bios/ruperteverett

FRANKIE GOES TO HOLLYWOOD

Formed in the summer of 1980, the group hit the headlines in 1984 with their top-selling hit 'Relax', which was famously taken off the air in mid-play by BBC DJ Mike Read for reasons of 'good taste' (thankfully, the BBC later got rid of Mike Read for the same reason). Although lead singer Holly Johnson and band member Paul Rutherford were unashamedly gay by any standards, it's astonishing to see just how many people now claim that they never realised that 'Relax' was essentially about gay sex. After breaking with the band, Holly went his own way, announcing that he had Aids in 1993, and he released semi-confessional autobiography *A Bone in my Flute* a year later. He has now effectively retired. Remember those 'Frankie Says' T-shirts? What were you thinking about?

Link

www.fgth.org.uk

STEPHEN FRY

Actor, writer, comedian and all-round fabulous person, Stephen first achieved major public recognition as half of a two-man comedy act with Hugh Laurie, and he became a popular figure on British television throughout the 1980s and beyond. Openly gay, Stephen never dodges round the homosexuality subject – he grabs hold of it, wrings it out and laughs at it. He told us when he was celibate and he told us when he got a boyfriend. He even told us when he started having sex, and you've got to admire a man who can do that in front of a national television audience and still make everybody roar with laughter at the same time. With a charming personality and the kind of wit that you'd happily chop off a limb for, Stephen is a latter-day Oscar Wilde. Little wonder that he played Oscar's part so beautifully in the eponymously titled 1997 movie. With more film, play and television show credits than you could comfortably imagine, Stephen Fry's career continues to steam ahead, and yet you can't help feeling that you still want just a little bit more.

Link

www.stephenfry.com

DAVID FURNISH

It's not often that anyone gains celebrity status simply for being somebody's partner, but David Furnish is, for good or bad, ultimately doomed to be forever known as Elton John's other half. But don't imagine that David stays home and washes all those frocks, because he's an accomplished film maker, as witnessed by one of his first projects, the fascinating *Tantrums and Tiaras*, which finally showed Elton John as a real person, rather than the media-created singing doll which we had all become so familiar with. David's also very handsome.

Link

www.davidfurnish.com

JUDY GARLAND

She's etched into our gay history almost like no other celebrity, and yet, if you ask just about any gay man under the age of about 25 who Judy Garland was, they'll probably not have much of a clue, other than that she 'did movies'. Such is the effect that time has upon a legend. Born Frances Ethel Gumm in 1922 in Grand Rapids, Judy was raised in a vaudeville family, and made her stage debut at the tender age of two. She auditioned for MGM in 1935 and earned the distinction of receiving a contract without even taking a screen test, making her movie debut in *Broadway Melody*. A recording contract quickly followed, as did her classic performance in *The Wizard of Oz*.

Judy's career blossomed, although her ego grew in similar proportion, and her on-screen performance contrasted with the temperamental and moody character which took over when the cameras stopped. Her reliance on drugs stemmed from her childhood, when her mother supplied her with endless uppers and downers to keep her going on the MGM set, but things began to spiral out of control, and she was eventually fired from movie contracts no less than three times, and divorced for a second time.

Switching to stage roles, she found even more success in London and on Broadway, eventually concentrating on her singing talents with concerts all over the world. Famously, she was warned to abandon her performing career in 1959 when she found herself in hospital with hepatitis, but a year later she was back on stage, belting out her overemotional renditions of torch songs which her (largely gay) audiences loved.

Her roller-coaster personal life only served to add to the drama, indeed some less kind commentators insist that she consciously milked it for all it was worth. More movies, concerts and television were to come, and then she married yet again, this time to actor Mark Heron, who she later divorced when she found out (yep, you guessed it) he was gay. Finally, she married again in 1969 but died on 22 June of the same year in London, after having taken an accidental overdose of barbiturates. Ironically, a tornado hit Kansas on the same day.

More than thirty years on, it's difficult to know exactly what it was about Judy that made her possibly the biggest gay icon of all time, but it's worth remembering that she came from an era when movie stars were perceptibly even more glamorous than they are now, and when television was still in its relative infancy. It was a time when concerts and show tunes were huge, and Judy was the unrivalled queen of every medium. Little wonder then that, when her body was flown back to New York, more than 22,000 people filed past her glass-covered coffin to pay their respects. You can only stop to wonder how many of them were gay. Probably most of them. And it's important to remember that her death was a seminal moment in all our lives, as the sadness of her funeral (on 27 June) provided the catalyst which sparked the infamous Stonewall riots, leading to the very beginnings of gay rights. May she indeed rest in peace – indirectly we owe her a lot, even though most of us might not even know it.

Link

www.judygarland.net

LESLEY GARRETT

The Madonna of opera they call her, a glamorous girl with a down-to-earth charm (she's from Doncaster, bless her, so what do you expect?) and a voice that could blow your socks off. The supreme soprano songstress loved by the whole nation, but, with a wardrobe like Lesley's, a marvellously camp personality and the simple fact that she sings opera, well, you can see why more than a few queens love her. Check out her CDs 'cause there's more to life than trance and house. No, really.

JEAN PAUL GAULTIER

Forever famous for designing that big ol' pointy bra for Madonna, Jean Paul is the campest and gayest face in fashion. He's been behind some of the biggest influences in gay clothing culture, and things like fellas in frocks or the lycra-with-Doc-Martens look have all been down to Jean Paul's tongue-in-cheek style. He's a good friend of Mrs Ritchie's and he proposed marriage to her no less than three times, and who could blame him? Like he says, she's the kind of gal that any gay man would want to tie the knot with, but, as we know, she graciously declined his offers. Beyond his clothing design, Jean Paul was also a familiar face on early series of Channel 4's *Eurotrash*, back in the days when the whole show was funny, rather than just the odd few minutes. Sad to reflect on how *Eurotrash* has become so tediously straight since our little French friend left. How many tits do you want to see in half an hour?

Link

www.jeanpaulgaultier.com

GILBERT AND GEORGE

The two icons of all that is bizarre and wonderful first met in 1967 and set up a studio in London's Spitalfields a year or so later, offering their services as 'living sculptures'. A London exhibition of new minimal and conceptual art opened in 1968 but conspicuously failed to include any of their work, and so, like any self-respecting queens would do, they painted their heads and stood motionless inside the gallery on opening night. It got them attention and it also got them a show at the Dusseldorf Kunsthalle, effectively launching their international career.

Gilbert and George almost defy description. Their work shocks, disturbs or simply amuses, depending upon your attitude and disposition towards works which often make generous use of shit or sperm as a main constituent. It's the art of annoyance, but gloriously enjoyable nonetheless. Paul McCann in the *Independent* commented that 'the surrealist duo have hit back at the Rev. Ian Paisley, after their latest exhibition in Belfast was branded a work of "Sodom and Gomorrah". Mr Paisley as an art critic is an image to conjure with. The idea of him crusading against Gilbert and George is a conflict to warm the heart of any lover of the absurd.' Precisely.

Link

www.Artcyclopedia.com/artists/gilbert_and_george.html

LARRY GRAYSON

After years of unrecognised acting work, Larry Grayson got his television break in 1971 when he appeared on ATV's Saturday variety show. Appearing on the *Lesley Crowther Show*, Grayson was spotted by Lew Grade and offered his own show *Shut That Door* (based on his famous catchphrase) and he became the *TV Times* Funniest Man of the Year. When Bruce Forsyth decided to leave the BBC hit show *The Generation Game*, Larry Grayson took over as host, boosting ratings to over 18 million. He was a huge star, but he decided to leave the show in 1981 when it was at its peak of popularity. After that, he returned to a mixture of stage and television appearances, but, as his health deteriorated, he gradually disappeared from our television screens, and died in 1995.

How does history judge Larry Grayson? He was outrageously camp and effeminate, but he never openly admitted to being gay, and avoided the subject whenever it was raised. On one occasion gay activists demonstrated outside BBC studios as Grayson recorded *The Generation Game*, protesting that he stereotyped gay men but was firmly closeted himself. But that was the whole point of Grayson's act. He was gay but only if you knew what being gay was all about. It was all about innuendo and the delivery of seemingly innocent remarks which were loaded with homosexual overtones, made all the more comical by his body language and carefully crafted facial expressions. He didn't have to say that he was gay – it was already too obvious to even mention. He was possibly the ultimate example of everything that today's 'straight-acting' homo would despise, but no matter what you thought about him, he was undeniably hilarious.

Link

www.bbc.co.uk/dna/h2g2/alabaster/A758072

FRANKIE HOWERD

Think of *Up Pompeii*, the odd *Carry On* film and a whole string of top-of-the-bill stage appearances. Frankie had a unique style all his own, and a way with double entendres that just left the audiences laughing, even though you knew the punchlines way before they were delivered. There was an inevitability and predictability about his act which might have made any other celebrity a major bore, but with Frankie it was all part of the fun. Somehow he got us all to join in on the joke. An outrageous old queen, he'll forever be a part of our vocabulary. Ooh, no, missus.

Link

www.frankiehowerd.com

ELTON JOHN

Reginald Kenneth Dwight, better known to you and me as Elton John – the Grand Dame of British pop celebrities. To say that Elton has enjoyed an eventful and successful career would be a major understatement. He's been singing hit songs since the early 1970s and he's still a major international A-list star, with a reserved and endearingly shy nature which contrasts starkly with the glittered, feathered drag colossus that used to wow the audiences across the globe, in those wild days before Elton found himself a boyfriend and cooled down. In partnership with writer Bernie Taupin (an immensely talented fella from Lincolnshire who has consistently avoided the media for thirty years, despite being capable of turning out internationally famous hit lyrics almost without any effort, in less than an hour on some occasions) Elton has become a national institution, as safe and comfortable as fish and chips.

His years of fame haven't been without some colourful episodes; he stayed married (to Renate Blauel) for some four years, even though he knew he was gay, and had already partially announced the fact to the nation through an interview with *Rolling Stone* magazine in 1976 (when he said that he was bisexual). He also developed a serious drugs habit, a reputation for temper tantrums, a constant battle with hair loss and a liking for outrageously over-the-top costumes that sometimes defied description, if not belief. Eventually he did regain control of his life, after separating from his wife, drag and drugs, and in 1992 he launched the Elton John Aids Foundation – now one of the world's largest Aids organisations which receives the royalties from all of his singles.

Famously, he sang a rewritten version of his hit 'Candle in the Wind' at Princess Diana's funeral (having been Diana's friend for some time) and, as a result, the song became (and remains) the biggest selling single of all time. He also met his long-term partner David Furnish, who produced a fascinating fly-on-the-wall documentary tracing Elton's off-screen life (*Tantrums and Tiaras*) which revealed that Elton was, in real life, a moody, bitchy, selfish and often downright rude old queen. Not surprisingly, we suddenly loved him even more.

Musically, his career has slowed in recent years, and his song partnership with Bernie Taupin has occasionally been exchanged for other projects, most notably the creation of a soundtrack for the musical *The Lion King*. Good, family-favourite stuff, but not the classic material that we traditionally associated with Elton. At his best, he gave us classics such as 'I'm Still Standing', 'Sad Songs', and 'Nikita', but it would be impossible to pick and choose from such a huge list of brilliant material ranging in style from the instrumental 'Funeral for a Friend' through to the downright bizarre 'Solar Prestige a Gammon' (no, really). He's done it all; he's a screaming queen; he's got talent like no other British artist, and he's a major supporter of Aids charities. Elton John truly rocks. His knighthood seems hardly sufficient.

Link

www.eltonjohn.com

GRACE JONES

Described on a fan site as 'the most feminine man alive', Grace is a legendary big ol' bird with an evil sense of humour, wicked fashion sense, great looks and a pretty useful right hook. Performance artist, model, singer and celebrity, her music career has been chequered but who cares? She rocks. Famous for having a swipe at Russell Harty, Grace is a feisty gal, but you just so want her at your party, don't ya?

Link

www.theworldofgracejones.com

BILLIE JEAN KING

Tennis girl par excellence but firmly in the closet until her ex-lover tried to sue her for half of her savings. Trouble was, she was married at the time. Having been outed so publicly, Billie became the dyke icon of the early 1970s and to this day she's still a much-used media buzz-word for lezziness (and an active pro-gay campaigner). But she could sure hit those balls . . .

Link

www.wic.org/bio/bking.htm

KD LANG

Super-dyke with oodles of talent (think 'Constant Craving') and classy lezzie style, KD Lang is a country girl turned bad. Defiantly refusing to conform to the Nashville notions of sweet cowboy niceness, KD was shunned by the Country Music Awards, but by 1988 she had made her mark and, like her or not, she was good. Always open about her sexuality, she announced in 1992 to *The Advocate* magazine that she was (in case you didn't already know) a lesbian, and her iconic status was cemented.

Grammies, MTV music awards and even some attention from Madonna ('I have seen Elvis, and she's beautiful'), KD has enjoyed success and recognition, but more recently she's been out of the spotlight, and whether she'll be making a comeback, we'll just have to wait and see. Never a major gay campaigner ('I don't feel political about my preference. I just don't. I'm sorry to disappoint you hard cores but I don't'), KD is openly gay, but not one for screaming it from the rooftops.

Link

www.kdlang.com

DANNY LA RUE

The Grand Dame of drag, there's nothing you can teach this gal about big hair, big frocks and a big personality. Nobody does it better. The only slightly disappointing aspect of his sequin-studded career is that he keeps his private life completely private, even though you'd almost expect someone like Danny to be so out of the closet that the door rusted shut behind him.

But he's from another era, and everybody agrees that he's a nice guy, so maybe we shouldn't expect any more from him other than his reliable ability to show lesser mortals how to deliver a double entendre and how to look totally glam. The ultimate cock in a frock.

Link

www.dannylarue.com

NIGELLA LAWSON

One of the best of the ever-increasing breed of television cooks, Nigella is a gay man's dream. She's a whiz in the kitchen; she sticks her fingers in the food for a taste; she's a lush with the ol' alcohol and she's not averse to a midnight fridge raid when she's feeling peckish (she's also slipped the odd bit of Palare speak into her commentaries too). And she's a good-looking gal with a posh house in a fancy bit of London, with some very well-connected friends and relatives. She's also learned (with a bit of television production help) how to make the whole cooking thing look quite erotic – she can make a soufflé sound like the best shag you've ever had (try not to think of cheese though).

But get this – the gay media (and some of the more mainstream rags) tried telling us that Delia Smith was (or is) a gay icon. In what universe? OK, Delia's good, and she seems to be a nice old stick, but she's not exactly sex, is she? Worse still, she supports football clubs and she's discovered God. Nah, it's just not happening there. You can forget Delia, and Jamie Oliver with his Mockney falseness, and you can forget about Ainsley (oh, per-lease, if only we could forget about him). Nigella's our girl. She rocks.

Link

www.channel4.com/life/microsites/N/nigella

LIBERACE

'He reeks with emetic language that can only make grown men long for a quiet corner, an aspidistra, a handkerchief and the old heave-ho . . . this deadly, winking, sniggering, snuggling, chromium-plated, scent-impregnated, luminous, quivering, giggling, fruit-flavoured, mincing, ice-covered heap of mother-love . . . he is the summit of sex, the pinnacle of masculine, feminine and neuter, everything that he, she and it can ever want.' So said *Daily Mirror* columnist William Connor back in 1956. Everything he said about Liberace was probably right, but the star sued and insisted that he was not in any way homosexual. He won an apology and £8,000.

That was the whole gag with Liberace. He made a career out of playing the piano (and playing it very well), but he became bigger than the act, until it was his clothes, his stage set and his personality that the crowds came to see. He had the knack of not taking himself seriously – after building the start of his career as a classical pianist, he famously ended a classical performance in 1939 with a rendition of 'Three Little Fishes' (followed by a smile and a wink). No wonder that the audience were spellbound.

He became more outlandish, more colourful and more camp, until he couldn't climb any higher and by the 1970s he was the world's highest-paid performer, with five gold million-seller albums under his sequinned belt. The media hated his popularity and his effeminate act, but Liberace just took the money and shrugged his feather-covered shoulders, giving the world his much-used phrase: 'I cried all the way to the bank'. He later capped that one with 'You remember the bank I used to cry all the way to? Well, now I own it.'

The only sad side to Liberace's glittering career was his life-long struggle with his sexuality. Despite his much-rumoured liking for younger men (his chauffeur did more than drive the car), he defiantly continued to deny that he was gay, even up until his death, and even then his family tried to keep up the pretence until the local coroner insisted upon an autopsy which revealed that the cause of death had been cardiac arrest due to congestive heart failure, caused by subacute encephalopathy. Liberace had died of Aids.

What a shame that one of the world's biggest stars couldn't have just come clean.

But he didn't really need to make any big coming-out speech – his whole style, personality, dress sense and lifestyle said it all for him. Camper than Christmas.

Link

www.liberace.org

MADONNA

If ever there was a clear definition of the term 'gay icon' then Madonna Louise Ciccone is without doubt the lady who wins the title hands-down. Love her or hate her (and she probably wouldn't care which), she's been a seminal part of gay culture almost since the day when she first burst into the world of pop music, back in the early eighties. Why? Well, it's not difficult to see why gay men identified with her when you look at the things she's done and the things she's said. Where do you start? From humble beginnings (when she first appeared on *Top of the Pops*, there were no clues as to how the dumpy little songstress would become an international superstar) she blossomed into the in-your-face monster which the media still loves to hate, but which gay men just love. For twenty years the pundits have waited for her fall but, like every fickle queen, she refuses to lay down and die.

The story goes that she ran away from her home town of Detroit at the tender age of nineteen with only $20 in her pocket and, after arriving in New York City, she reportedly told a cab driver to take her to 'the centre of everything'. After being deposited in Times Square, she managed to talk her way into a stranger's apartment (you can see how so many gay men would relate to all this?) where she stayed until she got herself her own room on the Lower East Side. Whether the various facts are strictly true is irrelevant – you've just got to admire her balls. With an ambition to become a dancer, she worked her way through waitress and nude modelling jobs, while she auditioned her way around the city, eventually becoming a familiar face in New York's clubland. Inexplicably ('cause let's face it, she wasn't the world's best singer) she even managed to get herself a recording contract, and the rest, as they say, is history.

Madonna has always been more than just music however. Her musical tastes have evolved (sometimes they've made quantum leaps) but the music only tells part of a much bigger story. In retrospect, her music can be seen as a key with which she unlocked something much bigger than just a singing career. Madonna is, in every sense of the word, a true icon. After becoming Queen of the pop music genre, she moved her attention to the movie industry, where she enjoyed (and continues to enjoy) considerable success as a good (if not great) actress in a growing list of flicks which have consistently failed to live up to the magical status of their star. But then, even the world's most accomplished actress would have faced an uphill struggle to impress the Hollywood critics, faced with baggage of the kind which Madonna carries with her.

Undaunted by her lukewarm movie reviews, she turned her attention to the publishing industry and created *Sex* – a book which literally laid her bare in a series of erotic and often gratuitously pornographic images which shocked, amused and irritated the world of celebrity which she had so swiftly conquered. Critics slated the book and the media confidently crowed that, as they had so often predicted, Madonna had finally gone too far. But, of course, that was the whole point. In the lyrics of the single 'Erotica', she replied to her critics with style. She wasn't sorry and she wasn't anybody's bitch.

It wasn't over either. Only Madonna could confidently get away with a whole movie which documented her bizarre life on the road during a world tour. *Truth or Dare*'s success probably owed more to careful planning and skilful editing than Madonna would ever have us believe, but it did provide some fascinating glimpses of Madonna's real personality, as observed by Warren Beatty while attempting to hold a conversation with her during a medical check-up, which (of course) was being filmed for the movie. As he commented (either in jest or in despair), what's the point of doing anything if it's not on camera? Simulated oral sex with a coke bottle or simulated sex on a bed in front of a concert audience while policemen wait to arrest her in the wings, it was Madonna at her worst and, therefore, her best.

Now in her mid-forties and married with two children, Madonna is certainly no longer the wild woman she once was, and her ability, or at least her ambition, to shock seems to have gone. Maybe she'd simply taken a swipe at everyone she could think of, or maybe she just got bored (in the lyrics to 'Substitute for Love' she whispers, 'and now, I find . . . I've changed my mind') but she's still stays firmly on the A-list, managing to produce some top-class music while appearing in a James Bond movie and even appearing as the leading actress in a West End play, where those who were lucky enough to enjoy such a long and surprisingly intimate audience with Madonna will testify that her star quality certainly hasn't faded. It takes some serious charisma to stand on a stage, in complete silence, hands in pockets, and still bring the house down.

To list all of Madonna's achievements would be pointless. We already know who she is and what she's about. Throughout her career she has tirelessly taken on establishment beliefs and traditions, shaking them up often to the point of destruction. But she has also freely given her support and time (which by any standards doesn't come cheap) to gay people and, even during the darkest days of the Aids crisis, her outspoken views always included the strongest defence of gay rights. Unlike so many celebrities who embraced the gay community after it became fashionable to do so, Madonna was there right from the start, and even now she clearly still knows who her friends really are. Taking a bow at the end of her West End play, she walked forward and saluted to a pair of T-shirted queens on the front row. Class!

Link

www.madonna.com

MAPP & LUCIA

Classy mid-eighties drama series with lots of light humour and a marvellous camp tone which made the show compulsive viewing. It's possible that Her Majesty tuned in too, as she is known to be an avid reader of the novels on which the series was based. Geraldine McEwan played the magnificent Lucia, while Prunella Scales played her frumpy sparring partner, Miss Mapp. The best performance, however, came from Nigel Hawthorne, as the delightful fop Georgie, complete with limp wrist, dodgy wigs and perfect snooty attitude combined with outrageous campness. Sometimes you miss quality productions such as these.

Link

www.epguides.com/MappandLucia

DAVINA McCALL

She's the kind of gal you'd want to go drinking with. A girl with laddish humour, good looks, humour and personality. She was brilliant on MTV and she is still outstanding on *Big Brother*. But somebody should stop her before she goes too far. Even Davina can't sound convincingly enthusiastic after the tenth week of *Pop Star Poop*.

Link

www.starpulse.com/Actresses/McCall,_Davina

FREDDIE MERCURY

With a real name (Farok Bulsara) almost as colourful as his on-stage persona, Freddie Mercury was a magnificent contradiction – an outrageously camp performer easily identified as gay, but worshipped by predominantly straight rockers all around the world. Queen (created in 1971 when Freddie joined a band called Smile) was for many years the ultimate expression of mainstream rock culture, with a seemingly endless stream of unforgettable hits, all fronted by a man that would have looked more at home in a Tom of Finland book. Nobody ever seemed to question Freddie's sexuality even when he regularly appeared on stage in cat-suits, angel wings or in full regalia complete with crown; it was the music that mattered and, while Freddie produced the hits, nobody was going to raise their eyebrows too high.

In fact, it was fascinating to observe how Freddie consistently avoided announcing his sexuality to the world, even though his on-stage performance hardly left anyone in any doubt as to where he was coming from. It wasn't until the whole band appeared in drag for the 1984 video of 'I Want To Break Free', that the public (and the media) really started to grasp that Freddie wasn't exactly the typical hettie rock dude you might have expected, but, by then, nobody wanted to try and dismantle the image of an icon; Freddie had famously got away with it.

He maintained a six-year relationship with close friend Mary Austin but in 1985 he began a long-term relationship with Irishman Jim Hutton and his years of infamous partying effectively ended (Freddie openly admitted to being 'extremely promiscuous' and regularly held wild after-show parties with strippers and drag queens), in exchange for a quieter life 'growing tulips' (as Freddie famously commented).

Queen began to fade from the charts, and rumours began to circulate that Freddie might be ill – he appeared weak and lost a huge amount of weight. The does-he-have-Aids gossip started, but no word was forthcoming from Freddie until 23 November 1991 when he issued a statement: 'Following enormous conjecture in the press, I wish to confirm that I have been tested HIV-positive and have Aids. I felt it correct to keep this information private in order to protect the privacy of those around me. However, the time has now come for my friends and fans around the world to know the truth, and I hope everyone will join me, my doctors and all those worldwide in the fight against this terrible disease.'

Freddie died just one day later. Nobody can ever know why he strove to keep his sexuality a secret, even though his stage persona made it impossible to imagine that he was anything other than gay. A true contradiction and a true talent.

Link

www.queen-fip.com

GEORGE MICHAEL

Yorgos Kyriatou Panayioutou, but George Michael to you and me. Despite a string of international hits, George will forever be the man who was arrested in a toilet. Both gay media and the music press claim that his career was ruined by that little incident, but the truth may be more prosaic; he's just run out of good songs. But whether George's talent has ultimately dried up remains to be seen.

What is certain is that he's more than made up for his many years in the closet. He's openly and defiantly gay, although when asked on an internet chat site whether he regarded himself as a role model for gay youths, he replied, 'Not unless gay youths are looking for advice on how to get arrested.' He's laughed loudly at the whole arrest saga, however, notably through his deliciously sarcastic video for 'Outside', in which a seedy toilet is transformed into a glittering disco, and American policemen are seen kissing in an embrace. The police officer who arrested George in the infamous toilet incident (Marcelo Rodriguez) is now busting his arse trying to sue George, to compensate for alleged 'emotional distress'. The humourless media hate George for refusing to express remorse for his deed, while we love him for it.

Link

www.georgemichael.com

BETTE MIDLER

Who? Well, anyone younger than twenty might imagine that Bette Midler's career revolves around endless re-runs of *Down and Out in Beverly Hills*, but of course the Divine Miss M is so much more than that. Long before Madonna had even begun to climb her way to her status as a true gay icon, Bette Midler was already out there being outrageously funny or just plain outrageous – filthy, in fact, at a time when ladies just didn't do that kinda thing. A perfect mix of New Jersey attitude and Jewish wit, Bette first made her claim to fame in the seedy Continental Baths (and, as you'll appreciate, very little bathing went on there) where she would perform her stage routine in front of a host of towel-clad homos, accompanied by (and it gets even camper here) Barry Manilow on piano! It was a drag show without the drag and, despite the fact that her act became so notorious that even major celebrities started making visits to the bath house to see her perform, there's no doubt that Bette Midler's showbiz career was created thanks to her gay fans.

Bette's act got bigger, more polished and even more outrageous as she took on a world audience, wowing fans with bizarre musical numbers which included some of her more famous tableaux, such as her performance in a full-body mermaid outfit (which she performed from a wheelchair) and her all-time classic-impersonation of Shelley Winters swimming (in *The Poseidon Adventure*) atop a tea trolley. You couldn't make it up.

Mixed with a successful 'mainstream' recording career, Bette Midler was hot property, but somehow the anticipated glittering career just never quite happened. Whether through ill-judgement or bad advice, her career has largely rested upon celebrity appearances, ill-conceived television shows and a number of popular but less than worthy movies. Apart from the much-acclaimed *Beaches*, Midler's movie career stalled, with only a hint of what could have been in films such as the delightful *First Wives Club* in which she was undoubtedly on top form, together with co-stars Diane Keaton and Goldie Hawn.

Although now rarely seen on British TV, Bette Midler does occasionally grace our screens with her presence. She reportedly failed to understand French and Saunders' humour when she appeared with them (exactly why is still a major mystery) but she can still produce some genuinely camp moments when she gets the opportunity. Those who saw her perform 'How I Want to Deserve You' while on an escalator in Harrods will know that The Divine Miss M can still deliver the goods. But no matter where her career may now be heading, she does have the good grace to remember where she came from, and makes no apologies for sticking like glue to the gay community. Her famous quote (made to a gay audience) 'Open your mouths, for Christ's sake, don't you ever get tired of being stepped on?' will probably stick with her. Quite rightly too, because although Bette may be a married mother, she's still, undoubtedly, one of us.

Links

www.experiencethedivine.com

www.wbr.com/bettemidler

KYLIE MINOGUE

The diminutive Kylie – a pocket-sized version of Madonna, every bit as glamorous and fabulous, Miss Minogue first came to our attention as the pint-sized mechanic Charlene in the BBC soap *Neighbours*, before springing to fame with her first chart hit, penned by the mighty Pete Waterman, who claims that, when Kylie first came to his office to discuss a recording deal, he thought that she was one of his staff's kids on a tour of the building. After almost ignoring her for most of the day, one of his colleagues reportedly mentioned that Kylie was still waiting and that they'd better think about creating a song for her, to which Pete Waterman replied, 'She should be so lucky'. . . Whether it really happened like that is open to question (Waterman has recently claimed that Kylie's hit had more to do with classical origins than his off-the-cuff remarks) but it's a sweet story, and the record catapulted Kylie to fame and fortune.

Almost by definition, any graduate of Pete Waterman's 'Hit Factory' can be expected to become a hit with gay fans (Pete Waterman is arguably the gayest straight man in the music industry) but Kylie was always something exceptional. Combining a string of foot-tapping hits with stunning good looks, she hopped from one classic disco single to another until, inexplicably, she decided to abandon PWL Music and reinvent herself as an indie artist. It was, by any standards, a mistake of epic proportions and, despite the release of the superb 'Confide in Me', there was no doubt that even Kylie's sweet voice couldn't make hit songs out of a series of proverbial lemons. Her career slipped even closer towards oblivion after making a disastrous movie debut opposite Jean Claude Van Damme, and the media could almost hear the sound of nails being banged into Kylie's coffin. But it wasn't over. Not even nearly.

Suddenly, almost from nowhere, Kylie was back and 'Spinning Around' quickly reminded both fans and critics that, when she had something worth singing, Kylie was good. Damn good. Even more surprising was that she'd suddenly become sexy – the little teen idol was suddenly a woman, in a pair of impossibly tight hot pants. But not just a straight man's object of desire – this lady knows how to camp it up too. Witness her appearance at the closing ceremony of the Sydney Olympic Games, surrounded by ten-foot-tall stilettos, sat atop a thirty-foot flip flop. It doesn't get any camper than that. And then, just when everyone was wondering if 'Spinning Around' was a fluke, a last-gasp lucky break, she came back even bigger and better with 'Can't Get You Out of My Head', the song that is forever going to be Kylie's. Never was a song title more appropriate; you just couldn't escape it and Miss Minogue finally crossed that almost indefinable threshold from being a pop singer to becoming something rather bigger – a star. From soap opera fame to obscurity and all the way back again.

But does she still remember how so many of her fans are gay? Does she still appear at events in support of gay people? You bet she does.

Link

www.kylie.com

MORRISSEY

Dark but fascinating songs which (unusually) contained intelligent thought, rather than just rhymes. Classic tracks which are now consigned to history. Is Steven Morrissey gay? You'd imagine so but he insists on avoiding any direct answer, relying on the old don't-pigeonhole-me line. Will The Smiths ever re-form? Probably not. Shame.

Link

www.shoplifters.morrissey-solo.com

MARTINA NAVRATILOVA

Another girl with balls, in more ways than one. Tennis dyke (well, bisexual, she says) of the eighties, Martina was adored, and now that she's retired from the sport, she devotes more of her time to gay campaigns and fund raising. Go girl.

Link

www.martina.globalweb.it

ANNA NOLAN

Love it or hate it, you can never escape from the phenomenon that is *Big Brother*. It's brought us hours of entertainment and even more hours of tedious boredom. But it also gave us an insight into some unusual and interesting characters, some of whom turned out to be, shall we say, less than conventional. Although most of the *Big Brother* contestants have thankfully faded into history (but wouldn't you just love to see a few of them again?), one or two have survived to continue their television careers elsewhere. Among the lucky few has been Anna Nolan, a former nun who came out to the nation as a lesbian during *Big Brother* and went on to present her own television series on BBC Choice (now BBC3).

Starting in March 2002, the six-episode series of *Anna in Wonderland* seemed, at least on the face of it, to be just another tedious excuse to find work for a vaguely familiar face. But it turned out that Anna had a personality, which made the series strangely fascinating.

The concept was simple enough – you wander off around the world interviewing mad people. But Anna had a special style, a convincing appearance of naivety and genuine interest which encouraged the show's victims to foolishly believe that Anna gave a damn. It was only the occasional glint in her eye that reassured you that, even though she was never so impolite as to actually say it, she knew just as well as we did that everyone she met was completely barking mad. From the insanity of the Christian fundamentalists who insisted they could cure her of her liking for girls, through bizarre people that get sexual kicks from dressing up as rabbits, and on to the delights of clairvoyant dating, Anna smiled stoically as the lunatics dug themselves into their proverbial graves. Good television and hopefully Anna will be back and, who knows, maybe the Beeb might even transfer her on to a proper channel.

Link

www.bbc.co.uk/1/hi/entertainment/tv_and_radio/1351751.stm

GRAHAM NORTON

Our hero. The man that delivered the acceptable face of effeminate homosexuality on to our television screens and into the hearts of (almost) everyone in the country. Graham made homos funny and fashionable in a way that they had never been before. Suddenly, it was cool to be queer, and all thanks to a manically funny Irishman with a girly manner and a twinkle in his eye which just makes you want to hug him.

An accomplished stand-up comic, Graham first captured our attention as a character in the *Father Ted* comedy series, where his few appearances were short but hilarious (remember the Irish dancing in the caravan?), although he increasingly popped up on TV as a comedian in his own right.

But it was his weekly television chat show that pushed his personality into the nation's living rooms, and all we could do was sit back and marvel at the way that Graham could deliver the smuttiest double entendres and get away with it. He talked about fucking and about sucking cock, about bottoms, about sex; he shoved a camera down a man's pants; he listened to a man wanking by telephone; he was outrageously gay, and yet nobody seemed to mind this time.

How did he do it? Part of the reason has to be his undeniable charm and his soft, non-threatening personality. He's the sort of guy that comes across as 'safely gay' with a liking for men and a dirty mind, but he doesn't look like the kind of fella that would actually, you know, do that sort of thing. He treats everything as a joke and so homosexuality becomes a joke, making it safe to handle. A cynic might conclude that Graham is therefore a sell-out to mainstream tastes, and that he's unconsciously made homosexuality 'nice' just to make himself (and therefore the rest of us) acceptable.

But it would be unfair to carp. Even if the whole 'loveable homo' act does leave some of us with a feeling that somebody is fooling somebody, somewhere, we have to accept that Graham Norton has helped to reshape our society for the better. In a society that is ruled by television and media, it's inevitable that what we see and hear changes our perceptions and our outlook. Graham became part of the furniture because he's a nice guy, he's funny and he's cute, and the fact that he's gay became unimportant. By a process of association, being gay has become less of an issue for everyone.

Link

www.grahamnorton.co.uk

JOE ORTON

Talented playwright from the sixties, responsible for shocking productions such as *Entertaining Mr Sloane*, Orton was a notorious gay boy, famous for his cottaging antics which presumably continued long after he'd met his long-term partner Kenneth Halliwell when he was just eighteen years old. Tragically, their turbulent (but artistically productive) relationship ended in 1967 when Halliwell (who remained an unpublished author while Orton achieved huge success) murdered Orton, bashing his skull with a hammer, in a fit of jealous rage before taking an overdose of sleeping tablets to kill himself. Drama queens par excellence.

Link

www.sbu.ac.uk/stafflag/joeorton.html

DOLLY PARTON

Country and Western singers rarely earn themselves much street cred, and winning over a gay (male and female) audience is harder still, but the legendary Dolly did it in style. She had a good deal going for her before she opened her mouth, what with the biggest pair of boobs this side of the international date line and a dress sense that a semi-sober drag queen would probably identify with. But when she did open her mouth she had the voice of an angel. From seriously humble beginnings up in Them Thar Hills, Dolly conquered the country music charts before seeking more fame and credit for acting appearances in movies such as *Nine To Five* and *Steel Magnolias.* Apart from the delicious fact that she even has her own theme park (you can't get much more camp than that), Dolly also recorded an excellent duet with Boy George, and more recently hosted Miss Graham Norton for a television documentary. Good actress, great singer, talented writer and, by all accounts, a very nice person. We like.

Links

www.dolly.net

www.dollywood.com

PET SHOP BOYS

Almost unheard of these days, the Pet Shop Boys were the very best of Euro-electronica, producing some top-class hits such as 'West End Girls' (their first single) and 'It's A Sin'. Although never officially 'out' the duo have always been overtly gay, their lyrics and costumes pretty much saying it all for them. As if their own talent wasn't enough, they also produced magnificent collaboration hits with both Dusty Springfield and Liza Minelli. Their latest project has been a seriously gay West End musical (*Closer to Heaven*) which received mixed reviews, so whether the boys will stick with the theatre remains to be seen. Wouldn't it be nice if they treated us to a few more hit singles?

Link

www.petshopboys.co.uk

BRAD PITT

OK, it's probably a cliché to perpetuate the notion that every gay man wants to get Brad Pitt into bed, but then it would be dishonest to suggest that there are many gay men that wouldn't. With a face and a body like that, who's looking for talent or personality?

CHRISTOPHER PRICE

The untimely death of Christopher Price in 2002 was tragic on many levels, not least the fact that he had just started to gain national attention as a great talent, and was rapidly becoming the gay face of the year. Everybody loved his wit, his charm and his cheeky, self-deprecating sense of humour. A journalist by trade, Price began his career with BBC local radio before moving to Radio Five and then to BBC television, presenting the nightly news show *Zero30* which became *Liquid News* in 2000. He signed a contract worth £280,000 causing a media outcry from pundits who dismissed him as a 'little-known newsreader'. But for once the BBC had spotted a real talent and, when you compared Christopher's camp, sarcastic and incisive presentation with some of the more run-of-the-mill BBC faces, you could see how he was going to earn his salary. Who knows where his career would have gone. What a waste. Really.

Link

www.bbc.co.uk/choice/liquidnews/christopher

SPICE GIRLS

There's not much you can say about this famous five that hasn't been said too many times already. We know who they are and what they did, but the jury is still out deciding whether us gay folks loved them or hated them. OK, they turned out some good hits (and a vaguely funny, if slightly pointless, movie), but in retrospect they aren't half as good as people pretended they were. The whole Girl Power thing was very amusing, and it did have some appeal for lots of younger lesbians, but it's still a mystery as to why the crop-topped skinny queens in G.A.Y. found the group so damned fascinating. Maybe it was because they just thought everybody else did too.

But they're gone now, cast into the bottomless pit of pop has-beens. Geri Halliwell could probably be rated as the most celebrated successful survivor of the band's demise had it not been for Posh Spice, and her virtual abandonment of all things musical in favour of a lush millionaire's life with David Beckham; and who could blame her? Meanwhile Melanie B just tried too hard and ultimately failed on the music front, but she defiantly clings on as a C-list television personality odd-jobber. Melanie C famously had her musical spot in the limelight but then she kinda lost it and . . . well, she came back again. Whether she is actually a dyke or not, she insists that she isn't, even though it might have made her a little bit more interesting if she had been. As for Emma Bunton? Er . . . um . . .

Link

www.spicegirlsforever.co.uk

DUSTY SPRINGFIELD

Mary Isabel Catherine Bernadette O'Brien, born in 1939 and forever a legend as the great Dusty Springfield, possibly the best British voice ever to cut a disc. Always a great dyke icon, Dusty never quite got her sexuality sorted, and rarely talked about the subject, even though she did drop the odd hint, such as in an interview with Ray Coleman when she said her affections were 'as easily swayed by a woman as by a man'. However, history records that most of her relationships were with women.

When her huge success of the sixties ended, she moved to Los Angeles and withdrew from the public eye, doing little recording work but spending much more time with drink and pills. In the 1980s she moved to Toronto but, despite a few recording projects (and an attempted come-back financed by Peter Stringfellow), it wasn't until the Pet Shop Boys invited her to duet on their classic single 'What Have I Done To Deserve This?' that Dusty finally stormed back into the charts. After a spell in the USA and the Netherlands, she returned to the UK for cancer treatment in 1994 but died in 2000, shortly after having been awarded an OBE. A big talent wasted.

Link

www.dustyspringfield.co.uk

STEPS

Famously described as being like 'Abba on acid', Steps became permanent gay property. The list of dance hits seemed unstoppable and while the papers printed their cosy reviews of how all the little girls just loved the wholesome sweetness of the Steps phenomenon, we all knew that Steps were much more than just a kiddie band. They were ours. The gay pundits tried (and still try) to rubbish Steps as being superficial, predictable, shallow and vaguely embarrassing, but they're blind to the sell-out lines of homos outside the Astoria every time Steps appeared at G.A.Y. They're blind to the nightly image of a half-empty dance floor suddenly filling to capacity with waving arms when a Steps hit gets played. The unpalatable truth is that the so-called trend-setters of the gay music scene just can't accept that the vast majority of gay boys and girls ultimately don't give a shit about progressive house, trance, jungle, garage, shed, hut, tent or whatever else we're force fed. We actually like good, old-fashioned songs with a tune you can remember, a beat you can dance to and words you can sing. Steps provided the perfect recipe – music that you couldn't help dancing to, while never pretending to be anything that they weren't. They were selling us dumbed-down, bargain basement pop and, at the end of the day, that's all we wanted. We wanted a good time. What a Tragedy that it all ended so abruptly. We wait for the comeback concert with eager anticipation.

Link

www.pop-music.com/steps

BARBRA STREISAND

Major megastar, adored by gay fans everywhere, forever. Or something like that. Unleashing a series of classic albums back in the 1960s Barbra dabbled with television appearances before returning to Broadway to star in *Funny Girl*, from which her first hit single 'People' came. The eponymously titled movie followed and Barbra was, at last, a huge star. More success was to follow with movies such as *A Star Is Born* and *Yentl*, plus sell-out concert tours. In terms of pure gay appeal, it was a mixture of her wild humour and attitude which first got her noticed, but duetting with Donna Summer ('No More Tears') and supporting Aids charities clinched the deal. When her son Jason came out as gay, Barbra was forever enshrined in our girly hall of fame.

Having largely disappeared from the celebrity circuit in favour of family life, Barbra still holds great affection in the hearts of many gay men and quite a few girls, but mention Miss Streisand to today's gay teens and you shouldn't be surprised to hear the word 'Who?' in response.

Links

www.barbra-streisand.com

www.jennifer-too.com/tides/home.html

DONNA SUMMER

You know the one 'Ooh, I feel love, I feel love . . .' well, that's Donna, a true disco diva from the seventies, responsible for classics like 'Dinner With Gershwin', 'McArthur Park' and 'No More Tears' with Barbra Streisand (how gay is that?). She was big on the gay scene for a long time but these days you don't hear much about her. In fact, she lost a whole lot of gay respect when the gay media spread a story about her spouting some religious garbage about Aids being God's punishment for being gay. Whether she really said it is now a subject of historical speculation, but Donna insists that she didn't ('I just thought people knew me better than that') and that she's always supported gay rights. OK, she has done her bit for lots of gay causes but most people couldn't help feeling that she'd got just a little bit too close to the Church to be completely whiter-than-white on this story, and we all know what they say about mud sticking . . .

Link

www.donna-tribute.com

TINKY WINKY

Is he or isn't he? The nation was momentarily gripped when the media realised that one of the BBC's Teletubbies was looking a little suspect. What did this mean? What a fuss. Maybe they should have asked us gay boys what the significance was of a man dressed in a purple suit, with a triangle on his head and a handbag in his hand. It doesn't take much analysis to conclude that there's something queer going on there. The show's creators kept a brave silence and offered some vague excuses but we weren't convinced even for a minute. Tinky Winky must be.

Link

www.pbskids.org/teletubbies

SANDI TOKSVIG

Lesbian lady with a sense of humour, Sandi first hit our television screens on the Saturday morning television show *No. 73* – an entertaining little production which would have received more favour had it not been doomed to follow the huge success of *Tiswas* (and how could anything top that?). But it had its moments – remember The Sandwich Quiz? After her spell with children's television, she moved to the comedy circuit and then back to television, most notably as a regular on *Call My Bluff.*

Although never in the closet, the papers feasted on the revelation that Sandi had (apparently) impregnated her (then) girlfriend with a ten-pence plastic syringe with sperm donated by a close friend. Quite why this would be of any consequence to anyone is hard to imagine, but then the papers do have an agenda all their own. Sandi does believe, however, that she did lose potential jobs through the exposure. Where Sandi's wit and one-liners will take her for the future, only time will tell.

Link

www.author.co.uk/toksvig/interview.htm

SHANIA TWAIN

A fairly recent addition to our list of ladies-we-love, Shania had been around on the country music scene for a long time before she hit our airwaves with 'That Don't Impress Me Much' but, following that hit, and a superb album, she's earned a place in our hearts. With a brand of foot-tapping music which is somewhere between country and pop, she manages to annoy both country enthusiasts (who bemoan the fact that her songs are just . . . well, they're just too mainstream and nice, with absolutely no mention of any dogs dying, divorces or even the odd orphan) and the so-called 'serious' music aficionados who think anything sounding even slightly cowboy-ish has got to be frowned on by definition. But for anyone with a liking for music that is just fun, catchy and great to dance to, she's got the recipe just right. When the guys started line-dancing to her first hit outside the Rembrandt pub in Manchester, you just knew that Shania truly had arrived. Oh, yes, and she's stunningly beautiful too. Don't you just hate her?

Link

www.shania-twain.com

VILLAGE PEOPLE

Although they're now regarded as probably the gayest thing to ever hit the pop charts, it's interesting to recall that at the height of their success, the Village People weren't perceived as being 'gay' by the public and media. They managed to remain ambiguous while churning out campery such as 'In the Navy' and their legendary 'YMCA', which (it seems) most people believed to be all about the worthy nature of youth hostels. Go figure. These days we all know what the Village People were all about, but strangely it doesn't stop every straight guy in the country getting up to do the moves whenever 'YMCA' gets some air play.

Link

www.ymca.multimania.com

KENNETH WILLIAMS

Like so many of our great comedy actors, Kenneth first trod the boards during his years of national service, before embarking upon a successful theatrical career. After becoming friends with Joe Orton, Kenneth starred in Orton's play *Loot* in 1965 and went on to star in countless *Carry On* films. But it was the BBC radio show *Round the Horne* which cemented his name in celebrity history, and the infamous characters Julian and Sandy became part of British (gay) culture. He died in April 1988 and after his death his diaries revealed that he'd lived a troubled life torn between homosexuality, caring for his mother, dealing with the few friends that he liked or trusted and handling an acting career which had pigeon-holed him as a comedian rather than an accomplished actor. How sad that such a talented, entertaining and intelligent man should have lived such a dark and depressing personal life.

Link

www.kennethwilliams.org.uk

BARBARA WINDSOR

Good ol' Babs is a British institution. The familiar face in so many *Carry On* films, she's a sort of living saucy seaside postcard, but with even bigger tits. Camp seems hardly an adequate word to describe her, and just to make her even sweeter she's a first-class fag hag, spending her time with the likes of Dale Winton or kick starting the Pride March in London. Famously, she was the only person in the *Carry On* cast that Kenneth Williams had any time for, and that pretty much says it all. Gawd bless ya!

Link

www.carryonline.com/carry/babs.html

XENA: WARRIOR PRINCESS

Talk about Lesbian icon – you couldn't invent anyone more dyke-ish. Six foot of rippling womanhood with a pair of hefty hooters and an appetite for killing fellas like they were . . . well, fellas really. Added to this, there was an unspoken thing going on between Xena and her sidekick Gabrielle, although nothing ever overtly came of it, and there you had it – the perfect lesbian fantasy show. Not surprisingly, one of the production team turned out to be, ahem, one of the girls and, as the show's creators began to realise just who was lapping up every episode, they mercilessly played up to the dyke angle even more. It's all over now though, and all that's left is a blood-soaked sword and a pile of overplayed video cassettes all around the country.

Link

www.mca.com/tv/xena

Then of course, there's another special breed of celebrities that we're either just not too sure about (you know the ones where you want to hate 'em but you can't . . . or the ones you want to love but somehow . . .) and the ones that we just love . . . to hate.

ANT AND DEC

Sometimes they're vaguely amusing but most of the time they're just too busy trying to be just too damned funny for their own good. Come on, boys, remember *Byker Grove* and 'Let's Get Ready to Rhumble'? We haven't forgotten even if you have. Nor have we forgotten your snotty attitude when Scott Capuro tried flirting with you. Get over yourselves please. And no, they're not cute.

ATOMIC KITTEN

Not our favourites. It would be nice if they could even be bothered to show up at the gay events they're booked to appear at, don't you think? Besides, they're crap anyway. Leave 'em to the hetties.

MICHAEL BARRYMORE

There's not much that you can say about Michael Barrymore that hasn't already been said far too many times. A vaguely amusing family-orientated comedian, Barrymore found his way to television success through work as a warm-up man, before becoming a compere for crappy Saturday evening entertainment shows. His act wasn't exactly sophisticated – it basically revolved around a flimsy impersonation of Basil Fawlty without all the carefully crafted humour that went into Cleese's character, but no matter, the public loved it and by the 1990s he was picking up awards for ITV Personality of the Year.

But all was not what it seemed with this family favourite; although he was married, he frequented the White Swan pub – a notorious East End gay bar, where to everyone's astonishment he climbed on stage one night in 1995 and announced that he was gay. The media lapped it up, but Barrymore's supposedly 'sensational' revelation was just one of many similar coming-out stories that left the public unmoved. While the papers anticipated cries of horror (the front-page headlines would have been three-foot high if the papers had been big enough), the public's reaction was basically 'so what?' and the Barrymore-is-gay furore fizzled out.

But the newspapers, like dogs with a bone, were on a mission, and the trickle of anti-Barrymore stories continued, culminating in a gift from heaven when a man was found dead in Barrymore's swimming pool in March 2001. We've all heard the lurid details time after time of how a supposedly innocent straight man was lured back to Barrymore's house after a drinking session and, the next thing anybody knew, he was face-down in a swimming pool with severe anal injuries. It didn't need much imagination to guess how he got the injuries, but the victim's family (egged on by the media) insisted that he was a good, wholesome straight boy, and ultimately it was all somehow Barrymore's fault. Go figure.

Love him or loathe him (and let's be honest – his on-screen antics have absolutely nothing to do with this story), Barrymore became the media's scapegoat, and why? Well because he was gay, of course, and the newspapers just couldn't bear the thought that, after having got hold of this supposedly earth-moving fact, the public just didn't care. They were determined to destroy Barrymore as an act of pure spite, and the man-in-the-pool incident was a deliciously perfect way to get their man. The whole saga leaves a bad taste in your mouth. It's tragic when anybody is found dead, but throughout the whole saga nobody ever accused Barrymore of actually having done anything to the victim, other than some anecdotal reports that he might have offered the victim some drugs some hours before. Barrymore's crime (if we exclude the whole unfortunate swimming pool business) according to the media, is that he got drunk a lot and took drugs a lot, which makes him unfit to be a 'family entertainer'. If that's all it takes to be banished from television, we ought to have some pretty blank screens in the future. But the darker truth is that the papers just couldn't forgive Barrymore for being gay or, to be more precise, for being gay and getting away with it. Some things never change.

BOY BANDS

And still they keep on coming (if you'll pardon the expression). It all started with the Beatles back in the sixties, but if you ignore both them and the likes of the Bay City Rollers (if you don't know, don't ask), then it was Take That which kicked off our national obsession with boy bands. Bless their little hearts, they're sweet and pretty, and they all dance in time to the music. Some of them can even sing, but, of course, the songs have little to do with their popularity. It's a commercial enterprise all about sex, and the need to cater for the tastes of randy pre-pubescent girls who don't really have a clue what it's all about, but they know that it's cool to drool . . . at boys. Of course, there's a little more to the story and, even though nobody is ever going to admit it, the unspoken truth is that whatever sells to little girls will probably sell to gay boys too, so if you really want to maximise your returns, your shiny new boy band has to dress gay, act gay and generally camp it up as much as possible. But never, ever say you're actually gay – that would upset the little girls.

Recently, however, the cynical gay-but-not-gay ploy has started to wear a little thin. First of all, Boyzone's Stephen Gateley suddenly announced that he was a homo and guess what? The girls didn't run away crying, they just kept on loving him. Then the biggest pop star sensation in the country, *Pop Idol* winner Will Young revealed that he was also gay and, while the papers waited with baited breath for the public reaction, the fans just shrugged their shoulders and said, 'So what?' Clearly, being gay is not the big commercial flop that the music moguls thought it was, so maybe they will now finally get over this nonsensical sexual ambiguity and actually tell the fans who is really batting for which team? Wouldn't it be fascinating to know?

THE TOP TEN BOY BANDS

① TAKE THAT

Long gone but still the ones that created the whole genre. They started their career doing gay clubs but then they went all commercial and, er . . . straight. Well, in a ridiculously camp sort of way.

② N*SYNC

An overseas import but hugely popular. Very Michael Jackson too, but their popularity has more to do with sexy lead singer Justin Timberlake than their music. Hell, who was listening to the tune?

③ BACKSTREET BOYS

More Americana, but a whole string of surprisingly decent songs. The singers scrub up pretty well too but they're just a little bit last year now. Singing with Shania Twain isn't very street cred.

④ BOYZONE

They were huge at the time but now they're gone. Nobody ever quite worked out why they disappeared but it might have had something to do with Ronan Keating thinking he was too fabulous to sing in a group (so wrong), or that Stephen Gateley's gayness was too much for the girls to handle.

⑤ WESTLIFE

A sort of new-look Boyzone but with crappier songs and uglier singers. Why they were ever popular remains unclear but it's probably fair to say that just about any boyband would have been popular at the time.

⑥ 5IVE

Funky stuff, very street and at least one of the group was seriously hot. But the old 'let's try and be black' thing got just a little bit tiresome, so it was a relief that they broke up when they did.

⑦ EAST 17

It all seems so long ago. They were everything that Take That weren't. But even their faux straightness just didn't quite convince us, did it? They still looked like straight boys who shagged behind the bike sheds.

⑧ NORTHERN LINE

Aww, we had such high hopes for them. The tunes were OK and they looked pretty good, but somehow they just never quite took off. Shame.

9 *BLUE*

Proving that the boy band thing is still very much alive, another so-so bunch of lads in search of something original. What the hell was Elton John thinking about?

10 *ONE TRUE VOICE*

Even Pete Waterman can have a bad day. Cute faces but they need a song too.

BASIL BRUSH

Sweet ol' Basil, the dapper fox from the seventies that so many of us boys and girls grew up with. Now we're told (by the gay media and a few other people who should know better) that our Basil is leaning a bit towards the gay side of the fence. What's the evidence for this? Well, he's back on children's television now with a posh suit (but then he always had that, didn't he?) and a rather high and slightly effeminate voice. No question then, he's gay. Per-lease, sometimes these stories are so ridiculous it's not even worth commenting. Basically, it's the old gags with a new puppet (which looks like it was made in China) and a distinctly more attractive 'friend'. Not even slightly gay really. On the other hand, he's spent his entire working career with a guy's hand up his arse . . .

TOM CRUISE

Oh dear, whatever happened to Maverick Mitchell, the sexy F-14 pilot in *Top Gun*, all dangling hoses and hard helmets? Somewhere it all went horribly wrong, and our lust, sorry, our love affair with Tom just ended abruptly. A great deal had to do with the rise to fame of another spunky young actor called Brad Pitt (who easily outshone poor Tom in the 'phwoar' category), but his marriage to Nicole Kidman didn't help either, as that slim possibility that he might be as gay as he looked was the thing that kept us interested. Then he got into the whole religion thing and it just got plain worse. Next came a series of lurid allegations by newspapers, each met with successful lawsuits. Then he and Nicole got divorced. Tom defiantly insists that he is one hundred per cent a red-blooded heterosexual, and he'll sue the pants off anyone who claims otherwise, as even mere suggestions of homosexuality would ruin his film career. So we certainly wouldn't suggest any such thing.

EMINEM

Is there any point in even discussing this mega-famous arsehole? White trash desperately trying to be a black rapper, oh dear, sweet Miss Mathers is a one-trick pony gone wild, a huge career built on the ability to string together words which rhyme. Big deal. Maybe we should admire him, as there aren't many people who have made so much money out of so little talent, but whatever the merits of his deep and meaningful lyrics (like we even care), the inescapable fact is that he's jumped on the black-rappers-hate-fags bandwagon. Damn it, if he's so bright, witty and intelligent, then why did he just have to go and spew out the same old cliché-filled hatred which the rappers and hip-hoppers have been peddling for years? No matter how many times he whines about how people have misunderstood him, or misinterpreted what he says, it's all patently a load of bollocks; he writes about hatred towards homos (we know this because we can read . . . duh!), and by doing that he makes it acceptable. End of story, there are no excuses. Let's not waste any more media space on this muppet. Although his brother's rather sexy . . . now, wouldn't that be a twist if . . .

JOHN INMAN

One of the country's grand old dames of pantomime, John will forever be remembered as the mincing fairy Mr Humphries in the BBC sitcom *Are You Being Served?*. Undoubtedly hilarious, it's only in more recent years that some gay observers have tried to criticise Inman's performance as a bad stereotype which set back gay rights and social acceptance by years. Actually it did nothing except give us a good laugh. Besides, as Inman points out, Mr Humphries never, ever actually said he was gay. Seriously.

IVAN MASSOW

Big on the posh side of the gay scene, Ivan was closely associated with his eponymously titled financial company but moved into the world of politics, becoming close to the big names in the Conservative Party. Then he astounded everyone by switching sides. He upset even more establishment figures when he resigned as the Chairman of the Institute of Contemporary Arts, after describing conceptual art as 'craftless tat' (well, he did have a point). More recently, he's been the man behind Jake, the posh bloke's version of Gaydar.

Link

www.jaketm.org

POPSTARS/POP IDOL/FAME ACADEMY etc.

Oh dear, they just wouldn't let it die. They should have called it quits after Hear'Say but, no, they had to force feed us more and more until we just couldn't take it any longer. The Beeb tried to cash in on the idea too in their usual stuffy, not-quite-getting-the-plot kind of way until . . . well, basically until we just switched off, figuratively and literally. The age of the instant pop star or group is over. Once was amusing, twice was OK, but no more please. We've moved on.

JOSH RAFTER

He made it to the 2001 series of *Big Brother* mid-way through the series, raising a few eyebrows as the first person to enter the *Big Brother* house who was in any way attractive. Things got even more exciting when he announced that he was gay. Would Brian Dowling and Josh get it together? Well, they were both gay so of course they would (that was the tone of most media coverage at the time). In fact they didn't get on all that well, and Josh's daily dose of semi-nudity did get a little tiresome after the first week. But the most interesting aspect of Josh's stay in da house was that the public loved Brian (he eventually won the show) but never quite got their heads round Josh. Why? Well Brian was your typical safe-and-cuddly gay man that the public likes. Josh, on the other hand, was good looking and (worse still) sexual. The idea of gay men actually having sex still takes some swallowing in some households. While Brian has moved on to the banal world of children's television, Josh remains firmly at the helm of his gay accommodation agency.

Links

www.outlet.co.uk

www.joshandpecs.com

FRANK SKINNER

Tiresome and tedious; the straight man's idea of comedy. Often reliant upon cheap, outdated gags based on hopelessly stereotypical notions of homosexuality. Throw in Rory McGrath and pretty much the whole crew from *A Question of Sport* and you have a recipe for guaranteed nausea.

ROBBIE WILLIAMS

Enough already. He was cute-ish when he was in Take That (well, he took his clothes off a lot and that's the main thing), but his cocky attitude has worn just that little bit too thin. He turned out a few hits but his more recent stuff really isn't very impressive if you stop to actually listen to it, instead of simply believing what the papers say. And what the hell was all that pseudo-Sinatra thing all about? As if.

But what really matters is the endless 'Is Robbie gay?' thing; a story which comes and goes, fuelled by Robbie's carefully crafted comments and his conspicuous refusal to just stand up and say, 'I'm straight, thank you very much.' OK, he almost certainly is a one hundred per cent red-blooded heterosexual, but isn't it time that he stopped trying to do this coy act which is supposed to whip us gay boys into a frenzy of speculation? Even more tiresome is the gay media's constant 'we love Robbie' predictability, and the endless lines about how wonderful it would be if Robbie came out, because he's just hinting at his true feelings, blah di blah . . . If Robbie Williams did suddenly announce that he was queer, the really offensive bit would be the fanfare of gay magazine features on how 'we've always loved him really' and how we always knew he was one of the gay boys. You can bet that nobody would dream of saying 'thanks for hiding in the closet while you milked your career prospects Robbie dear' now, would they?

DALE WINTON

Finally he released his autobiography and announced to the world that he was, in fact, gay. Who knew? Dale is everywhere, loved by many, hated by many others. Devoid of any specific talent, camp ol' Dale is famous for being famous, but it's hard to hate him, even though you want to. By all accounts he's a nice bloke, and he does hang out with Cilla Black and Babs Windsor (and that tells you a lot). Besides, he did give us *Supermarket Sweep* . . .

WILL YOUNG

OK, we all thought Gareth Gates was going to win, but it was the slightly more indie style of Will Young that clinched the winning position on *Pop Idol* – you know? That dial-a-celebrity marathon, the one that we actually bothered to watch, unlike all the similarly themed garbage that has been churned out ever since. Poor old Gareth, he looked so queer, what with his puppy dog eyes and his gay-boy hair (let's ignore the sphincter lips, OK?) but what a monumental twist of fate – it was Will that suddenly announced that he was the one that was batting for our side.

Who would have thought it? A huge celebrity suddenly tells the world that he's a homo, and right at the beginning of his career, rather than at the end of it (when any publicity is better than obscurity). But that's where the potentially exciting story ends. After coming out of the closet (and let's be brutally honest and accept that he only did that because the papers were going to out him in any case), he went back in and locked the proverbial door. He never mentions his sexuality now, other than to spew out a totally unconvincing line about how it's not important to him, and that it's his private life, blah, blah, blah. So, er, since when did fame-seeking wannabes want privacy or even expect a private life anyway? Wasn't wanting to become a pop idol all about becoming public property?

So what do we learn from this story? We learn that it's OK to be a young pop star and also be gay, providing that you don't bang on about it, so that the little girls (who buy the records) can listen comfortably to the 'girl I lurve you' songs and convince themselves that ol' Will actually wants a taste of minge, not cock. What a charade. Wouldn't it be a real sign of progress if he suddenly got himself a boyfriend and turned up at all the glitzy showbiz events with a fella stuck on his arm? But don't hold your breath 'cause that won't be happening until the record sales start to slump.

TOP TEN DIVAS

A word almost as over-used as 'icon' but, when appropriately applied, we all know the gals that we're talking about; those big, shining, larger-than-life ladies that we either just love to see and hear, or would quite fancy actually being (or just plain fancy if you happen to be a girl too). Oh go on, pass the lipstick, you know you'd just love to be . . .

① SHIRLEY BASSEY

Big voice and big personality, plus all the right mouth and hand movements that make imitating her oh-so easy (and that counts for a lot). Fabulous frocks too, but she's not exactly a fag hag so don't get too giddy.

② EDITH PIAF

Ah the little sparrow, with the voice of an angel. Oh whatever, she was a French gal who knew how to belt out a good song with her own unique pronunciation. Try it after a few pints. *Je ne regrrr-et rien . . .*

③ CHER

That hair, that voice, that surgery. Just fabulous.

④ ARETHA FRANKLIN

She's all voice; a former gospel singer who went soul, giving us classics like 'R.E.S.P.E.C.T.' and 'You Make Me Feel (Like a Natural Woman)'. Where the hell is she now though?

⑤ *DIANA ROSS*

OK, she was in the Supremes but she was always out there on her own. All-time-classic songs and always with plenty of style and presentation. And even though Steps did it just great, don't you think Diana's 'Chain Reaction' is still way better?

⑥ *WHITNEY HOUSTON*

Another big voice behind some great songs but, boy, has she lost her way. And some of those Whitney tunes have become just a little bit too straight recently. Seems like every straight bloke wants to sing 'I Will Always Love You' once he's had a couple of pints.

⑦ *DUSTY SPRINGFIELD*

Was she or wasn't she? No matter, whatever side of the bed she slept on, she was one of Britain's best that we just let slip though our fingers. Thanks to the Pet Shop Boys for giving us a reminder of her talent before her untimely demise.

⑧ *LIZA MINELLI*

It's not like she does much these days (maybe she's busy looking through her new husband's Judy Garland collection?), but her very presence is enough. A unique personality with more than enough talent, plus the little extra bonus of being Judy's daughter. How cool is that?

⑨ *JUDY GARLAND*

Forever Dorothy, a legend who endures. Songs, concerts, movies, drugs, alcohol, failed marriages, the whole deal. One of that rare breed of celebrities who could bring the house down just by standing there. That's real charisma.

⑩ *MADONNA*

OK, she might be in her forties and busy bringing up her kids, washing the car and doing the shopping, but she's still Madonna. The ultimate diva, gay icon, megastar, call her what you will. She's bigger than any epithet. She just is.

AND THOSE ALMOST-DIVAS?

① MONSERRAT CABALLE

Hell, she can sing. Best known to us for her partnership with Freddie Mercury, but subsequently she's sort of slipped back into the more obscure parts of the opera world. Shame 'cause she's good. We like – let's keep her!

② LESLEY GARRETT

Great singer, great personality too, but she doesn't exactly chase the gay scene, does she? Pity really, as she'd be a big hit, but maybe not at G.A.Y. Find a gay niche, girl.

③ KYLIE MINOGUE

She's become a sort of handy-sized version of Madonna. You can't get away from her and who would want to? She's sweet and beautiful, with a huge list of gay favourites under her arm. But just look at how the breeders are trying to get their claws into her. Keep your grubby hands off; Kylie has (gay) history and she's ours.

④ GLORIA GAYNOR

Fabulous undoubtedly but how long can you remain an icon on the back of just one song? Time she hit the club circuit maybe.

⑤ BARBRA STREISAND

A gay icon she may have been, but this particular star has faded. Is she dead? No, she's just retired, or has she? Either way, she's old news. Bless. Come back and remind us what it was all about.

⑥ BRITNEY SPEARS

So much promise but she's kinda lost it, don't you think? The looks, the songs, the outfits but it's all getting a little bit stale. Don't drop the ball again, Britney, giving Justin the boot was bad enough . . .

⑦ CHRISTINA AGUILERA

Britney wannabe, but slightly downmarket, so we weren't impressed. And then she released 'Beautiful' and overnight she changed everything. What is there to say? A modern gay anthem complete with drag queens and man-on-man action. We are beautiful in every way, Christina, and so are you. Kisses!

⑧ JENNIFER LOPEZ

She's so last year. Jay-Low? Oh per-lease, it's over. And no, you're not black.

(9) *MARIAH CAREY*
God bless her. Never use one note where twelve will do. And does she love herself as much as she looks like she does? She might be big in the celebrity stakes but she's doing squat in the gay diva stakes. It could have worked but it didn't.

(10) *CHARLOTTE CHURCH*
No, not ever, not in her wildest dreams.

TELEVISION

As if you need telling, there are some TV shows that have a certain appeal to queer tastes. You know the ones.

ABSOLUTELY FABULOUS

Without doubt the gayest and campest television programme ever, *Absolutely Fabulous* remains supreme as a must-see series, destined to be repeated, re-told and re-digested until its classic gags and ludicrous situations have become part of everyday gay vocabulary. Developed from a relatively uninspiring comedy sketch in a *French & Saunders* show, the series is based upon the central character (played by series writer and creator Jennifer Saunders) – one Edwina Monsoon, a dysfunctional (and corpulent, as Saffy would put it) single parent trapped in a bizarre, vapid and meaningless (but frighteningly realistic) world of public relations, cushioned from the realities of life by an overreliance on alcohol, alimony and her closest (and possibly her only) friend, the legendary Patricia Stone, a predatory fifty-something beehived monster played by the maginificent Joanna Lumley.

Although the sparkling scripts make the show undeniably funny for virtually any audience, it's easy to grasp the show's immediate appeal for gay viewers. Edina and Patsy represent the ultimate expression of our collective ambition – a lifestyle of selfish non-stop indulgence, skipping from glitzy restaurants to equally fancy bars, via Harvey Nicks. Jet-setting from New York to Morocco, with a humble (but classically trendy) home in Holland Park. A no-regrets life of perpetual drug taking and alcohol abuse, interrupted by only the briefest interludes of attention towards the more mundane aspects of life, such as work and parenthood. It sounds absolutely fabulous but, of course (and this is the whole point of the show), it's actually rather sad and slightly ugly and, just like any real-life over-indulgers, Eddy and Patsy's fast-lane of drinks and drugs quickly becomes a rather embarrassing and squalid gutter from which Eddy's long-suffering daughter Saffy repeatedly (and thanklessly) tries to rescue them.

Almost anyone could relate to the show – the sight of two overdressed tarts trying to maintain their dignity as they skid and stagger from a late-night taxi is universally funny in any language, but it's the detail that makes the show so very gay – the bottle of Bollinger that Patsy is clutching and the Gucci purse on Edina's arm, or her blind belief that by wearing a label she will look fantastic, no matter how overweight she is. It's the references to facelifts, drugs, consequence-free sex, youth, image, style, fashion . . . and it's Patsy's deplorable chain smoking and her insistence that she's '39' . . . and that she proudly boasts that she hasn't eaten any solid food since 1974. It really doesn't get any more gay than that. Little wonder that so much of *Ab Fab* has become part of accepted gayslang. Referring to someone as 'sweetie' became almost compulsory during the nineties (Eddy constantly referred to her daughter Saffron as 'Sweetie Darling' chiefly because she was usually too drunk to remember her real name) and 'Bolly-Stolly' (a combination of Bollinger champagne and Stolichnaya vodka) became the standard drinks order on every gay wish list (Eddy's kitchen featured a marvellous self-reloading fridge filled with Bollinger). Christian LaCroix became an everyday name ('if it's LaCroix then I like it, sweetie') and Joanna Lumley – seemingly doomed to a post-*Avengers* world of unimaginative television dramas – became an international celebrity and a huge gay icon. Joanna later marvelled at the sight of hundreds of gay men dressed as Patsy in Sydney's Mardi Gras parade, commenting that most of them looked more like Patsy than she ever did.

Remorselessly lampooning the artifice of public relations ('I Pee-Are things, sweetie'), advertising, fashion, celebrity and media, *Ab Fab* went from strength to strength, and it was only at the end of three hugely successful series that Saunders announced that the *Ab Fab* party was finally over, after treating us to the truly deliciously hideous sight of Eddy and Patsy as ninety-somethings, still looking for sex, drugs and alcohol (and 'that dog that sniffs your crutch').

Jennifer moved on and wrote a completely new series based on the equally pretentious life of London's theatreland, but using the same *Ab Fab* cast (and almost the same gags) was not a wise move. *Glitterball* was funny, but following the brilliance of *Ab Fab* it seemed more than a little pale in comparison and it was quietly dropped by the BBC. Saunders later admitted that even she didn't think it was all that good, and that she'd found it very difficult to start afresh without Eddy and Patsy.

Despite protestations that she wouldn't write any more episodes of *Ab Fab*, Saunders eventually yielded to BBC and public pressure and created another series which was received as warmly as the previous episodes. But something of the early magic seemed to have gone and although the characters and situations remained as ridiculous and hilarious as ever, there was a sense that old ground was simply being re-covered. Saunders later confessed that she had become almost frightened of her own creation and could have done more with the fourth series had she not been scared of failing. She certainly didn't fail; in fact, the final series was still way ahead of any other comedy on the nation's television screens, but the first three series of *Ab Fab* were always going to be almost impossible to follow. Thankfully, she still maintains enthusiasm for writing occasional one-off episodes, so we can be gleefully reassured that we haven't seen the last of this comedy classic.

CAGNEY AND LACEY

Not just another cop show, *Cagney and Lacey* was a gritty New York story of two girls making it in a hard place. A big blonde with an alcoholic father (Christine Cagney played by Sharon Gless) and a struggling mother-of-two (Mary-Beth Lacey played by Tyne Daly), these two girls took on the hoodlums with style and determination, looking out for each other while they fought it out on the New York streets. Then they went home and had tea.

It's hard to put your finger on the reason why so many gay men and lesbians got so hooked on the show, but it was probably the characters that we warmed to. The dizzy cocktail of murder, alcohol and mashed potato fights over the kitchen table just forced you to watch. You felt like you were there in the police car with them, eating that burger and dropping those fries when the radio crackled.

When the shows ended we mourned. And yet, when they started reappearing for endless repetition on satellite and cable channels, they just didn't seem the same. Maybe you just had to be there at the time. But no matter, Sharon Gless returned as Michael's mother in the US version of *Queer As Folk*. Talk about inspired casting . . .

CHANGING ROOMS

What did the Beeb start with this show? The ultimate gay fantasy – an empty room and a pile of dosh to make it beautiful with. Little wonder that grinning Carol Smillie almost became the mere warm-up act for designer extraordinaire Lawrence Llewelyn-Bowen, the long-haired, flouncy dandy with a breathtaking capacity for transforming even the dowdiest of rooms into something akin to a bordello. Possibly the gayest straight man ever to grace our television screens, Lawrence has deservedly gone on to bigger and better (OK, other) things. While the *Changing Rooms* genre has spawned a whole family of let's-make-your-room-look-like-shit programmes, we've got slightly tired with the whole thing, save for the mornings-only *Garden Invaders* (some of those garden hands do like getting their kit off), and, well, anything that saucy Alistair Appleton appears in really.

DYNASTY

A glorious television mega-soap name from the past, a sort of gay version of *Dallas*, which lacked the latter show's compulsiveness, but had a trashy, camp overtone that made it a must-see for anyone with an interest in shoulder pads, big, big hair and more glamour than you could fit on to your television screen. Just don't pay too much attention to the script or the acting.

Actually, it's unfair to carp at all of the actors as our beloved Joan Collins was in there, right in the thick of it, but you got the feeling that even she knew it was too ludicrous to be taken seriously by anyone with an IQ higher than a chimp's, and she hammed it up for all it was worth. As if the show wasn't girlie enough as it was, Joan's on-screen son was (you guessed it) gay, and most of the fellas in the cast were more than keen to whip most of their clothes off at the drop of even the smallest hat.

Controversy briefly courted the show when guest star Rock Hudson had an on-screen kiss with Linda Evans, shortly before he was diagnosed with Aids. In the midst of the 1980s Aids paranoia, the media briefly raged about the possible implications for poor Linda but, of course, it was all nonsense, much like the show itself.

After nine series the show finally exhausted itself, only to spawn a spin-off (*The Colbys*) which tried all the same tricks (including the inclusion of another queen bitch character in the shape of Stephanie Beacham) but never quite worked in the same sequin-studded way as *Dynasty* did.

EUROVISION SONG CONTEST

What a turn-around. At one time the ol' Eurovision had become a national embarrassment which we were cringingly obliged to watch once a year, usually because there was nothing else to watch on the other television channels. But then, almost imperceptibly, we began to see that the whole event, the whole ensemble, had a sort of camp faux glamour that it was, in fact, quite entertaining. Now its popularity has reached such proportions that gay pubs hold Eurovision live coverage parties, and countless gay boys and girls stay home until late on Song Contest night, until they've seen who wins. Eurovision is a glorious pageant of European trash at its best – a jumbled line-up of the most ludicrous and laughable attempts at music imaginable, combined with a jury voting system which is so overtly politically rigged, it defies understanding. In fact, nobody knows how minor wars haven't been started over Eurovision voting. It's camp tomfoolery at its best – dressed in fake solemnity. It won't be as much fun when our commentator Terry Wogan retires from his annual festival of xenophobic sarcasm, but we can still hope that the show that brought us naff delights such as Brotherhood of Man and Bucks Fizz might one day deliver us another Abba. But maybe flukes like that only happen once in a lifetime. Let's hope Cliff Richard doesn't happen twice.

GIMME GIMME GIMME

Never has such a simple comedy show caused so much fuss. On the face of it, you'd think that everyone would love the idea of a screaming queen living with a fag hag, throwing increasingly smutty one-liners at each other. But it didn't work out like that. *Gimme Gimme Gimme* was just that little bit too close to reality. It reminded the ranks of po-faced, straight-acting guys that the world is full of limp-wristed, giggling, girly queens that bend over. It was hilarious to read the endless indignant complaints about the way in which James Dreyfus shamelessly played his character Tom as the campest, most effeminate stereotype imaginable. He was setting back gay rights by decades so we were told. What bollocks. Actually Richard's only crime was to be just too damned good. He crafted Tom's outrageous girliness perfectly and made Tom all too real, but our brave, shiny new gay community didn't like having a mirror held up to itself. How sad that we couldn't take it on the chin and laugh at ourselves because, politics aside, Tom is very funny, and teamed with the legendary Kathy Burke the show is patently hilarious. If only we could get over ourselves and get a sense of humour.

PRISONER CELL BLOCK H

Sometimes you just have to wonder about the love/hate relationship we have with Australia. The country that imposed *Neighbours* and Rolf Harris upon us also gave us Kylie, Edna, *Priscilla* and, of course, the legendary *Prisoner* – the all-time queen of dodgy soaps. Complete with ludicrous scripts, wobbly scenery and some questionable acting, *Prisoner* was compulsive viewing for anyone, but particularly gay boys with a sense of camp humour. But the dyke-ish undertones also made the series a huge hit with the girls too – think dungarees, top dogs, illicit goings-on under the sheets . . . Amongst the immensely entertaining garbage were some great performers too, however, including the magnificent Maggie Kirkpatrick as Joan Ferguson aka The Freak. She later came to England to join Lily Savage on stage for a hugely successful stage production of the series. Brilliant.

QUEER AS FOLK

Ground-breaking stuff back in 1998 when Channel 4 launched an exciting new drama series based on the lives of a group of gay men in the heart of Manchester's gay village. Even more surprising was that the shows actually lived up to their pre-publicity hype; believable characters in a realistic setting, and . . . they even have sex – gay sex that is! Not surprising that the series was warmly received by everybody, apart from the usual die-hard homophobes. The downside to the whole *QAF* experience was that Manchester's Canal Street became the latest must-see place for television addicts who wanted to surround themselves with the perceived excitement of gay nightlife and, to this day, the gay village is still embarrassingly full of straight people who seem to think that hanging around Canal Street makes them more interesting. As if. The format was sold to American television and rescreened for our pleasure on BBC Choice (now BBC3), surprising many viewers by revealing a series which is substantially longer, rather funnier, with distinctly prettier actors and just as much explicit sex. There's more episodes to come too if the BBC can be bothered to show them.

THE GOLDEN GIRLS

Ah, the happy, warm days of *The Golden Girls*, a seven-season hit show which began in 1985 featuring four of the funniest and bitchiest gals (well, they were old dears actually) you could ever hope to meet. Lead character was Dorothy, a character which had effectively been tried out in an earlier sitcom (*Maude*) but she reappeared in style as the dour, stern-faced daughter of the even more wrinkly Sofia – a sharp, one-line-gag lady par excellence played by Estelle Getty, who had supposedly been rescued from a nursing home, but is ultimately doomed to a life of constant threats of being sent back there. Meanwhile there's also the heroically good-natured but mind-numbingly stupid Rose (played by Betty White) and the magnificent Southern Belle (OK, tramp) Blanche, played perfectly down to the swishiest inch by Rue McClanahan. It was a recipe for success and the simple plots were overshadowed by the superb put-down gags and well-delivered sarcasm which any would-be drag queen would die for.

The show's producers knew that *The Golden Girls* had a huge gay following, and every series included more than a few references to our side of the fence. There were even some occasional gay and lesbian characters but, even without any overt gayness, the show was compulsive viewing. Episodes are regularly re-run on satellite and cable channels and, even nearly two decades on, they're still just as funny as they were the first time round. Enjoy!

THE LEAGUE OF GENTLEMEN

During late 2002, while the BBC shamelessly hyped up and promoted its funny-in-parts series *The Office*, another comedy show reappeared for a third series on the very same channel, and proved beyond any reasonable doubt that overpromotion can never compensate for quality. *The League of Gentlemen* was from the very start a true comedy classic but, like most shows which earn themselves the dubious 'cult' title, it never received anything like the amount of praise or recognition that it deserved. Likewise, from a purely gay angle, *The League* was hugely popular with gay and lesbian viewers all across the country right from the outset, and yet it consistently failed to get any substantial recognition in the gay press where (as we are constantly reminded) we're supposedly informed of what is fashionable, great and good.

Set in the fictional town of Royston Vasey (this being the real name of comedian Roy Chubby Brown, who even made a cameo appearance in one episode), *The League of Gentlemen* explores the bizarre and slightly dark lives of the town's residents, all of whom are played perfectly by the show's writers, Mark Gatiss, Steve Pemberton and Reece Shearsmith (together with Jeremy Dyson who sticks to writing rather than acting). To say that Royston Vasey's residents are a little unusual would be a major understatement but, in true comedy style, the characters are never played for cheap laughs – they are inevitably presented with hard-faced seriousness.

The League is one of those shows that you either get or don't get – a real love-or-hate series which *Daily Mail* readers evidently never quite grasped, but which many others, particularly in gay circles, embraced and still love. But what's the gay angle? In truth, there never was an obvious gay 'hook' but the ludicrous nature of the characters (and a sizeable dose of drag) gave the series a camp feel which wasn't difficult to appreciate, and it wasn't long before key catchphrases started to be heard in gay pubs and clubs. However, viewers of the most recent (third) series couldn't avoid the overtly gay feel to some of the colourful goings-on, not least when one character realised he'd fallen for his wife's lover (after wanking him off in a massage parlour – don't ask, it's too complicated) and the supremely ironic revelation that another of the show's most sinister characters was masquerading as a hideously overdisguised drama queen. Equally comical was the post-screening revelation that one of the characters had been based on gay scene celebrity Julia Grant. How mad could it get?

In truth, *The League of Gentlemen* was a seriously underrated series which should have reached a much bigger audience, but perhaps the BBC thought it wasn't sufficiently banal to occupy a prime slot on BBC1. The third series may well have been the last and, although it was a darker and more subtle series than the previous two, it was just as compulsively entertaining. Perhaps it was a slightly ill-judged decision to kill off the two main characters (Edward and Tubbs in their legendary 'local shop'), although some of the main characters did survive until the very end, most notably the Employment Service's worst nightmare, the magnificent Pauline, and her revolting husband-to-be Mickey. But without doubt the last series was perfected in the very last episode with the reappearance of the supremely sinister Papa Lazaro, played perfectly by Reece Shearsmith. A chilling black-faced gypsy serial killer with a passion for collecting 'wives' (all of whom he inexplicably calls 'Dave') and an over-reliance on heavily applied make-up. It's hard to imagine anything more camp.

There's talk of a movie, so even if a fourth series is not produced, there's the prospect of seeing the population of Royston Vasey on the big screen, preferably with all of the original characters raised from the dead, and viewed from behind a large cinema-sized sofa.

TIPPING THE VELVET

Ooh, the Beeb goes lezzie big time with their period drama lesbian love series. Quality acting and scripting, all hailed as sensationalism by the media, but as with so many gay stories of late, the public shrugged their shoulders and tuned in. A major success, and a classic example of how most queer television is no longer a big deal. Would have been interesting to see how the viewers would have reacted to a similar story but with male characters though, wouldn't it?

WILL AND GRACE

Proving that sitcoms can feature gay characters with all the stereotypical mannerisms and gags, but still be hilarious, NBC's *Will and Grace* is a huge hit on both sides of the pond. The only peculiar aspect of the show is how it was never renamed 'Jack and Karen' when you consider that the two supporting actors are way funnier than the leads. The whole fag hag thing with the strait-laced and rather grey Will and the slightly annoying Grace is OK, but you have to learn to simply smile your way through their lines, while waiting for the camper-than-camp Jack to appear, together with his truly fabulous sidekick Karen. In essence, the show is all about Karen, with her classy dress sense, piles of cash, dodgy marriage, adoration of gay men, obsession with liquor and sex, and a whole string of beautiful one-liners which any gay man would kill for. You can't help wishing Will and Grace would go honeymoon some place and leave the whole show to the people that matter. But then, too much of a good thing . . .

MOVIES

The big screen offers even more girly delights.

ALL ABOUT EVE

Bette Davis in one of her best bitchy performances in a movie which takes a sideways swipe at the world of show business. Marilyn Monroe's in there too, although you wonder why.

BEAUTIFUL THING

A 1996 movie based on Jonathan Harvey's stage production, *Beautiful Thing* traces the story of Jamie, Ste and Leah, a trio of teenagers kicking their heels in a block of seedy flats on Thamesmead Estate. Jamie doesn't fit in at school, and his mother is preoccupied with making ends meet and taking care of her (younger) boyfriend, an odd-jobbing painter. Ste, on the other hand, is a sporty lad who everybody gets along with, apart, that is, from his drunken father and his equally dodgy drug-dealing brother. One night, after another alcohol-induced fight, Ste runs from his house and jumps into bed with Jamie . . .

Meanwhile, Leah has been kicked out of school but pays no attention to the abuse she gets from all around her. She's got her Mamas and Papas records and her drag-like clothes, and she's hopelessly obsessed with Mama Cass. No, really, in fact she is Mama Cass.

Beautiful Thing is a gritty and up-front love story with a happy ending, and a seriously cute pair of young stars (Scott Neal and Glen Berry). Not the typical sort of flick you'd expect gay guys and girls to go for, as there's nothing more than a few fleeting fumbles sex-wise, but it has a real and down-to-earth quality and a funny charm that make it the kind of movie that you could watch again and again, if only to lust after the actors and laugh at Leah.

CABARET

Some movies are unashamedly camp, and some movies are dark. Few if any have ever managed to combine the two genres so magnificently as *Cabaret*, the 1972 Bob Fosse classic based on Christopher Isherwood's book *Goodbye to Berlin* (Isherwood moved from England to Berlin in 1930, famously enjoying a relationship with a man more than thirty years his junior until his death in 1986). A chilling snapshot of pre-war Berlin, *Cabaret* owes much of its deserved success (no less than eleven Academy awards) to what was undoubtedly Liza Minelli's greatest on-screen performance. Minelli's portrayal of Sally Bowles, a naive but predatory American with a capacity to light up the stage with her dazzling presence, illustrates what was effectively the very beginnings of drag and modern-day cabaret bars. The glitz and glamour of the on-stage acts are contrasted by the sinister presence of the violent Nazis waiting outside. Joel Grey's outstanding performance as the bizarre bowler-hatted and white-faced Master of Ceremonies easily overshadows Michael York's commendable performance as Bowles's teacher and (eventual) sexual conquest, but the movie will forever belong to Minelli and likewise Minelli will forever be *Cabaret*. A must-see for anyone, gay or straight.

CAN'T STOP THE MUSIC

A whole movie devoted to the Village People. And astonishingly the word 'gay' is never uttered. It's all about suggestion, but it's done so poorly and with such camp tackiness, it's great. In a trashy kind of way.

FLASH GORDON

Sci-fi gone hopelessly wrong in a hilariously camp sort of way. A cavalcade of dodgy outfits, a barely plausible script and some questionable acting, all saved by the heroic tendency towards semi-nudity displayed by the lead character.

FRIED GREEN TOMATOES AT THE WHISTLE-STOP CAFE

A movie based on a distinctly dyke-ish book, but strangely the lesbian overtones didn't really make it to the big screen, or at least not very overtly. No matter, it's still a great empowerment flick, a sort of road movie without the road.

HAIRSPRAY

John Waters at his best. Sixties nostalgia running wild with podgy Ricki Lake (long before she found the chat show circuit) in company with her substantially larger mother played by the late, great Divine. Tacky sets, but a great movie.

LA CAGE AUX FOLLES

A delicious extravaganza of drag queens and revue performances, with the added twist of a plot which involves lots of wigs, and lots of deception, in a completely tongue-in-cheek *Carry-On* sort of way. Far from politically correct, it's fun with frocks. The more recent reincarnation (*The Birdcage*) just didn't quite hack it. Maybe it was because you can't stop thinking of Robin Williams as Mrs Doubtfire.

MAURICE

Film of the book (written by E.M. Forster), set in the First World War, starring Hugh Grant as an English aristocrat with the hots for his close friend Maurice. Set in an era when homosexuality was illegal (and hardly even mentioned), the scandal is mixed with the emotion, with Maurice eventually showering his affections on the gardener. Isn't it always the way?

MY BEAUTIFUL LAUNDRETTE

Gritty working-class saga of mixed-race homo shenanigans in eighties London. Excellent film which looks at the subject honestly and entertainingly – and pretty sexy too. Almost enough to make you start visiting the laundrette again.

PHILADELPHIA

Big-name actors (Tom Hanks and Denzel Washington) in a big-name movie about Aids. Good script and good acting which won Tom Hanks an Oscar (and provided him with an opportunity to make a very moving pro-gay speech) but the film is conspicuously shy of dealing with homosexuality. Not so much as a peck on the cheek really. But it's a start.

PRISCILLA – QUEEN OF THE DESERT

You don't expect classic movies to come out of Australia all too often, and *Priscilla* might have been just another one of those samey television movies that crop up on Channel 4 on Sunday nights, had it not been for the fact that it's the gayest movie ever. Consequently, it ranks high on our relatively short list of classic movies which you've got to have on video and DVD and that, preferably, you can memorise word-for-word, so that you can re-enact the wittiest and campest bits at will.

Priscilla is the story of a bunch of drag queens in a road movie from hell. Bored with the gay scene in Sydney, they embark on a tour of Australia in a dilapidated Greyhound bus, which is appropriately covered in pink emulsion and named, that's right, Priscilla – Queen of the Desert. The ensuing antics are pure gay mayhem at its best – temper tantrums, huge performance drag costumes, lip-synching to Abba (one of the characters carries a secretly stolen Agnetha turd, pickled in a jar) and bitchiness of the grandest and most well-prepared kind. The movie even gave the gay scene some much-used and now commonly accepted throwaway lines such as 'Oh, Felecia, where the fuck are we?' and the even more well-known 'A cock in a frock on a rock' plus a whole new range of festival costume ideas (notably the flip-flop frock).

The actual storyline isn't anything too magnificent (they tour the country, get in a fight and climb to the top of Ayres Rock – then go home) but, like any good road movie, it's the getting-there that's the story, not the actual arrival. In fact, the only real message of the film is that we might like to slag off the gay scene, but we'd sure miss it if it was gone. The acting is brilliant (Terence Stamp as a drag queen – who would have thought it, and he's so damned good at it too), and you can't help but wonder how a straight actor like Guy Pearce can become the gayest, campest, most limp-wristed fairy you've ever seen, and be even more believable than the real thing. Better still, he keeps taking his clothes off.

SHOWGIRLS

Basically a shameless rehash of *All About Eve*, but without Bette Davis. The same cynical trudge through showbiz land, but with plenty of questionable talent and poor production. It was slated by reviewers so it's got to be good.

STRICTLY BALLROOM

A festival of frocks and glamour, tracing the story of a sexy young ballroom dancer (played by Paul Mercurio) who is set for dancefloor stardom until he abandons orthodox dance moves in favour of his own more exciting routines. Of course, the stuffy ballroom dancing elders are outraged, but he does his own thing, eventually partnering a timid amateur, after his sequinned dancing partner walks out. You can guess the rest – they dance hard until they take on the establishment and win the big award. No great surprises there, but it's the detail in the story which makes the movie a camp classic. It doesn't have any gay storyline as such but if you don't find this movie hilarious, you're just plain straight.

THEATRE OF BLOOD

Possibly the campest movie of all time. Vincent Price as the world's worst actor (although, of course, he thinks he's the best) taking revenge on his critics in the most venomous and ludicrous ways possible. Just brilliant.

THELMA AND LOUISE

Road movie par excellence. No great plot, just the odd murder and lots (and lots) of driving, but it works so well, you just want to be there with them (until the end that is).

THE ROCKY HORROR PICTURE SHOW

Camp and occasionally funny, but ultimately uninspiring. The concept is good and the performances are commendable but the whole movie is built on the one gag. Little wonder that it's straight people that have hijacked this movie and made it their own. Sadly, they still think a man in a dress is hilarious. It's just a jump to the left . . .

THE WIZARD OF OZ

We all know the story – poor little Dorothy is whisked up in a tornado and deposited in the land of Oz, where her black-and-white Kansas world is transformed into a technicolour land of talking scarecrows, munchkins and wicked witches. It's one of those movies that every homo just can't help watching, even though there's nothing particularly gay about it. Maybe it's the limp-wristed lion, or Dorothy's overoptimistic skip-through-disaster attitude that we locked on to, if not the oh-so-gay song 'Somewhere Over The Rainbow'. Who knows, but the movie will be forever associated with all things camp, finding acceptance and the typically gay notion of abandoning all things black and white in favour of a life more colourful, so much so that the term 'Friend of Dorothy' was (and to some extent still is) a much-used euphemism for 'homosexual'.

More cynical analysts suggest that the movie accurately describes a drug-fed hallucination, and that's something that more than a few of us can certainly relate to. When we all started dancing to Tampara's 'Can You Feel It' a couple of years back, there was another gloriously camp *Wizard of Oz* connection which made the hit all the more amusing; the line 'what's she gonna look like with a chimney on her' originally had another line attached which went 'gonna drop a house on that witch' . . . you see where it came from now?

TORCH SONG TRILOGY

The story of a forty-something drag queen, and his liaisons with various men, in a society steeped in homophobia. Slightly TV-movie-esque but nonetheless a good movie which was bravely released at a time when audiences were lapping up a diet of Schwarzenegger and Stallone.

WHATEVER HAPPENED TO BABY JANE?

Truly a must-see movie for anyone with even the slightest liking for camp humour. A dark tale of sibling rivalry taken to its extreme, this black-and-white 1962 flick stars Hollywood icons Bette Davis and Joan Crawford as the Sisters from Hell, embroiled in an endless bitch-fight over stage and screen stardom. Blanche (played by Crawford) is a major celebrity actress, stealing the limelight (unintentionally) from her embittered sister 'Baby Jane' Hudson, played by Bette Davis in one of her most memorable performances as the dumpy precocious child star whose on-stage adoration is in danger of being upstaged until a terrible car accident befalls poor Blanche. No prizes for guessing who is responsible.

The rest of the movie dwells on the scary and yet hilarious relationship between the wheelchair-bound Blanche, and the monstrously evil (and slightly deranged) sister Jane, as she clomps up the stairs to feed Blanche rat for breakfast (served on a silver tray, of course), and tries her best to thwart any attempts at escape or rescue from her imprisonment in the attic of their dilapidated mansion. It's fabulous stuff, packed with one-liners and scenes which you're compelled to relive and repeat for the rest of your gay life. An all-time camp classic.

Acknowledgements

Having compiled this book from a variety of sources, it would be impossible to thank every person who has contributed to its pages. To all the people I have interviewed, chatted to in pubs and clubs, or grilled remorselessly on the internet, I must extend my sincere thanks for your time and co-operation. I will however, extend a special thank you to both Craig and Leon whose generous assistance was greatly appreciated. Likewise, I could fill a page with acknowledgements of all those great and wonderful individuals and organisations who were ultimately incapable (or simply unwilling) to provide even the smallest amount of feedback. You know who you are.

On a wider theme, I guess this would be a good place to offer a thank you to my friends out there on the gay scene who have, either directly or indirectly, helped me to create this book, either by offering their own input, or by simply being there when the idea of a pint seemed way more inviting than a blank computer screen. It is to the following people that I dedicate this publication:

To Daphney, Maureen, Ada, Miss Cawthorne, and of course Shaun for being yourselves.

To Miss Terrine for introducing me to the bizarre and fabulous world of the gay scene (yes lady, it was all your fault, you created a monster).

To Miss Roacha for being the feisty, moody, evil bitch of a drag queen that she's always been (and hopefully always will be).

To my long-suffering partner Marsha for teaching me that being gay or straight ultimately isn't about who you fuck; it's about who you love.

Index